CANADA'S FORGOTTEN SLAVES

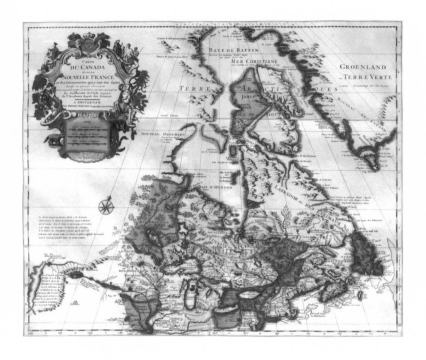

"Carte du Canada ou de la Nouvelle France" from *Atlas Nouveau*, 1708
by Pierre Mortier, after an earlier 1703 map by Guillaume De L'Isle.

Canada's Forgotten Slaves

TWO CENTURIES OF BONDAGE

Marcel Trudel

WITH THE COLLABORATION OF

Micheline D'Allaire

TRANSLATED FROM THE FRENCH BY

GEORGE TOMBS

Véhicule Press

Published with the assistance of the Canada Council for the Arts, the
Canada Book Fund of the Department of Canadian Heritage, and the
Société de développement des entreprises culturelles du Québec (SODEC).

We acknowledge the financial support of the Government of Canada
through the National Translation Program for Book Publishing
for our translation activities.

Cover design: J.W. Stewart
Typeset in Minion by Simon Garamond
Maps and graphs by Irving Dardick
Printed by Marquis Printing Inc.

Originally published in 1960 as *L'esclavage au Canada français*. This
edition was published as *Deux siècles d'esclavage au Québec*
by Marcel Trudel with the collaboration of Micheline D'Allaire,
Les Éditions Hurtubise HMH, 2009.

LIBRARY AND ARCHIVES CANADA CATALOGUING IN PUBLICATION

Trudel, Marcel, 1917-2011
Canada's forgotten slaves : two centuries of
bondage / Marcel Trudel ; translated by George Tombs.

(Dossier Quebec)
Originally published under title: Deux siècles d'esclavage au Québec.
Includes bibliographical references and index.
ISBN 978-1-55065-327-4

1. Slavery–Québec (Province)–History. 2. Slavery–Canada–
History. 3. Indian slaves–Québec (Province)–History. I. Tombs,
George II. Title. III. Series: Dossier Québec series

HT1051.T7 2012   306.3'6209714   C2012-901923-2

Published by Véhicule Press, Montréal, Québec, Canada
www.vehiculepress.com

Distribution in Canada by LitDistCo
www.litdistco.ca

Distributed in the U.S. by Independent Publishers Group
www.ipgbook.com

Printed in Canada on FSC certified paper

Contents

Translator's Preface

Canada's Forgotten Slaves is a classic of historiography. In this bold, highly original work, Marcel Trudel flies in the face of the nationalist historians of previous generations, who portrayed French Canadians either as swashbuckling heroes, virtuous missionaries in black robes, or victims crushed under the boot of British conquerors.

Here, Marcel Trudel gives a voice to the voiceless, to the most humble, powerless people in society, putting a human face on a phenomenon long denied in Canada, and all but forgotten: namely, that Canadian masters and mistresses exploited over four thousand aboriginal and black slaves between 1632 and 1834.

Canadians have long seen slavery in terms, above all, of the Underground Railway, that clandestine network of forest and waterside paths by which Quakers, black freedmen and other human rights advocates smuggled runaway American slaves northwards to liberty in the early nineteenth century. As many as a hundred thousand slaves escaped to Canada. But for some strange reason, while congratulating Canadians for offering refuge to these fugitives, generations of historians maintained a virtual conspiracy of silence about slaves owned and exploited, bought and sold, by Canadians themselves.

In fact, as Marcel Trudel points out, several prominent French Canadian historians, François-Xavier Garneau among them, deliberately misled their readers, skewing the historical record in order to exonerate the Roman Catholic Church (which held slaves), to perpetrate the vision of a French Canadian nation which could do no harm since it was more victim than victimizer, and to lay the blame for Canadian slavery squarely at the door of the British alone.

Actually, as this work demonstrates, men and women at every level of French and English Canadian society owned slaves, from farmers, bakers, printers, merchants, seigneurs, baronesses, judges and government officials to priests, nuns and bishops. This meant that slaves were not only an accepted feature of society, but were also acknowledged both in law and by notarized contract. Yet these slaves remained practically invisible, as if they had long been considered somehow sub-human.

One of the most remarkable parts of this work is in establishing that slaves did not passively wait to be freed by others: some slaves researched their own condition, filed lawsuits, challenged their master's ownership rights, sought to negotiate their release or simply ran away. Slaves suffered for being slaves. In the most poignant case of a slave escape, 1732, the black Angélique set fire to the home of her mistress on rue Saint-Paul in Montreal, to create a diversion in order to run off with her white lover. The fire ended up destroying forty-six houses, and Angélique was caught and executed for this crime, although her lover, being white, was acquitted of any charge.

Marcel Trudel passed away on January 11, 2011 at the age of ninety-three. I remember discussing my translation with him in his lovely riverside home near Montreal. Even in his nineties, wearing eye-glasses as thick as fishbowls, surrounded by an impressive library of first editions, he was passionate about a historian's duty to establish facts, grounding them rigorously in statistical and documentary evidence, and bringing them together in an appealing although balanced narrative. He was passionate above all, in a subversive, irrepressible way, about going against the grain, defying conventional wisdom in his native Quebec, making a contribution to the history of human rights. He was also proud to have brought out this work for the first time in 1960, although he was ostracized as a result and had to leave Quebec for the more open-minded academic setting of the University of Ottawa. He brought out an updated edition of the work in 2004 and a slightly shorter pocket edition in 2009. By and large this translation follows the 2009 edition, while restoring some passages from the 2004 edition. Going back to original sources, Trudel's endnotes were researched and corrected.

In speaking to Marcel Trudel, I could see he referred to "Canada" the way an authority on seventeenth- and eighteenth-century history would: "Canada" for him was another name for New France, which at its peak in 1712 stretched from Newfoundland down to the Gulf of Mexico, and encompassed Acadia (present day Nova Scotia, Prince Edward Island and New Brunswick), southern Quebec and Ontario, and lands in the heartland of the continent, along the Missouri and Missisippi rivers, all the way to Louisiana. For this reason, a few of the slaves described in this work fell under Canadian jurisdiction, although physically they lived in what is now the United States.

Marcel Trudel's history of slavery starts with New France, then continues under the British military regime after the Conquest of 1760, when English-speaking masters joined the dark company of Canadian slave owners; then moves in time to the province of Quebec from 1774 to 1791 (which included Michigan and other lands around the Great Lakes, although the Ohio River Valley was ceded to the United States in 1783) and across what is now southern Ontario to today's Quebec; and finally comes to a close in Lower Canada from 1791 to the formal abolition of slavery in the British empire in 1834.

It is important to remember that by "Canada," Marcel Trudel generally means "French Canada" and even when he examines British slave owners, such as James McGill, the founder of McGill University, he only considers those non-French slave owners living on the former territory of New France. This means he sometimes leaves out other parts of modern-day Canada, from British Columbia to Newfoundland and Nova Scotia.

Moreover, he generally uses the term "Canadian" to refer to French Canadians, and "Québécois" to refer to residents of the province of Quebec, whether or not they were French Canadians; in several cases, he refers to "us" in addressing his French-speaking readership, and I have removed these references; he often uses "English" in referring to people we would call "British," especially since the Acts of Union resulted in the establishment of Great Britain in 1706, so I have sometimes replaced the term "English" by "British" for this reason.

Trudel also uses the word "we" in two different ways. First there is the royal "we", when he proudly announces the result of his ground-breaking researches. Then there is the French-Canadian "we", the sense that he belongs to (and is perhaps speaking on behalf of) a people with common descent, history, culture, language and territory. It should be clear from the context which "we" he is using.

The term *pays d'en haut* (literally "Upper Country") which appears in the text refers to the vast North American hinterland, upstream from Montreal, which mainly included territory around the Great Lakes region, as well as various river basins where French explorers, fur traders and missionaries were active.

He also uses the racial terminology originally found in the historical record – terms such as "Negro and Negress, mulatto, savage, redskin, Montagnais and Eskimo," although he is careful to use less pejorative modern-day terms such as black and Amerindian in developing his interpretation of the original documents. I have decided to use the French term "Panis" for Amerindian slaves, rather than the modern-day "Pawnee" (the name of an Indian tribe in the Midwest) since "Panis" was used generically to refer to any aboriginal slave in New France, whatever their origin. It has been a challenge finding equivalents for all these terms nowadays: as translator I faced a choice between modernizing all racial references, or of sticking to Marcel Trudel's original text. For example, black slaves were sometimes referred to euphemistically as *bois d'ébène* or "ebony wood," and the expressions "ebony" and "ebony slaves" appear frequently in this translation.

I opted to remain true to his original intention, which imparts a somewhat archaic flavour to some passages in the book. Readers should take note that Marcel Trudel provides footnotes for short quotations, but not for longer passages. He often refers to leading authorities providing eye-witness accounts of New France simply as "Lahontan, Lafitau, Charlevoix and Bougainville," as if they were second nature to every reader nowadays. Louis-Armand Lom d'Arce, Baron Lahontan (1666-1716) was a military officer, explorer and precursor of the Enlightenment who wrote admiringly of the Hurons; Joseph-François Lafitau (1681-1746) was a Jesuit ethnologist and naturalist who wrote extensively about the Iroquois, comparing them to the Greeks of Antiquity; Pierre-François-Xavier de Charlevoix (1682-1761) was the author of a multi-volume history of New France, published in 1744; and Louis-Antoine de Bougainville (1729-1811) was a French naval officer, mathematician and explorer who wrote about his experiences during the French and Indian War, and went on to circumnavigate the globe three years after the British Conquest of Canada.

I remember asking Trudel why this pioneering work had only just begun to spawn new studies and fiction about slavery in Canada. He shook his head wistfully, replying that this subject had long been a blind spot in the French Canadian psyche. But what of English Canada, I asked? Why had no comparable work on slavery in English Canada ever come out? Could there be some way of adapting my translation, so that it included as many references to slaves belonging to English Canadian as to French Canadian owners? Otherwise, readers of my translation might get the mistaken impression that slave owners in Canada had mainly been French-speaking, and rarely English-speaking! He seemed daunted by the amount of research such an adaptation would involve.

It is to be hoped that some future historian will be inspired by this translation to provide a more complete history of slavery in what is now Canada. Such a history would reconstitute the way aboriginals on the Pacific and in the Eastern woodlands sometimes enslaved other aboriginals; it would mention the revolt of Celtic slaves against their Viking masters on Baffin Island, in 997 (as recounted in *Thorsigl's Saga*); it would show how the Portuguese explorer Gaspar Corte-Real seized sixty Beothuks or Mi'kmaq in Newfoundland in 1500, later selling them as slaves in Portugal; and it would recount how the Patuxet Squanto, taken from New England to Spain in 1614, to be sold there as a slave, eventually managed to return to his native Massachusetts via England and Newfoundland, ultimately settling with Pilgrims in the new colony of Plymouth.

A history of slavery in what is now Canada would indicate that white people could also be slaves: after all, Barbary pirates seized a fleet of fishing vessels off Newfoundland in 1625, taking their crews back to North Africa and throwing them into bondage there; when the Marquis de Tracy brought soldiers of the Carignan-

Salières Regiment on the ship of the line *Le Brézé* to New France in 1665, by way of French Guiana, they had first to fight off Barbary pirates intent on enslaving them, in a fierce naval battle off Portugal; when Louis XIV began condemning French Protestants to be galley-slaves in 1685, Huguenots had a new incentive to abjure their faith, convert to Catholicism and resettle in New France; finally, when approximately 1500 New England captives were taken by aboriginals in the seventeenth and eighteenth centuries and spirited up to Canada, some were called "slaves" by their captors, and treated as such, although there was little chance an Abenaki or Mohawk captor would register slave ownership before a notary!

A word about currency. In terms of exchange rates, one écu in the late seventeenth century was worth three French livres. In the late eighteenth century, one pound Quebec currency was worth about twenty-four French livres, or just under one British pound one shilling, or one guinea. (There were twenty shillings to the pound.) The value of currency was naturally affected by the gradual introduction of card and paper money, differences in the value of money between Paris, London and the colonies, and inflation, which began rising particularly under the French regime in the 1720s.

Of course, any future history of slavery in Canada would have to explain the distinction between captives, debtor and chattel slaves, indentured servants, prisoners, hostages, kidnap victims – these are not just semantic gradations, but distinct realities for people deprived of their liberty. In the meantime, Marcel Trudel's work is the most complete history of Canadian slavery we have.

In doing this translation, I have benefited from the wise counsel of Frank Mackey, author of *Done with Slavery: The Black Fact in Montreal*, and Sue Peabody, co-author of *Slavery, Freedom and the Law in the Atlantic World*. I hope it will give a voice to the voiceless, contributing more generally to a debate in Canada about liberty, the universality of human rights, as well as "man's inhumanity to man."

George Tombs

Preface to the 2009 Edition

More than forty years ago, I brought out *Histoire de l'esclavage au Canada français* [The History of Slavery in French Canada]. At the time I promised to follow that work up with a biographical dictionary providing details about Amerindian and black slaves held in servitude here in the seventeenth and eighteenth centuries. Unfortunately, I lost the 900-page manuscript and much of the accompanying documentation in a devastating fire. Many years later, I took up the research again and finally brought out a *Dictionnaire des esclaves et de leurs propriétaires* [Dictionary of Slaves and Their Owners] in 1990, which has gone through two editions in French, but has not appeared in English.

In 2004, my publisher brought out a completely updated edition of *Histoire de l'esclavage*, on which Micheline D'Allaire worked assiduously, under the title *Deux siècles d'esclavage au Québec* [Two Hundred Years of Slavery in Quebec], an edition accompanied by a CD-ROM containing the *Dictionnaire des esclaves et de leurs propriétaires*.

Micheline D'Allaire prepared the 2009 edition [from which *Canada's Forgotten Slaves* is derived]. The 2009 edition still covers slavery in what used to be called "French Canada" – in other words, the current territory of the province of Quebec as well as those colonial territories which formerly fell under Quebec jurisdiction.

To make chronological sense of the history of slavery, I refer to today's Quebec and its inhabitants as "Québécois", but in describing French North America before 1760 I refer to "New France" and the "French regime." Moreover, in dealing with the period from 1760 to 1791, I refer to the British regime, since from 1764 onwards "the province of Quebec" only consisted of the North and South Shores of the St. Lawrence River, but was then greatly expanded in 1774, and stretched from Labrador to the confluence of the Ohio and Mississippi Rivers. This huge region was populated mainly by francophones with a small anglophone minority, and I call these people "Canadians." Subsequently, in dealing with the period from 1791 to 1840, I felt it more appropriate to speak of "French Canadians" than of "Québécois" since the latter appellation has only come into use quite recently, in referring to residents of the current province of Quebec. However, it is hoped the reader will understand that when I refer to Quebec before 1867, I am referring to a State that exists nowadays, and that has nonetheless lived through various historical periods and seen its territory expand and contract at different times.

In presenting this book to the reading public, I would like to pay tribute to the magnificent work of the historian Micheline D'Allaire. Without her tireless devotion, and given my own state at this point in my life, the updated work you are holding would never have seen the light of day.

Marcel Trudel

Introduction

Slavery was formally abolished in 1834 throughout the British Empire, yet it is hard to say exactly when it disappeared in Lower Canada: all we can say is that no further documented trace of slaves can be found starting in the years 1810-1820. But when did slavery begin here? The first slaves were few and far between, and the practice of slave-holding only became a common practice starting in the 1680s. A few individual slaves appeared first of all. Gradually servitude became a recognized institution in the society of New France, and it remained so up to the first quarter of the nineteenth century.

GUILLAUME COUILLART's NEGRO

The first slave we can positively identify in New France was a Negro boy brought here by David Kirke in 1629 during the English occupation of the St. Lawrence Valley. According to one account he was from Madagascar, according to another from Guinea: whatever his place of origin, there can be no doubt he was a slave. This Negro boy belonged to one of the three Kirke brothers, and was sold for the sum of fifty écus to Le Baillif, a French trader who had gone over to the English (fifty écus, or 150 livres, was the equivalent of six months' wages for a skilled person). When the English left Quebec in July 1632, Le Bailiff gave the young black slave to Guillaume Couillart.

The slave's new master sent him to a school run by Le Jeune, a Jesuit missionary, who wrote in 1632: "I have become a regent in Canada. The other day I had a little Savage on one side and a little Negro[1] or Moor on the other, whom I taught to read and write. After so many years of regency, I have finally come back to teaching ABCs, but with such contentment and satisfaction that I wouldn't give up these two pupils for even the most prestigious audience in France."

Father Le Jeune was the first Jesuit educator in the St. Lawrence Valley, and his first pupils were an Amerindian and a Negro boy.

Le Jeune found this little black boy's naïve attitude amusing:

We took him in to instruct and baptize him, but he does not yet understand conversation very well, so we will have to wait awhile longer. When he spoke of baptism he made us laugh: when his mistress [Guillemette Hébert, Guillaume Couillart's wife] asked him if he wanted to become a Christian, and be baptized, so he could be like us, he said yes: but he also asked whether we would flay him during the baptismal ceremony: he must have been truly afraid, because he had seen poor Savages flayed. And when he saw us laughing over his question, he replied in his gibbering patois. [...] 'You say that through baptism I will become like you: I am black and you are white, so you will have to flay my skin so I become like you,' whereupon we began to laugh even more, and seeing he had been mistaken, he laughed along with us.

Then, in 1633 this Negro boy was baptized, just like a white man, although no flaying of his skin was involved: he was given the name Olivier, in honour of the general clerk Olivier Tardif, and it may have been from this moment onwards that he took the surname Le Jeune, after his spiritual father, the Jesuit Le Jeune.

This black boy does not seem to have learned much more than the rudiments of the Catechism. He had to testify in court in 1638, and only managed to sign with an X, which does not seem so bad considering that his master Guillaume Couillart's signature consisted of a drawing of a man lying on his back. Why did Couillart's Negro have to appear in court? He had been placed under arrest, after claiming that sailors arriving from Tadoussac had informed him the interpreter Nicolas Marsolet had received a letter from the traitor Le Bailiff. Marsolet had already got into enough trouble for having collaborated with the English, and had no desire to compromise himself further: he took the black boy to court. An investigation took place, and witnesses maintained that no one had seen Le Baillif's ship. The slave was forced to admit before Guillaume Couillart and Guillaume Hébert that he could not substantiate his claim. The court ordered him to seek Marsolet's forgiveness, and to spend "twenty-four hours in chains." So here was the first black boy in Canada, already clapped in irons!

This slave only turns up in official records one more time, when he was buried in Quebec City on May 10, 1654. The priest recorded his name as Olivier Le Jeune, and noted him simply as Guillaume Couillart's servant, without mentioning his age, although he must have been in his thirties by then.[2]

This was the first recorded death of a black person in the St. Lawrence Valley. He lived with the Couillart family, but we cannot say for sure in what capacity. In the seventeenth century, any black person was considered a slave wherever he might be found in Canada, unless he had been formally emancipated. We found no evidence of Olivier Le Jeune's emancipation. It is conceivable that he had been freed, although this is not indicated in surviving records. Moreover, the fact he was described in burial records as a servant did not alter the fact of his bondage: the records tell us of many servants who were actually slaves in fact and in law. We should recall that in the seventeenth century, servants were considered to form part of their master's household. However, we are inclined to think that Kirke and Le Baillif's former slave was no longer a slave by the time he reached Couillart's household. Perhaps this was simply a case of adoption. The fact remains that for twenty years, a young representative of an enslaved race lived among the earliest French inhabitants of Canada. And it is impossible to imagine Couillart's household from 1632 to 1654 without the presence of Olivier Le Jeune, this living memory of the English occupation.

WERE AMERINDIANS TREATED LIKE EBONY SLAVES?
When the Negro Olivier Le Jeune died in 1654, we believe he was the

only one of his kind in Canada, and the next black slave only turned up a quarter of a century later. Elsewhere in the Americas, however, slave traders preyed on native Amerindians. In 1493, Christopher Columbus was the first explorer to propose enslaving Amerindians to his fellow Europeans. Addressing the Spanish monarchs, he wrote: "I can provide as much aloes and [Amerindian] slaves for the navy, as their Highnesses require"; writing further about slaves, he noted he would send as many as were desired. Europeans must have found it tempting to treat the indigenous population of the New World the same way they had treated Africans since at least 1444.

The temptation was all the greater because Amerindians were slave-holders themselves. Alluding to islanders he had just met, Columbus wrote on October 11, 1492: "I thought, and I still think that [Amerindians] come here from the mainland to take them and enslave them." On settling in Acadia, the French also found that native people traded in slaves; when Lescarbot pitied the prisoners who had long been subjected to all kinds of exactions, he suggested that we simply "make them our slaves the way the Savages do, or hold them to ransom."[3] Lafitau described in great detail the treatment of prisoners captured by native Amerindians: when the captives were not tortured to death, they were subjected to such awful living conditions that death by torture almost seemed preferable. The enslavement of prisoners was so common among Amerindians, Lahontan noted, that the two terms were practically synonymous.[4]

Even when resident Amerindians settled in villages along the St. Lawrence Valley, they held other Amerindians in bondage. The Jesuit Nau wrote of the Iroquois mission of Sault-St-Louis: "Most of the adults we teach in the village are slaves taken in wartime."[5] There were slaves in other villages too: Quicinsik, chief of the Algonquins of the Lake of Two Mountains, had a "savage" slave about thirty-five years old who was buried in Montreal on May 4, 1750; on August 15, 1762, at Michilimackinac, the old Amerindian Angélique baptized her "savage" slave Antoine, who was about eighteen years old.

Gradually, slaveholders got into the habit of acquiring Amerindian slaves in order to sell them to the French, which profited both parties to the transaction. One incident illustrates how easily Amerindians could sell their fellow natives. An Amerindian hunter accompanying Bossu on his 1752 expedition in Illinois liked to get drunk, so to cure him of the habit, his wife got Bossu to say he had a lot of spirits but was reluctant to dish them out; the hunter offered Bossu a trade – his wife for an entire month of alcohol. "I remonstrated," Bossu wrote, "that the Chiefs of white warriors do not come among the red men to enjoy their wives, but as for his son, I would gladly accept him as my slave if the hunter wanted to sell him to me, and I would give him a barrel of spirits; we concluded the contract in the presence of witnesses, and he gave me his son." The Amerindian got comfortably drunk, and when he had recovered his wits, his family accused him of unnatural behaviour; he apologized, saying that Bossu would be good enough to hand his son back, "and he knew that the great Chief of the French and the Father of the Indians had no child slaves in his empire. I replied that this was the case, but I had adopted the boy as my son and as such would take him to France to become a Christian, so all the fur of his nation would not be enough to redeem him." The Amerindian was then advised to go see the missionary, and it was agreed that Bossu would hand the son back once he had been baptized and the father "had sworn off that drunkenness which had proven so disastrous for him"; the father agreed, and stayed sober.[6] In 1752, a member of the Illinois nation was willing to sell his son into slavery for drink, and this fact suggests that the practice of selling one's own kind into slavery had become something of a reflex.

It would take volumes to recount the slave trade between North American Amerindians and the French and English. In this work, we will only be dealing with that part of the slave trade involving the inhabitants of New France and the subsequent British regime. A separate study should be made of the slave trade that operated between native people and the English colonies. In 1492, Columbus noted that Amerindians took and traded slaves; this practice would continue until the late eighteenth century. Just as some black Africans served as intermediaries for slave traders, some native Amerindians bore a lot of responsibility for enslaving their fellow natives.

The French waited a long time, however, before trading in Amerindian slaves or in reducing prisoners to slavery. When Jacques Cartier took two natives from Honguedo back to France in 1534, and then Chief Donnacona in 1536, it was by no means with the intent to enslave them: in the first case, he wanted the natives to learn French so they could serve as guides and interpreters, and in the second, Cartier wanted to remove from Stadacona a native leader who could endanger the French-Amerindian alliance. It has sometimes been claimed the French of Acadia took or wanted to take Amerindian slaves starting in 1607, in order to operate a flour mill, but we believe this to have been a misinterpretation of a document by Lescarbot.[7]

Nor can we speak of slavery in the case of three young Amerindian girls (Foi, Espérance and Charité, or Faith, Hope and Charity) given by the Montagnais to Champlain in 1628: they said he had expressed the wish "to take our girls back to France, and educate them there in matters of faith and morality"; Champlain "took such care that he had them rigorously instructed not just in matters of faith but also in little exercises for girls and in weaving tapestries which he traced himself." But in 1629, Kirke refused to allow Champlain to take two remaining native girls back to France.[8]

The same kind of adoption was involved when Chomedey de Maisonneuve received a little girl from an Amerindian mother: the nine-month-old girl was baptized in Montreal on August 4, 1658. According to Dollier de Casson, the Sisters of the Congregation of Notre-Dame also adopted young native girls, the first of whom may have been the one given to Chomedey de Maisonneuve:

On 11 August [1663] a most promising little Indian girl named Marie des Neiges died at the Congregation. Sister Bourgeois had looked after her from the age of ten months, taking a great deal of pains and trouble with her, and was repaid by the pleasure the child gave her. By reason of the affection felt for the child, her name was kept alive by being passed on to another little Indian girl that we had here who was baptized with the same name. When this second child likewise died, they took a third little girl and in the same way gave her this name [according to the baptismal register of Montreal].

The French had not yet begun to reduce Amerindians to slavery, and we believe this was still the case in 1668 when two slaves escaped from the Iroquois country and found refuge with the French. On October 2, 1666, when Dollier de Casson and Gallinée left Lachine enroute for the Quinté mission, in a bay of Lake St. Francis, they met "two poor savage women, quite emaciated, who were going down to the French settlements to escape the bondage in which they had been held for some years. They had set out forty days before from the village of Oneida, in which they were slaves, and for the whole of this time they had lived on nothing but squirrels which a child of ten or twelve years killed with arrows made for him by those unfortunates." After many difficulties, the Sulpicians got their Iroquois guides to let one of these women continue on to Montreal with her little boy, while the other woman was entrusted to the Hurons who would be trading in Montreal. Finally, the two fugitive slaves reached Montreal, which Dollier Casson described as "the old asylum for such miserable fugitives." [9]

THE FIRST AMERINDIAN SLAVES
So far, we have seen French colonists adopting Amerindians with Ville-Marie serving as a refuge for fugitive slaves. But starting in 1671, the French settlers of Canada began to acquire Amerindian slaves. It is true that once the French acquired these Amerindians, they do not always seem to have formally regarded them as slaves. What matters is that these slaves were given to the French as slaves, and that the French accepted them as such, at least for a time.

In order to appease the wrath of Governor Rémy de Courcelle in 1671, the Iroquois brought him two Potawatami slaves, and the governor accepted both slaves and his anger subsided. Who were these two slaves, the first native Amerindians to come to Quebec officially as slaves? The governor placed them with the Sisters of the Congregation:

These two girls are with the Sisters of the Congregation [Dollier de Casson wrote], where they learned the French tongue and have been brought up in European fashion, so that the bigger, who was the later baptized, is ready to marry a Frenchman. But one wishes there were some small means of providing her with a dowry, so that once she was established, it would serve as an example to others and fill them with the desire to be brought up in the French manner. The smaller of the two girls of whom we speak, after being at the Congregation for some time, was carried off by her mother who had given her up, conjointly with the Iroquois. A daughter of the Congregation ran after her to get her back and the child left her mother, who held her by the arm, throwing herself into the hands of the daughters of the Congregation.

Female benefactors in France provided about 1200 livres for the education of these two girls.[10] Rémy de Courcelle had received them from the Iroquois as slaves, and accepted them as such, but they were soon treated more or less as persons of a free condition: one of the girls later married a French settler, and it was hoped other Amerindians would follow her example.

So Amerindians began giving Amerindian slaves to the French. The explorer Louis Jolliet received the same favour as Governor Rémy deCourcelle. During his Mississippi expedition, Jolliet brought back a young slave he had received from native Amerindians, but in 1674, within sight of Montreal, the canoe capsized and Jolliet lost the young slave, two men and his personal papers. He wrote to Bishop Laval: "I really miss a slave boy of ten who had been given to me. He had a lot of spunk, was witty, diligent and obedient, he could express himself in French, he had began to read and write."[11] Buade de Frontenac mentioned this young slave, adding something Jolliet had left out: the Amerindian boy had been intended for Frontenac. The governor wrote to Colbert: Jolliet "lost all his papers and a young Savage from those lands, whose death fills me with sadness."[12] To our knowledge, this was the first slave to come to Canada from as far afield as the Mississippi and there would be many more.

In 1678, the explorer Daniel Greysolon Dulhut found himself in the same situation as Jolliet: he was about to leave on a large expedition to Lake Superior when Amerindians gave him three slaves in Montreal.[13] According to the documents we have consulted, the first Amerindian specifically referred to as a slave was an unnamed girl belonging to Buade de Frontenac, whom the Ursulines of Quebec signed up as a boarder for schooling on July 23, 1679, and who left the convent on October 7, 1680.[14] It is impossible to say what became of her.

Several years went by, and historical documents do not provide us with any substantial leads. In February 1681, according to the registry of civil status, Marie, a twenty-eight-year-old native of the "Loup" or Wolf nation, was buried in Lachine: she was from a tribe associated with the Iroquois, she was certainly a prisoner of war and her presence in Lachine suggests she was in bondage. In 1685, an Amerindian woman named Agnès, daughter of Mathieu Houlacous, died at the home of Nicolas Juchereau de Saint-Denys, seigneur of Beauport; communion was administered and she died after "having led a worthy life." According to the registry of civil status, Joseph Giffard and Nicolas Juchereau de Saint-Denys attended her burial. Since the French did not use resident Amerindians (Hurons, Algonquins, Abenakis and others) as servants, we are inclined to include Agnès, in service at the Beauport manor, among the slave population.

THE ARRIVAL OF AMERINDIAN SLAVES

Trafficking of Amerindian slaves truly began in earnest in 1687: it was on a modest scale at first, but then became more generalized and continued until the early nineteenth century. In 1687 the first two Panis[15] to reach the St. Lawrence Valley were brought all the way from outlying tributaries of the Missouri basin: Pierre, aged about ten, was buried in Montreal on October 15, while Jacques, aged nine, was buried there on December 19. In 1688, another Panis, Louis, was confirmed a Catholic by the bishop in Lachine. In 1689, an anonymous Panis (who may have been the one just confirmed) died in the Lachine Massacre along with René Chartier, whose slave he was. How long had these slaves been living among the French? It is impossible to say. It is clear however that they only appeared in the civil registry after arriving in the colony. The Panis Louis, for example, must have been living in French society for a fairly long time because he could not be confirmed before learning adequate French as well as the catechism.[16]

By the end of the seventeenth century, Amerindian slaves turn up almost each year in historical records. After René Chartier's Panis slave died in the Lachine massacre, Philippe, an Amerindian slave belonging to one Lalemant, was discharged from the Hôtel-Dieu de Québec on December 28, 1689. In 1690, three Amerindians lived at the same hospital: a Panis said to be from Illinois and belonging to an officer named Tonty died there on May 22; a certain Bernard, listed as a dependent of Bishop St-Vallier, stayed there in July and returned in August before dying on September 11, just eight years old; Pierre of the Illinois nation was treated by the Jesuits in August and stayed with them again from November 1691 to February 1692, at which time he was considered their servant. The Illinois came to the St. Lawrence Valley as slaves, yet we cannot say whether the Jesuits still held this particular Illinois as their slave. The same year, in November, an unnamed Amerindian owned by the officer Paul Lemoyne de Maricourt, was treated in hospital. In 1671, the Hôtel-Dieu patient registry mentioned the Panis Nicolas, aged between thirteen and fifteen, belonging to one Doyon: he stayed there in April and November; this Panis married a Canadian in 1710, adopting Doyon as his surname. In the registry, we also find an unnamed Amerindian belonging to Pierre Moreau de Lataupine: he was ill in July, and died the following month.[17] On May 24, 1692, an Amerindian named François, about eight years old and belonging to Jean Mailhiot, was baptized in

Montreal: the baptismal certificate states that he had come from about 300 leagues (900 miles or 1440 kilometres) beyond Illinois. This child had been obtained through tribal slavery. He was not held in bondage for long, since he died the following July. In February 1695, the twenty-three-year-old Amerindian François, belonging to Lamontagne, stayed at the Hôtel-Dieu de Québec. The Panis Ignace died in this same hospital on April 24. In November 1695, Jeanne Wannanemim of the Mohican nation, who had been captured near Deerfield by the Iroquois of Sault Saint-Louis, was brought to Montreal: as a prisoner of Amerindians she was held in bondage; she was baptized on May 1, 1698 at about fifty years of age. On June 9, 1696, the officer Louis Dailleboust de Coulonge baptized Philippe-Marie-Louise, a fourteen- or fifteen-year-old Panis girl he owned. On September 27 that year, five-year-old Louis, an Arkansas boy, was baptized at Sainte-Anne-de-la-Pérade: the owner was not specified, but this little Arkansas boy from the Mississippi Valley was certainly a slave, just like other Amerindians imported from the Midwest. In 1698, another Arkansas boy – Jean, aged ten – was baptized in Montreal: he belonged to Jacques Picard, who had brought him to New France the year before; in December, Jean-Amador Godefroy de St-Paul's Panis Jean-Baptiste died in Trois-Rivières. Finally, we learn of a third Arkansas in 1699, nine-year-old Jean-Baptiste, belonging to the fur trader Pierre Trutaut; this Arkansas boy was baptized in Montreal on April 21, and was later buried there on February 18, 1709. Another Panis, thirty-six-year-old Jacques, was admitted to the Hôtel-Dieu on May 22, dying there on June 2; given his age, this Panis must have been in Quebec for some time[18]

These are the native Amerindians identified as slaves in historical records, but it would also be worth knowing which slaves were held by officers at the trading posts of the *pays d'en haut* (the Great Lakes region); since these officers were geographically closer to the slave market, they must have owned slaves during the seventeenth century just as they later would in the eighteenth; it had always been customary before any trading ceremony for Amerindian hunters to exchange gifts with French merchants, and slaves were often presented as gifts to these merchants. In the eighteenth century, there was trading in both furs and slaves.

For the period before 1700, our research on the Great Lakes trading posts produced few results, apart from a Shawnee slave given in 1699 to Juchereau, commander at Michilimackinac, who immediately ordered the slave shot. Why? According to Lahontan, a group of Iroquois on a mission to the French had been captured by the Hurons, led by the famous Le Rat who had every interest in derailing Governor Denonville's peace initiatives. Among these prisoners was a Shawnee slave. Le Rat handed the slave as a gift to Juchereau, but according to Lahontan, Juchereau no sooner received the slave than "he amused himself having the slave shot." Le Rat fully expected this outcome, and immediately released an Iroquois prisoner so the latter could tell his people how the French treated embassies.[19] If Lahontan was telling the truth, Juchereau must have had a peculiar way of enjoying gifts!

During his Mississippi expedition, Lahontan also received Amerindian slaves from an Arikara chief, to serve as guides in their country; he was hoping to bring four of them back to Canada: "I thought I could return to Canada with more valuable booty. So I proposed to them that I would obtain their freedom from the Grand Chief, and I promised such a sweet and honourable condition, and benefits so great, that I would have been hard-pressed if they had taken me at my word." But love of their country prevailed, and the four slaves preferred to return home.[20] And it was just as well, since Lahontan was not sure he could fulfil his promises.

If we bring together a list of the Amerindian slaves who lived among the French population at the end of the seventeenth century, we find twenty-nine Amerindian slaves over a twenty-nine-year period, three from Arkansas, ten identified as Panis (the Panis lived in the Upper Missouri), one from the Illinois Country, two from the southern shores of Lake Michigan, and two from the land of the Mohicans, south of the Iroquois. It is however impossible to say where the rest were from, although they must have come from far away, because the resident Amerindians of the St Lawrence Valley were not enslaved.

The age of only fourteen of these slaves is known, and of these, ten were under fifteen years of age. Some were very young, like the five-year-old boy who came from the Arkansas country. And this is the point when a new characteristic of native Amerindian slavery emerged in New France: slaves were young, and those slaves drawn from the tribes farthest away were mostly children.

Historical records do not always indicate the owners of these first twenty-nine Amerindian slaves, and when they do, it is not always possible to determine the profession of the owners. Two governors accepted Amerindian slaves, and subsequent governors would follow their example. Bishop Saint-Vallier had a young Amerindian slave, and was by no means the last bishop to be a slave owner, just as the Amerindian belonging to the Jesuits was hardly the last slave owned by a religious community. The explorers Jolliet and Greysolon Dulhut held slaves, and so in turn would Gaultier de Lavérendrye. Tonty, Lemoyne de Maricourt and Dailleboust de Coulonge were the first officers heading a list that would continue to grow during the following century. The same can be said for fur traders. Our list of seventeenth-century slave owners in Canada thus includes colonial officials, military officers, explorers and fur traders: indeed, these are the key groups that defined the heyday of slave-owning, and they were also the groups most intimately involved with native Amerindian nations.

We are here talking about slaves. Aside from men, women and children explicitly identified as slaves or said to belong to an owner, it is not certain that the other Amerindians who entered New France as slaves actually appear as such in historical documents. A colonist may have acquired an Amerindian slave, but even when the Amerindian remained attached to the colonist, he did not necessarily continue on as a slave. For our purposes, it is enough to count the native person as a slave once he or she entered the French population as such. Moreover, documents are not always explicit and sometimes require us to make inferences. For example, before 1709, when Intendant Raudot intervened to provide a legal basis for slavery, civil registries rarely used the word "slave"; in the fifteen civil acts of this period relating to slaves, only one directly used the word "slave"; in a Lachine document dated October 28, 1694, referring to the burial of victims of the 1689 massacre there, René Chartier's Panis is referred to as a slave. This was the first time prior to 1700 that civil registries used the word slave; up till then, those maintaining records had usually written "savage belonging to..." a specific free person.

CHAPTER ONE

"Give Us Negroes!"

Before 1700, few Amerindian slaves and even fewer blacks were brought to New France. The black Olivier Le Jeune was acquired by Guillaume Couillart in 1632 and died in 1654. It was not until the year 1686 that the next black person appeared in New France, a man named La Liberté whose presence was duly recorded in the census of Acadia. Yet black slavery was already flourishing by this time in other French colonies. In 1640, Jean Aubert had introduced sugar cane in the French West Indies. Given the shortage of Amerindian and European labour, the French followed the example of the Spaniards who had started importing African slaves in 1611. The Compagnie française des Indes occidentales was founded in 1664 and undertook to supply Aubert with black ebony. In 1673, the Compagnie du Sénégal specialized in the slave trade, so that by 1687 there were already 27,000 black slaves in the Caribbean. In March 1685, an edict of Louis XIV known as the *Code Noir*, sought "to settle issues dealing with the condition and quality of the slaves in said islands," officially sanctioning black slavery in the Caribbean.[21]

NEGROES FOR CANADA
Blacks were needed to harvest sugar cane in the Caribbean, and the labour supply argument was also put forward in Canada. In 1688, the governor of New France Brisay de Denonville and Intendant Bochart de Champigny wrote to the king that workers and servants were so hard to find in the colony, and so expensive, that they ruined anyone engaged in any enterprise: the best way to remedy this situation would be to introduce black slaves.[22]

That autumn, the attorney general of the Conseil souverain, François-Madeleine Ruette d'Auteuil, sailed to France, to present the case of the Canadian authorities: in April 1689, the king was presented a brief drafted by the attorney general, containing various suggestions about justice, commerce and war.

Ruette d'Auteuil was primarily concerned about commerce, but nearly half of what he wrote on commerce involved black slaves. He listed a few undertakings likely to promote the development of Canadian trade, and added:

> In order to succeed in these kinds of undertakings, one needs some advantage, whereas servants are so extraordinarily scarce and expensive that they will ruin anyone who dares to embark on any enterprise.

So how could cheap labour be obtained?

> If it please the King, Ruette d'Auteuil wrote, to grant permission to have Negro or other slaves in that country [New France], as He has been pleased to approve in the islands of America [the Caribbean], this would be the best guarantee of success in all sorts of manufactures, together with the graces He would have the kindness to bestow on those striving for the good and increase of the said country.

Ruette d'Auteuil anticipated the objection of the climate:

> If it be objected that Negroes will not live there any longer because of the cold, experience shows the opposite, because some Negroes have borne themselves well for several years and the English have had large numbers [of such Negroes] in New England and there are many in [New] Holland.

It was worth citing the example of the neighbouring colonies of New England and New York: by 1680 New England already had about 200 blacks, although Ruette d'Auteuil neglected or avoided to mention that New England's climate was milder than Canada's. To buttress his argument, he said that there were several blacks in Canada "who have borne themselves perfectly well for several years." He did not provide any hard numbers, however, perhaps as a way of avoiding ridicule, given the tiny number of these blacks: Olivier Le Jeune died in 1654, and had been in good health since 1632 (at least we hope so); La Liberté had been living in Acadia, and there may have been a few others. It was better for Ruette d'Auteuil not to base his argument on statistics.

He also found an argument stronger than mere numbers. He seized on the most ingenious schemes to address the climate problem to the benefit of one and all. To keep blacks warm, he wrote, "their clothing will be beaver skin, whose fur will prevent them from feeling the inconveniences of winter and will moreover be inexpensive, because in wearing it they will fatten it, thereby increasing its value." It should be recalled that New France traded in two kinds of pelts: dry beaver, which according to an expression current at the time consisted of "the pelt of the beaver as it is drawn off the animal," and fat beaver, worn by Amerindians whose sweat and bodily oils made the long hairs fall out. Fat beaver was a particularly fine fur highly prized in the clothing industry and usually brought twice the price of dry beaver.

According to Ruette d'Auteuil, not only would blacks be well protected from the cold, but by staying warm, they would double the value of the clothes they wore. Once their beaver pelts were fat, the blacks would put on new pelts and the whole operation would be repeated. Money could be made simply by dressing slaves warmly!

LOUIS XIV GRANTED AN AUTHORIZATION
Did the king find this idea persuasive? Whatever the case, he granted his authorization. On May 1, 1689, he wrote to Governor Brisay de Denonville and Intendant Bochart deChampigny as follows:

The attorney general of the Conseil souverain of Quebec, who has come to France to inform His Majesty that the principal inhabitants of Canada are resolved, if His Majesty so consents, to bring Negroes to that country for the purposes of cultivating and clearing land, as a way of avoiding the heavy costs of resorting to workers and labourers of that country. Whereupon His Majesty is pleased to state that He consents to such importation of Negroes as they propose, but He must at the same time warn them that Negroes may die in Canada because of the difference of the climate there; this warning being needed so that the people there only execute this project in gradual steps, and do not take on large expenditures which may in due course prove useless, doing considerable harm to their affairs and consequently to the Colony.[23]

By royal permission, Canadians could acquire blacks, but the king advised caution: the climate could prove harmful and Canadians would then have incurred large expenditures in vain. The effectiveness of Ruette d'Auteuil's scheme was questioned. Once Brisay de Denonville's tenure of governor came to an end, the king reaffirmed the authorization and repeated his advice in instructions he gave to Governor Buade de Frontenac in the same month of May 1689:

His Majesty wishes him [Frontenac] to carefully consider the proposal made by some residents of Canada who would like to bring in Blacks for the purposes of cultivating and clearing land; upon which he must observe that in the event that such people are resolved to go forward with this undertaking, he must not allow them to take on considerable expense for the purchase of said Blacks, lest the loss of them, which could result from the difference between the climate of the Blacks and that of Canada, result in very considerable losses; but he should allow them to acquire Blacks gradually, increasing their purchase with each indication of success; if the establishment of these Blacks were to succeed, then it is certain that the colony would derive a great advantage in terms of cultivating and clearing land.[24]

With the authorization and appropriate advice in hand, there was nothing to do but wait for the blacks to turn up. But on May 17, 1689, war broke out between France and England, and under terms of the League of Augsburg, a European-wide coalition of Protestant and Catholic countries lined up against the France of Louis XIV. The metropolitan powers of Europe were at war, so the colonies followed suit. Slaves could only be sent to Quebec from trading posts in Guinea once the war was over.

Slave-traders could not sell off their black ebony directly: but could prospective owners in New France find others way to ensure a supply of slaves? The war lasted eight years, and during this time only four blacks turned up in Canada. On May 26, 1692, two blacks were baptized in Montreal: Pierre-Célestin, about twenty-four years old, belonging to the merchant Leber (father of the famous recluse); andLouis, about twenty-six years old, a native of Madagascar living with the merchant Louis Lecompte-Dupré.[25] On April 10, 1694, Bishop Saint-Vallier confirmed the black Jacques, a native of Guinea about thirty-six years old, who had been living with the same merchant Jacques Leber, and who had been taken from the English. In September 1696, the black François, aged thirty-two years and owned by merchant Louis Lecompte-Dupré, was admitted to the Hôtel-Dieu de Québec. These were the only four blacks documented to have reached New France during the War of the League of Augsburg. It would appear from the civil registries that two of them had been in New France at least since 1692 and one of them had been taken from the English. With no slave market then in operation, prospective owners resorted to the spoils of war.

With the Treaty of Ryswick in 1697, the war came to an end after eight long years. Did this mean prospective slave owners could finally take advantage of the royal authorization granted in 1689? The next mention in the royal mail of the problem of sending blacks to Canada was in 1701, when the king wrote to Governor Callières and Intendant Bochart de Champigny: "His Majesty has no objection to granting the people of Canada permission to own Blacks, but as the only way to effect this is to bring in a ship laden with Blacks, they must give assurances they will pay the costs of transportation, and Messrs. Callières and Champigny must ensure that precautions are taken to make this happen."[26] In 1689 the king had given permission to own blacks; by 1701, transporting blacks was still at the discussion stage. To minimize any losses, it had to be made clear first of all whether Canadians were actually in a position to pay for goods from abroad, and the authorities of New France had to ensure "that precautions are taken to make this happen." There was no question of a ship bearing Negroes to Quebec for the time being. In any case, war broke out again in 1702 between European powers, when a grandson of Louis XIV succeeded to the throne of Spain. This incurred further delays, and it would be eleven years before a new peace treaty was signed.

Not Even One New Black Slave Each Year

In the meantime, a few more individuals were added to the black population (if the word "population" can be applied to a group of just four people): one in 1700, two in 1704, one in 1705, one in 1706, one in 1707, then another in 1708, an eighth in 1711 and a ninth in 1713. This did not amount even to one new black person each year. What became of these individuals? In 1700, Philippe, a black from Barbados was bought from the Abenakis who had taken him as war booty: he was considered a slave, although surviving documents do not indicate who his owner was; he was baptized at Pointe-Lévy on January 18, 1700 at about sixteen years of age.[27] In 1704, the Hôtel-Dieu de Québec registry indicates that an unnamed black was admitted, belonging to the wife of the treasurer of the Marine, Georges Regnard-Duplessis.[28] In this same hospital was a twenty-one-year-old black man belonging to Governor General Vaudreuil: since his name was Joseph Hisme, he may very well have been taken from the English. Pierre, another black slave aged thirty-one belonging to the same Governor General, was admitted for treatment in 1705; further traces of him can be found in documents dating to 1706 and 1708. In 1706 and 1707 another slave belonging to the same owner, the black Louis, about twenty-two years of age, was also admitted to the hospital. More black slaves belonging to Governor General Vaudreuil followed: in 1707, he sent his slave Antoine "Flesche" to the Hôtel-Dieu de Québec; this would likely have been a slave taken from the English colonies. In 1709, Pierre, the black slave of the merchant Pagé-Carcy was admitted to the same hospital, followed, two years later, by another prisoner of war, Titus Jones.[29] Finally, the ninth black slave of this period, Claude Antoine, was found in the service of the Governor of Montreal, Claude de Ramezay, and was baptized on March 15, 1713. Of nine blacks newly arrived in New France, four likely came here as war booty.

Given the uncertain supply of black slaves, prospective owners naturally turned to Amerindians, who continued arriving in the country as slaves, slowly at first, but then at an ever greater pace from 1700, as the following table shows.

	Amerindians	Blacks		Amerindians	Blacks
1689	2		1702	2	
1690	4		1703	12	
1691	2		1704	6	2
1692	1	3	1705	3	1
1693	2		1706	7	1
1694			1707	3	1
1695	1		1708	8	
1696	2	1	1709	5	1
1697	1		1710	12	
1698	1		1711	10	1
1699	2		1712	20	
1700	7	1	1713	26	1
1710	6				

Between 1689 and 1713, thirteen black and 145 Amerindian slaves reached New France. In fact, these latter Amerindian slaves far outnumbered blacks, and they would maintain their lead over time. Amerindian slavery stood at a relatively high level from 1710 onwards, largely because of an ordinance issued by Intendant Raudot in 1709, to the effect that people who bought Panis and blacks as slaves owned them outright.[30] Given the proximity to the Amerindian slave market, this ordinance was likely to encourage people who needed slaves, but it could do nothing for prospective owners who preferred blacks. Canadians who preferred ebony slaves had to wait till the war was over: added delays came when metropolitan authorities in France had to figure out how to ship slaves to Quebec.

Louisiana was only established in 1699, but acquired blacks far more quickly than New France. Louisiana had the advantage of being closer to the Caribbean market, but it also exploited the Amerindian market of the vast Mississippi Valley. In fact, Amerindian slaves were put to work in the first years of the Louisiana colony, although these slaves could always wander back to their nearby tribes. This is why, in 1706 and in 1708, Governor Lemoyne de Bienville proposed a swap with the French West Indies: two Panis would be sent from Louisiana to the islands, for every black who was sent back. This would ensure that French colonists in Louisiana had less trouble holding onto their slaves.[31] We do not know whether this two-for-one swap was put into practice. One thing is certain: in granting Crozat the Louisiana trade monopoly in 1712, the king opened the way to voyages each year to the coast of Guinea, where blacks were acquired for resale to colonists.[32] Louisianan slave owners got the slaves they wanted, whereas the people of Canada had been waiting since 1689 for the blacks they had been officially authorized to buy.

The war ended in 1713 with the Treaty of Utrecht. Wouldn't the Canadians now finally get their cargo of blacks? Louis XIV had granted his authorization in 1689 and had reaffirmed this authorization in 1701. In 1709, Intendant Raudot had established the legal existence of slavery. Crozat was thus in a position to buy slaves in Africa. But no shipment of Negroes reached Quebec.

Was Ebony Too Expensive for Canadians?

The cause was likely economic. Canadians had racked up one victory after the other during the war, but under terms of the treaty, they lost trading posts on Hudson Bay and saw the value of paper money go up in smoke. As a result, they may have been in less of a position to acquire expensive merchandise from Africa than they had been in 1689.

Still, in 1716, Intendant Bégon returned to the charge. Governor Vaudreuil was prevented by illness from writing to the king, so Bégon took it upon himself to plead the urgency of acquiring black slaves. Taking up the same arguments that had worked in the past, he wrote: "There are few inhabitants in Canada, and many enterprises suffer from the difficulty of finding workers and day labourers whose wages are excessively high." Importing blacks would "lead to an increase in the colony and its trade." Why not use this resource profitably, the way English colonies did? "This was the means by which all of New England was established in such short order. Most English and Dutch people living under the government of Manhattan, close to Montreal, take no part in farming, since their slaves do all the work, and this government alone provides all the flour needed to support England's southern islands. If there were Negroes in Canada, the same results could be obtained. Our colony also has iron mines from which the King could derive significant benefits if workers were available to exploit them."

As a result, according to Intendant Bégon, black slaves would help New France flourish just like the English colonies, the land would be cultivated and iron mines could be exploited. The problem was paying for them:

An objection could be raised, the intendant continued, about the difficulty of payment, whereas the promissory notes that must be issued for the extinction of playing-card money, the free trade in beaver pelts, and the funds that the King is kindly committing for the colony's expenses, will provide the means to pay real value for these Negroes, and it is certain that all those capable of acquiring them will do so.[33]

Governor General Vaudreuil did not agree. According to a marginal note in this same memorandum, he believed "it is inappropriate to bring them to [New France], because the climate is too cold and it would cost too much for people to dress them in winter and he believes it would be better to bring in salt workers." The problem of how to clothe Negroes had already been raised in 1689. But was Vaudreuil unaware that Ruette d'Auteuil had come up with an ingenious scheme: dressing blacks in beaver pelts, as a means of doubling their value? Or had his personal experience as slave owner made him pessimistic? By 1716, his two Amerindians and four blacks had been admitted to the Hôtel-Dieu de Québec: at that time, entering the hospital meant being on the verge of dying. Indeed, records show that black slaves under the French regime died young – on average before reaching their twentieth birthday.

Word from the French government came back: "it does not seem appropriate at present to send Negroes to Canada."[34] Vaudreuil's prudence had won the day, but it is worth noting that the government refused to send a shipment of blacks to Canada, while continuing to allow Canadians to own slaves. As a result, in 1719 Intendant Bégon asked once more that blacks be sent to Canada, and the regent replied in 1720 that he "wants to know beforehand what price people will pay for Negroes, *pièce d'Inde*."[35] Acccording to the *Dictionnaire de Trévoux*, the expression "*pièce d'Inde*" referred to a black slave between twenty and thirty who was well built, healthy and had all his teeth.

Bégon supplied the information requested, sending the regent a "submission made by the communities, senior officers and *habitants* of the Colony to pay the sum of 600 [livres] for Negroes, *pièce d'Inde*, or as established by mutual agreement at Quebec with the captains of slave ships." This submission, the intendant added, "was signed only by those to whom he has had the opportunity of proposing it, and there are already subscriptions for 101 Negroes and Negresses, which leads him to believe that if the Compagnie des Indes wanted to send a vessel to Quebec in 1701 laden with 200 Negroes or Negresses, sales would be brisk and the slaves would be sold just as advantageously as in Martinique."[36]

There was nothing random about Intendant Bégon's request: he had taken the trouble to get religious communities, officers and *habitants* to sign purchase orders. In so doing, he had collected subscriptions for hundreds of blacks, which is why he believed a cargo of 200 blacks could be sold off quickly enough in Canada. Subscribers were willing to pay 500 livres each, or as agreed with the slaver-traders.

Who were those subscribers? We did not find a list of buyers. We can only say that at least a hundred individuals wanted to acquire blacks. In the absence of a list, we can only rely on notarized deeds of sale, references in the civil registries or other documents. Subscribers included religious communities, clergymen, officers, merchants and even ordinary *habitants* or tillers of the land.

Bégon Called for a Cargo of Negroes

According to Intendant Bégon, if 200 blacks were sent to Quebec, sales would be brisk, and they would be even more so "when money is more common in Quebec and people know the usefulness of having Negroes on their land." And he saw fit to write a memorandum to colonial authorities on the need for blacks in Canada. In 1689, the main argument had been the scarcity and high cost of domestic servants. The argument had developed over time. Bégon now developed a series of important arguments: the cultivation of hemp and the general progress of agriculture, assistance to the elderly, the dearth of domestic servants, defence in time of war, the experience of other colonies.

Bégon began his plea by urging that blacks be brought in to grow hemp, drawing inspiration perhaps from the role sugar cane had played in the introduction of black slavery in the Caribbean. He then referred to a social problem that black slavery could help solve – that of parents who became infirm or who had no children.

"Widows and the elderly who have no children fit to work would no longer be forced by their powerlessness to abandon their homes or sell them for a pittance." If black slaves could work the land, then elderly parents would no longer depend on their children in conditions that caused all sorts of tragedies:

> Fathers and mothers who have cleared a lot of land and established their homes could, on reaching an advanced age or becoming infirm and being incapable of working any longer, maintain control of their assets and continue exploiting them. By means of their Negroes, they would no longer be forced to depend on their children, nor be exposed to abuse from them. Instead, their children would always show them respect and submission, hoping thereby to show themselves worthy of an eventual inheritance, whereas at present, because there is not enough labour to work the land, ageing fathers and mothers are forced to place themselves at the mercy of one of their sons, and to induce him to help them in their old age, making him a donation of all their property so they can be [properly] fed, housed and supported.

However, the intendant noted, the terms of these donations were not always faithfully fulfilled, which led to lawsuits or conflicts about anticipated inheritances, with as many as ten or twelve children quarrelling over terms of the donation of property.

The presence of black slaves would not only make the elderly independent of their own children, it would help solve the problem of domestic servants. Officers, merchants and city-dwellers in general could take land and have blacks work it for them. Blacks could be taught essential trades, thereby increasing the number of workers. In addition, blacks would be very useful for home defence, and were more obedient: this meant no longer relying solely on Amerindians, who did whatever they pleased and withdrew from battle as soon as they felt their position weakening. Finally, the

English colonies had started thriving once blacks were introduced there. Intendant Bégon recalled that other French colonies had been granted authorizations to import blacks, and hoped the same favour would be accorded to Canada.[37]

A Cargo of Negroes Authorized Once Again

This was the line of argument Bégon submitted to the Conseil de la Marine in January 1721. It was a more elaborate argument than the one Ruette d'Auteuil had developed in 1689. On the margins of the document, the Conseil wrote this favourable note: "Send a copy of this notice and the submission to the Compagnie des Indes, underlining the fact that if it commits to sending a shipment of Negroes this year, sales will move quickly and it will reap considerable profit." Bégon's project of importing 101 blacks reached a milestone when the regent sent his consent to the Compagnie des Indes.

The Conseil de la Marine informed Bégon of a new delay, which "has arisen because of the need for a restructuring of the Company governance, which is being addressed at the moment, so the shipment cannot be sent this year,"[38] but the Council would ensure that its promise was kept.

This, it seemed, meant only that a postponement of the project was in order: the Company had to be restructured, the Conseil de la Marine would hire the Company to send a shipment of blacks to Quebec, and so the purchase order would be fulfilled in 1721.

In fact, no shipment ever reached the colony. Word of this new delay was the last time Bégon's project was ever mentioned. How can this be explained? The Compagnie des Indes was in a new situation: it held the monopoly of the slave trade, but had constantly to defend itself from private ship owners while being unable to profit from its own monopoly. The council of the Compagnie proposed to abandon the monopoly; then, in 1724, its monopoly privilege was restricted to the territory of Senegal alone – a huge victory for private ship owners, but a great loss for the Compagnie. Bégon's project seems to have got lost in the shuffle.

People in Canada could always rely on private initiative: but could a ship owner profitably transport a few hundred blacks from Africa to Quebec? There were many closer colonies to sell off a regular cargo of 500 or 600 Negroes.

No slave ship ever came to Quebec, as we know from statistics between 1714 and 1760 on total black slave arrivals each year.

1715	7	1730	4	1746	11
1715	3	1731	3	1747	18
1716	1	1732	5	1748	16
1717	2	1733	4	1749	8
1718	2	1734	2	1750	12
1719	–	1735	4	1751	7
1720	–	1736	3	1752	10
1721	2	1737	6	1753	6
1722	1	1738	7	1754	5
1723	1	1739	4	1755	16
1724	2	1740	5	1756	9
1725	–	1741	5	1757	15
1726	2	1742	3	1758	9
1727	3	1743	15	1759	12
1728	3	1744	21	1760	6
1729	2	1745	11		

The annual number of new blacks arriving was ridiculously low, even when we count a few black infants born here. Canadians had received official authorizations in 1689, 1701 and 1721, yet there was no massive import of blacks to Quebec. Prospective slave owners would have to make do with a few individuals.

CHAPTER TWO

The Legalization of Slavery

Slaves show up in historical records in Quebec from the 1670s up till the 1830s. We located documented traces of eighty-six slaves before 1709 (eleven blacks and seventy-five Amerindians), although slavery had not yet been formally legalized. The civil registry of Lachine (an official state document) referred to a Panis as a slave, and in 1700 the civil registry of Pointe-Lévy identified a black man as a slave. In church and hospital registries, meanwhile, blacks and Amerindians were described as belonging to particular individuals. Slavery was not yet an established institution.

WAS THERE ANY GUARANTEE OF SLAVE OWNERSHIP BEFORE 1709?
When a Canadian *habitant* owned a slave, he had, or believed he had, some basis for the right of ownership. Yet before 1709, it was hard for owners to demonstrate that they could indeed exercise such a right. In March 1685, Louis XIV published the *Code Noir*, which settled issues in the Caribbean, "dealing with the condition and quality of the slaves in said islands." The *Code Noir* specified that particular slaves were "personal property" duly belonging to their owners,[39] but the edict only applied to the French West Indies and was neither promulgated in Canada nor even recorded by the Conseil souverain. When the time came to settle issues related to blacks in Louisiana, the King of France issued another edict, in much the same terms, but for Louisiana alone. Nothing in the *Code Noir* of the French West Indies or of Louisiana applied to Canada.

Could slave owners find some basis for the right of ownership in the Treaty of Whitehall, concluded between France and England in November 1686? This treaty concerning the neutrality of American

43

colonies stipulated in Article 10 that citizens of one nation could not give refuge to slaves belonging to citizens of the other nation.[40] The article came into force in 1686, but only applied to jurisdictions where slavery was formally recognized, which was not yet the case in Canada.

However, starting in 1689, owners of blacks could rest easy: Louis XIV had authorized Canadians to import blacks for the purposes of working and clearing the land. This royal authorization served as a guarantee of ownership of blacks, but could not be applied to Amerindians held in bondage, even though most slaves in New France were actually Amerindians.

Bishop Saint-Vallier referred directly to slaves in his *Catéchisme de Québec* of 1702 and his *Rituel du diocèse de Québec* of 1703. The *Catéchisme* outlined impediments making a marriage null and void, in question-and-answer format. The second of these impediments was "the error of condition: marrying a slave who was believed to be a free person would result in a marriage that was null."[41] This is what the *Catéchisme* taught Catholics of the diocese of Quebec, which then covered all of New France (all the way down to Louisiana). The 1703 *Rituel* of the same diocese, published by Bishop Saint-Vallier in France, contained another passage on slavery: the bishop listed categories of persons ineligible for the priesthood, the second of which was "those born out of lawful wedlock or who are slaves."[42]

On the basis of these church documents from 1702 and 1703, we were tempted to conclude that slavery, whether black or Amerindian, already had a legal foundation in New France. But a few pages later, the *Rituel* contains a confusing passage. Saint-Vallier repeated a passage from his catechism: he noted that if a party contracting marriage believed the other party to be free whereas that other person was actually a slave, then the marriage was null; he added that "there are no grounds for such an impediment in this kingdom [of France], where all persons are free."

The confusion did not stop there. Was the bishop denying there were slaves in Canada? When he left Quebec in 1694 for a stay in France, there were at least fifteen slaves in Canada, including three blacks. Ownership of these latter black slaves was guaranteed by the authorization Louis XIV had given in 1689; in April 1694 Saint-Vallier himself baptized and confirmed the black Jacques, who was in service to the merchant Leber; what's more, an eight-year-old Amerindian boy, named Bernard, died at the Hôtel-Dieu de Québec in July 1680, and was recorded as "My Lord Bishop's little savage."

But Saint-Vallier was referring to the *kingdom*. It should be noted here that the official term "the kingdom of France" applied to continental France, a distinction made clear in the edict of October 1716. Slavery was illegal in continental France: if a slave found refuge there, he became free. If the slave were only passing through France (for example in the case of slaves accompanying masters temporarily residing there), this did not automatically mean the slave lost his slave status. The apparent inconsistency arose from the fact that Saint-Vallier published his *Rituel* in France, whereas he was addressing the faithful in his diocese of Quebec.

INTENDANT RAUDOT AND THE LEGALIZATION OF SLAVERY IN 1709
The situation was all the more confusing because even within Canada there were people (we did not manage to identify them) who encouraged slaves to desert, on the grounds that slavery had no rightful place in the colony. As Intendant Raudot wrote, masters "are frustrated because they have laid out considerable sums" to acquire Amerindians, "who hear about the idea of liberty from people who have not purchased them, and as a result [these Amerindians] almost always leave their masters, under the pretext that in France there are no slaves."[43]

On April 13, 1709, the intendant put a stop to this situation. His ordinance began with a statement on the usefulness of slaves in Canada: "Having certain knowledge of the benefits that the colony would obtain if it were possible, through purchases made by the inhabitants themselves, to have Amerindians called Panis, whose nation is far removed from that country, and who can only be acquired from savages who sell them most often to the English of Carolina and who have sometimes sold them to people in this country." To those who claimed that "in France there are no slaves," the intendant replied: "this is not always the case, when one thinks of the colonies belonging to France, such as the islands of this continent [in the French West Indies], where all Negroes that people purchase continue to be viewed as such." Moreover, "since all colonies should be treated on the same footing, and since the people of the Panis nation are needed by the people of this country [New France] for the cultivation of land and other tasks that could be undertaken in the same way as the Negroes are needed in the islands [the French West Indies], and since these kinds of undertakings are useful to this colony," and given that it is necessary "to ensure the ownership of those who have bought and who will buy [such slaves] in the future," the intendant concluded: "We, at His Majesty's pleasure, order that all Panis and Negroes who have been bought and who shall be bought hereafter shall belong in full ownership to those who bought them as their slaves; and we hereby forbid said Panis and Negroes to leave their masters, and anyone else to tempt them away, under penalty of a fine of fifty livres." This ordinance had to be read out in Quebec City, Trois-Rivières and Montreal.[44] In Quebec the ordinance was read out on Sunday, April 21, 1709 before the church of the Lower Town, after the seven o'clock mass, and then before the door of the church of the Upper Town, at the end of the high mass.

Here we have the first official ordinance on slavery in Canada. It meant that blacks and Amerindians who had been purchased would remain in slavery, just like blacks in the Caribbean: whether Amerindian or black, slaves were the outright property of those persons who had acquired them. Raudot's ordinance served as the fundamental legal text establishing slavery in New France: in 1730, Intendant Hocquart would base his decisions on it, and in 1799, when the inhabitants of Montreal presented a petition to the House of Assembly about slavery, the first argument they invoked was this ordinance of 1709.[45]

Louis XIV had decided in 1689 that black slavery could exist in Canada, but 1709 was the first time that a specific ordinance was issued on slavery in the colony. The mere existence of such an ordinance was not that significant. More extraordinary was the fact that the ordinance marked the first official confirmation of the enslavement of an entire Amerindian nation, the Panis. Various tribes of the American West had traded in Panis with the English of Carolina, and then between Amerindians and the French. The Panis were now designated officially and legally for slavery. The very term "Panis" was generalized, and came to mean an Amerindian slave of whatever origin. This is why, in studying the history of slavery in Quebec, it is hard to determine exactly where Amerindian slaves were from, unless their origin was explicitly indicated: "Joseph, a Panis" or "Marie, a Panis" were not necessarily members of the Pawnee nation.

The immediate consequence of publication of this ordinance was that for the first time the sale of Panis slaves had to be notarized.

Two months later (on June 15), the notary Adhémar drew up the first known contract for the sale of a Panis: Madeleine Just, wife of the fur trader Pierre You d'Youville Ladécouverte, sold her Panis Pascal, aged about nineteen, for the sum of 120 livres to Lieutenant Pierre-Thomas Tarieu de Lapérade, husband of the celebrated Madeleine de Verchères.[46] Four months later, the same notary drew up another deed of sale involving a slave: on October 19, Jacques Nepveu living in Lachenaie sold an eleven-year-old Panis girl named Marie for the sum of 200 livres to his brother Jean-Baptiste, a merchant in Montreal; the young Panis was present at the transaction and gave her consent.

No notarized sales took place before 1709, but after that date they became increasingly common. In fact, Raudot's ordinance seems to have led to a speeding-up in the acquisition of Amerindian slaves, which is indicated by the total number of new slaves reaching New France each year.

Starting in 1710, the annual total of new Amerindian slaves could be counted in two digits: supply was relatively abundant.

Louis XV and Amerindian Slavery

When the intendant legalized Amerindian slavery, he only referred to Panis, but we should remember this was a generic term applied

SLAVE ARRIVALS 1700-1730

1700	7	1716	25
1701	6	1717	20
1702	2	1718	16
1703	12	1719	51
1704	6	1720	34
1705	3	1721	30
1706	7	1722	21
1707	3	1723	21
1708	8	1724	14
1709	5	1725	17
1710	12	1726	13
1711	10	1727	12
1712	20	1728	17
1713	26	1729	29
1714	34	1730	25
1715	32		

to Amerindian slaves more generally. Legalization targeted other tribes or nations, and the slave market soon included the Paducahs, Arkansas, Fox, Illinois, Sioux – in other words, any tribe that was not formally allied to the French. Missing from the list were the Algonquins, Montagnais, Abenakis and even the Iroquois, who signed a peace treaty with the French in 1701. There were exceptions: an Amerindian described as Montagnais was also considered a slave, whereas this was actually a slave who had lived for some time among the Montagnais, and was accordingly called Montagnais himself.

A distinction was drawn between allied Amerindians and non-allied Amerindians. Was there also a distinction between baptized Amerindians and pagan Amerindians? We should recall that according to an article of the charter of the Compagnie des Cent-Associés, a baptized Amerindian became a "French natural," in other words a citizen with full rights. The problem was raised in a civil lawsuit of 1733, between the fur trader Philippe You d'Youville Ladécouverte and

Captain Daniel Migeon de Lagauchetière. Ladécouverte owed 3,500 livres to Lagauchetière, who had therefore seized the Paducah Pierre, aged about twenty-six years. Pierre belonged to Ladécouverte and had been baptized in Montreal on September 11, 1723. In December 1732, the lieutenant general for civil and criminal matters in Montreal (the chief justice) endorsed the seizure, directing that the slave be sold in the market for Lagauchetière's benefit: the merchant Nolan de Lamarque bought the slave for 351 livres. Ladécouverte appealed to the Conseil supérieur, requesting that "the sale of the savage in question be declared void and dangerous for religion because it flies in the face of morality, given that [the person being sold] is a Christian." Ladécouverte even argued that the Paducah would enjoy "his freedom as he has done heretofore," which contradicted the Montreal judge's decision. In any case, Ladécouverte petitioned the judge for "having ordered the sale of a Christian on the market, where he was sold like some animal."

In attempting to nullify the seizure of his slave, and in petitioning the judge, Ladécouverte cast himself as the indignant adversary of slavery. But in 1709, his mother had sold a baptized Panis, and he owned a baptized Amerindian himself. In any event, his petition challenged the legality of Amerindian slavery.

What did the Conseil supérieur do? It referred both parties to Intendant Hocquart, who in 1730 had published Raudot's original ordinance, as a way of reminding people it was still in force. In fact, Hocquart based his own decision on Raudot's ordinance.[47] He upheld the decision of the court, declaring that the Paducah had been sold legally, and identified Nolan de Lamarque as the rightful owner. As for Ladécouverte, he could redeem the slave by paying 351 livres, plus court costs as well as the expense of caring for the sick Amerindian. Ladécouverte was already heavily in debt, and preferred to let things drop. When the slave was buried in Montreal, on August 5, 1747, he still belonged to Nolan de Lamarque.

Raudot's ordinance served once again as the guarantee of ownership, but was still subject to the king's pleasure, whereas Louis XV had neither endorsed nor condemned the practice. Intendant Hocquart therefore took advantage of this lawsuit to pressure the king to decide the matter once and for all. He wrote to the king explaining the nature of the lawsuit and requested a formal law on Amerindian slavery.

The minister wrote back from Versailles on April 20, 1734: the decision regarding the Paducah was upheld, but the king did not see fit to "issue any regulations on the state of this nation and others with whom the French neither trade nor are at war, but [His Majesty] wishes that customary practice in this regard be followed in Canada."[48]

The following year, 1735, the royal mail again referred to this subject, providing greater clarity this time. The king had explained the preceding year to the governor and intendant why "His Majesty has not approved the proposal they had made to promulgate a formal law on the Panis savages and others with whom the French neither trade nor are at war. [His Majesty] maintains the same position on the matter; but the judges of the colony may follow customary practice in considering these Amerindians as slaves. Regarding the manner in which they are to be freed," the intendant could issue an ordinance requiring masters to notarize any such emancipation; the king was willing to defer to the judgment of the governor and the intendant. The king responded in the same manner in 1736.[49]

The intendant asked the king for a law specifically applying to Amerindian slaves, but Louis XV did not see fit to grant this request even though blacks were officially considered slaves in the French colonies. How can this distinction be explained, since the royal mail gave no explanation of its own?

Louis XV may have based his decision on considerations of foreign policy. France had an interest in contracting the greatest number of alliances with Amerindian nations in the interior of the continent, as a way of extending its economic hinterland, but alliances were impossible as long as France treated tribes there as a source of slaves. The farther the French explored westward in search of "the Sea of Asia," the more they had to rely on alliances with Amerindian tribes. In 1720 for example, the Compagnie française des Indes complained about voyageurs trading furs on the Missouri and Arkansas rivers who "try to sow discord between the Amerindian nations and incite them to war in order to acquire slaves there, which is not only contrary to the King's ordinances, but also extremely detrimental to the Company's trading interests."[50] Gaultier de Lavérendrye suffered from the same problem; the fur trade suffered when western tribes raided to acquire slaves instead of peaceably hunting fur-bearing animals. According to the Jesuit Coquart, Lavérendrye "will bring in more slaves than packages" of furs.[51] Amerindians were potential suppliers of furs, but if France treated them as potential slaves it would upset the complex system of French-Indian alliances, and it could not afford to do this. However, we are inclined to believe that Louis XV abstained from taking a hard-and-fast position because of France's traditional Amerindian policy. Other European nations were bent on destroying Amerindians, or on driving them as far away from colonial settlements as possible; but France supported the work of missionaries fanning out into the interior of the continent, with a view to converting Amerindians and teaching them French. In 1627, France had even acknowledged that a baptized Amerindian became a French citizen with full rights, and this policy was best articulated by Colbert when he said that the French and Amerindians should "form only one people and one blood."[52] France was the only European nation to grant this preferential treatment to Amerindians. This helps explain why Louis XV refused to sanction slavery by statute, and accepted only that customary practice be followed. The colony's judges, the king wrote, could follow custom in regarding these savages as slaves. This custom had been established by the Raudot ordinance of 1709, subsequently reaffirmed by Hocquart in 1730 and 1733. It is therefore wrong to claim, as the publisher Hector de Saint-Denys Garneau did in his 1928 edition of François-Xavier Garneau's *Histoire* (vol. II, p. 92, n90), that Louis XV actually prohibited Panis slavery in 1736.

Louis XV did more than tolerate customary practice: he left it to Hocquart's discretion to decide whether Amerindians could only regain their freedom when the act of emancipation was notarized. It was up to the intendant, the king wrote in the same letter, to judge whether masters should emancipate their slaves before a notary, or simply by declaring their slaves to be free.

However, leaving it up to the intendant to decide involved a potential conflict of interest: Hocquart owned five Amerindian slaves himself, and Governor Beauharnois had owned a good twenty slaves. Hocquart decided to make things as clear as possible. In an ordinance dated September 1, 1736, he required owners emancipating slaves "to make a declaration to this effect before a notary, who will write minutes of the act, which will be duly registered in the nearest royal court." Any act of emancipation not following this procedure would be "null and void."[53]

WERE AMERINDIAN SLAVES DESTINED FOR EXPORT?
One point in the law still needed to be cleared up: if an Amerindian slave legally belonged to a master who had the right to sell him, could the master transport the slave anywhere else – for example to the Caribbean? This problem arose within a year after the first ordinance was published.

The merchant François-Marie Boüat had sold a Panis to Monsieur Mounier for the sum of 300 livres, apparently indicating to Mounier that he could transport the Panis to the Caribbean for resale. Mounier boarded a ship for the French West Indies with his slave, but the Panis had no desire to leave New France and so disappeared without trace. Mounier contacted Intendant Raudot to find out if he was really the owner and if he was allowed to sell a Canadian Panis in the Caribbean. Raudot replied on March 23, 1710: Mounier, owner of the Panis, was authorized to seize him wherever he could be found; as to the question of whether he had the right to sell the Panis in the Caribbean, if Boüat had claimed as much to Mounier, then Boüat should take his Panis back and reimburse Mounier. What basis did the intendant give for this decision? "Whereas our authority with respect to policy does not [extend] beyond the colony for whose benefit it was made ... the Panis can only be considered slaves as long as they remain here [New France] and it is therefore illegal to transport them anywhere else for the purpose of sale."[54]

Since the ordinance of 1709 applied to New France alone, the Panis were only considered slaves as long as they remained in the colony. If they left New France, they were free. Mounier had been told he could export his Panis, but this was not the case, so he was entitled to get his 300 livres back.

Despite Raudot's ordinance, Panis slavery was based on customary practice in Canada rather than a royal edict, so some slave exports did take place. During a trial of 1740, Chevalier Dormicourt said several owners had sent Panis to the Caribbean to serve as slaves.[55] Who were they? Our research has only turned up a few fragments of information.

In 1730, the Panis Charles took part in a mutiny while in military service at Fort Niagara. He was sentenced to deportation and was quickly transported as a slave to Martinique.[56] In 1734, when Louis XV learned that the Fox Indians had sent an embassy to Quebec, but had then attacked the French, he ordered the two emissaries and the woman accompanying them to be transported on the first vessel bound for the Caribbean, to be sold there as the king's property. One of the emissaries died before departure, the woman escaped and was retaken, and as a result a Fox man and woman were transported to the Caribbean, where they lived as slaves.[57] In 1747, a Panis was taken from the English along with four blacks: he fled with them and was caught again. For added security, the five were transported to Martinique, where they were sold on behalf of their owners.[58]

Despite Raudot's ordinance of 1710, this state policy of transporting Amerindian slaves to the Caribbean could encourage individual owners to do just the same. For example, in one famous case, Chevalier Marc-Antoine Huart Dormicourt owned a Panis slave, Marie-Marguerite Radisson *dite* Duplessis, but he became dissatisfied with her, and entered into a contract in 1740 with a certain Aubry to transport her to the "islands of America." While in prison awaiting her departure, the slave managed to file a lawsuit in which she tried to prove she was not a slave. At no time was Dormicourt's right to transport her to the French West Indies challenged. But the matter was referred to the provost of Quebec, the Conseil supérieur and Intendant Hocquart. The Panis slave's case was dismissed and she left for the Caribbean.[59]

This practice of sending slaves of unhappy masters to the Caribbean became so popular that Governor La Galissonnière and Intendant Hocquart proposed to the king that it be done systematically. Even when Amerindians were acquired at a young age, they did not always manage well in French; on reaching adulthood, many of them headed back west to become "savages" again. And these fugitives could become a danger for the colony, because they knew its geography so well. In 1747, Canadian authorities therefore proposed to the king that owners should not keep these Amerindians beyond the age of sixteen or seventeen years, after which they should be sold in the Caribbean, where they obviously had no means of escape. This closely resembled the plan Louisiana Governor Lemoyne de Bienville had proposed in 1706 and 1708, with the difference that he had proposed bartering two Panis for every black slave.

Government officials in metropolitan France objected to this proposal of 1747: they were particularly concerned about the effect any systematic transfer of slaves abroad would have on Amerindian nations. In 1749, these officials submitted the plan to the attention of Governor La Jonquière and Intendant Bigot,[60] but nothing further was heard about it. The export of Amerindian slaves to the Caribbean may have continued without any need for official state authorization.

Masters could get rid of Amerindian slaves by transporting them to the Caribbean, but could they also transport slaves to France? In principle, France was a land of liberty, so we might at first assume that masters could neither send slaves to France nor bring them back from there. But this would be jumping to conclusions, except in the case of permanent expatriation. In October 1716 the regent published an edict allowing people to send their Caribbean slaves to France to confirm them in the Catholic faith or to learn a trade: the slaves "cannot claim to have gained their liberty on the pretext of their arrival in the Kingdom, and they shall be required to return to the colonies when their masters deem it necessary." Slaves could not marry in France without their owners' consent, but once inhabitants of the Caribbean had returned to France, having sold their homes in the French West Indies, they would have to send their slaves back to the Caribbean the following year. The same applied to officers on leave from the Caribbean; once their leave was over, they had to send their slaves back. In either case, slaves who were not sent back became free. Furthermore, Article 14 of this edict of 1716 refused to grant some fugitives asylum: if black slaves left French colonies without the permission of their masters and settled in France, they could not claim to have gained their freedom and their masters could reclaim them wherever they settled, and send them back to the colonies.[61]

However, a procureur du roi, or Crown attorney, stated that a "flood of Negroes" was reaching France, hoping to free themselves from servitude. Slaves believed they were entitled to seek refuge in France, where they could regain their liberty, and take advantage of official negligence in enforcing restrictions. Louis XV tightened regulations by issuing a declaration in December 1733 that renewed his earlier edict. Slaves reaching France with their masters could stay no longer than three years, and they could not marry even with their owners' consent.[62] Despite this new measure, and given the lackadaisical application of the law, it seems that France, and more particularly Paris, "has become a public market where men have been sold to the highest bidder; every bourgeois, every worker has his own Negro slave." A measure in 1762 was adopted to stop such abuses: anyone owning black slaves had to make an explicit declaration to that effect, and the buying and selling of slaves was forbidden.[63] France was not exactly the classical land of liberty...

Slavery was tolerated up to a point in France, and as a result Canadian owners brought slaves there, and even Amerindian ones. We found a few examples. In 1720, Augustin Legardeur de Courte-manche's widow sailed for France with a slave. The lawyer Claude Le Beau wrote that he had seen a Fox chief who had been sent by Governor Beauharnois to serve his brother, an intendant at Rochefort, reduced to slavery at Quebec in 1730 or early 1731. The Panis Jacques was sentenced to the galleys in France for having sexually abused a girl. The Panis Constant, slave of Paul-François Raimbault de Simblin, was convicted of theft, banished for life, and placed on board a ship bound for France. Governor General Vaudreuil-Cavagnial left New France for good in 1760 with his black, Canon, who would serve him in the Bastille.[64] Were all these Amerindians or blacks still considered slaves, once they had crossed the Atlantic? Whatever the case, they were slaves on leaving New France.

"A Black is a Slave, Wherever He May Be Found"

In 1689, Louis XIV had granted permission to the people of Canada to own black slaves; in 1709, Intendant Raudot declared that blacks who had been purchased were slaves; the regent called on the Compagnie des Indes to send a cargo of blacks to Quebec. More official decisions were made. In December 1721, the king issued an edict preventing minors emancipated from wardship to sell blacks they owned. This edict came into force in Canada on October 5, 1722 when it was registered by the Conseil supérieur of Quebec.[65] In October 1727, the king issued another edict to regulate foreign commerce in the American colonies: blacks found on vessels trading abroad would be forfeited to the state; this edict came into force in Canada on September 17, 1728, when it was registered by the Conseil supérieur. On June 19, 1748, the Conseil supérieur registered another edict issued in 1745: blacks fleeing enemy colonies in order to take refuge in the French colonies, and any effects they brought with them, belonged to the king and proceeds from any sale thereof also belonged to the king. According to this latter edict, a black person who thought he had gained freedom by taking refuge in a French colony was mistaken; this edict registered by the Conseil supérieur put an end to any hopes that black slaves held by the English could become free simply by setting foot on French soil.

There was no question of denying the right of asylum – even when asylum was granted, a black person remained a slave! For example in 1732 a black slave ran away from New England. There was no state of war at the time, so the English came to Quebec to reclaim the slave, but Governor Beauharnois refused to hand him over. Instead of releasing him, the governor donated the black man to the nuns of the Hôpital-Général.[66] The right of asylum only prevented a slave's extradition, Governor Jonquière wrote, because of the principle acknowledged by the English just as much as the French, that "a black is a slave, wherever he might be found"[67] – unless he had been formally emancipated.

THE CAPITULATION OF 1760 AND THE MAINTENANCE OF SLAVERY

When the Articles of Capitulation were signed in Montreal in September 1760, they reasserted the legal character of Amerindian and black slavery, and extended it under British rule. Governor Vaudreuil-Cavagnial made a special request relating to slavery which became Article 47:

> The Negroes and Panis of both sexes shall remain in their quality of slaves in the possession of the French and Canadians to whom they belong; they shall be at liberty to keep them in their service in the colony or to sell them; and they may also continue to bring them up in the Roman Religion.[68]

General Amherst replied, "Granted, except those who shall have been made prisoners." Vaudreuil-Cavagnial requested that the slaves be recognized as the property of their masters and Amherst agreed to this request, which is hardly surprising, considering that both men represented slave-owning powers.

Whatever the numbers of these Amerindian and black slaves, there were evidently enough of them to deserve a special article in the treaty of capitulation.

And so the institution of slavery in Canada was first recognized and amply protected by French law, and was then extended under the British regime by another statute, the Articles of Capitulation of 1760.

CHAPTER THREE

Nearly 4200 Slaves in Quebec

In a letter to the minister Maurepas in 1744, Gaultier de Lavérendrye wrote about his toils in His Majesty's service for the good of the colony, citing three advantages in particular: "the great number of persons to whom this enterprise affords a living, of the slaves that are obtained for the country, and the furs of which formerly the English got the benefit."[69] If Lavérendrye considered slavery to be the second advantage in importance, ahead of furs, then slavery must have been a perfectly legal institution, accepted just as readily by the authorities as by the inhabitants of New France; and there had to be sufficient numbers of slaves for the minister to be impressed by the argument. We set out to establish the number of these slaves.

THE CHALLENGES OF COMING UP WITH A NUMBER

We combed the civil registries from the beginnings of New France to colonial Quebec in the nineteenth century, which involved thorough searches of Catholic and Protestant records. Since the Church required that slaves be baptized and buried in consecrated ground, this seemed a promising way to account for much of the slave population. In fact, these records provided us with the greater part of our documentation: of 4200 slaves we identified, over 3000 show up in civil registries. Additional information was obtained by going through patient records and death registries at the Hôtel-Dieu de Québec (the records for this period at the Hôtel-Dieu de Montréal have unfortunately disappeared) and in the general hospitals.

Census roles, particularly the one taken in Quebec in 1744, were also helpful, at least when census takers took the trouble to enumerate slaves. In rare cases, lists of communicants and confirmation candidates have survived. We also searched notarial records of the deeds of sale and the freeing of slaves, as well as those wills and inventories after death likely to mention slaves. What else? The official correspondence of colonial authorities, (extremely rare) private letters, travel narratives, accounts books, and finally newspapers that started appearing in the second half of the eighteenth century. In short, we hope to give a more or less representative view of slavery in Quebec by tapping all sources of information on the colony from its beginnings until the formal abolition of slavery in the nineteenth century.

The biggest challenge was identifying the slave's name, age, origin, condition, and the owner's name. For example, where the records indicate that Jacques, a nineteen-year-old Panis slave belonging to Mr. A, was baptized in 1740, then we know this was the same Jacques, a twenty-one-year-old slave belonging to the same Mr. A., buried in 1742. The civil registries were our most abundant source of information, but if they had identified slaves as completely as they did non-slave families, our task would have been far easier.

In actual fact, slaves were not generally identified as rigorously as non-slaves were. Civil registries do not always bother to give the slave's name. Some priests only noted they had baptized or buried a "Negro" or "Panis." Close to a thousand slaves in our *Dictionnaire des esclaves et de leurs propriétaires* remain nameless. Was the Panis Pierre, buried in 1750, the same as the anonymous Panis baptized in 1749? To give a really definite answer, we would have to compare ages and owners. But what if the age (in any case a guesstimate) or the owner's name were only given in one case? We could just as well be dealing with a single slave as with two separate slaves.

What of slaves with a first name: did the slave generally use the name he or she received at baptism or another more common name? In 1731, Louison, belonging to Governor Beauharnois, was admitted to the Hôtel-Dieu de Québec, but the following year this young Amerindian was baptized under the name of Charles-Louis, and nothing prevented him from reappearing in another document under the name of Charles.

What of a single owner with several slaves bearing the same name? In 1729, Governor Beauharnois owned two slaves named Charlotte, one of whom was identified as belonging to the Fox nation, while the other was variously identified as a Fox or a Panis: the nun at the Hôtel-Dieu de Québec noted in the burial register "the taller Charlotte." The voyageur Jacques Cardinal gave his first name to an Outagami slave he had baptized in 1718, and both were later buried under the name Jacques Cardinal. The Fox Gilles-Hyacinthe belonged to Intendant Gilles Hocquart, but documents give the slave's name variously as Gilles and Hyacinthe, while Intendant Hocquart had another Panis slave named Gilles: in this case we are able to distinguish between these two Gilles, because in each case we have their age, and the margin is quite significant.

In general, references to the age of slaves are remarkably vague. How could the age of a black or Amerindian be properly estimated when the slave had been born abroad and lacked identity papers? At the moment of baptism, the priest was only making an eyeball estimate, jotting down for instance "twelve years old." But such estimates were sometimes made by different people in different circumstances, leading to the most confusing results: a Panis was supposedly eight years old at baptism; when he was admitted a month later to the Hôtel-Dieu de Québec, he was ten years old; and when he died soon afterwards, a nun gave his age as seven years. So the researcher is faced with the problem of a single slave identified by name and owner, whose age nonetheless fluctuates in official records. Whenever we encounter a Panis or black slave in historical records, we can expect him to be attached to an owner. First, because this enables us to determine whether the Panis or black in question was still in bondage; and second because it may no longer have been considered important (for example at a burial) to include the owner's name. And when the owner's name is indicated, we would naturally hope to find both first and last names and the owner's occupation. But in that case, we would be excessively optimistic! Most of the time, the occupation is omitted, and we must consult other sources. We identified about 1500 slave owners, 1100 of them by their first and last names, even though these identifications may lead to confusion. An example is the Gadois-Mogé family, where father and son bore the same names. Even more confusion may arise in cases where only the last name of slave owners appears in the record.

For the purposes of identification, records of a particular slave's origin are not particularly reliable. A native Amerindian slave might be identified in different records as belonging to two distinct tribes. A single slave could be identified as a Fox in one record, and as a Panis in another, and indeed the term "Panis" could be used to designate any Amerindian slave, of whatever origin, which only makes things more confusing! Similar difficulties arise in records describing black slaves: an individual might not be identified specifically as black, although other sources identify him as black.

We would have had felt more confident about our results, if all slaves or former slaves were designated as such in the documentary sources. But of 4200 slaves, we found that only 456 Amerindians and 228 blacks were either indicated as slaves or were subject to a commercial transaction. In Quebec, people were reluctant to use the term "slavery" although the reality was there for all to see. The priest making entries in the civil registry hesitated to use the word "slave" or could not be bothered to use it. We repeatedly found cases where an Amerindian or black was baptized and had been acquired by purchase, but was nonetheless still not specifically referred to as a slave. In most cases, the record-keeper merely noted that a given Amerindian or black belonged to a given owner.

Nearly 2700 Amerindian slaves

Our *Dictionnaire* contains nearly 2700 Amerindian slaves, although we came across a good hundred more we could not include in that work. For example, we came across Amerindians in the historical record, about whom few details were known, although they lived in parishes where slavery was thriving: they were bound to be slaves too, although the lack of more detailed information prevented us from counting them among the slave population. We included the following aboriginal people, without counting them in the above-mentioned figure: 24 Ojibwa (living at Sault-Sainte-Marie and the entrance of Lake Superior), a Sioux ambassador, six Montagnais, two Miamis, five Foxes (held hostage), an Eskimo, a Métis and a Papinachois: we had no proof they were held in bondage, but we included them because members of their nations were already in bondage. We included fifteen Amerindians from Detroit and Michilimackinac after 1796, without counting them in the above figure, since these two places ceased to be part of Canadian territory after 1796, and were transferred to the United States; moreover, Amerindians too young to have experienced slavery under Canadian rule could not be incorporated into this study. For these reasons, we ended up with a total of 2683 Amerindian slaves.

How does this slave population of 2683 break down? We included 456 Amerindians explicitly described as slaves in historical records, 251 of whom were Panis. The next group consists of Amerindians described as belonging to specific owners, which by basing ourselves on historical records we interpreted as being equivalent to actual property; this second group consists of 1431 Amerindians, of whom 1011 were Panis. A third group consists of 106 other Amerindians, identified in records as domestic servants, whether because they were Panis (all Panis entered the colony as slaves) or because they were from nations deep in the interior of the continent. A fourth group consists of 129 Amerindians described in our sources as residing with one Canadian or another: we included these eighty-nine Panis and forty more Amerindians of various origins as slaves, either because they came from nations far afield or because of the family they lived with. A fifth group consists of twenty-seven adopted Amerindians, twenty-three of them Panis, and four more Amerindians of unknown origin, all of whom had come from far-away territories, and entered the colony as slaves. Finally, a sixth group consists of 269 Panis without specific details, and fifty-four more Amerindians, who most likely were or had been in bondage because they belonged to the Fox, Paducah or other Amerindian tribes that were frequently enslaved.

This total of 2683 Amerindians includes 339 children (265 of them Panis) who were subjected to the same conditions of servitude as their parents: according to established practice, the children of a slave mother were slaves just like their mother, irrespective of the father's status. To sum up:

Amerindians described as slaves	465	17.3%
Amerindians belonging to an owner	1440	53.7%
Amerindian servants or domestics, who were most likely slaves	106	4.0%
Amerindians residing with particular Canadians and who were probably slaves	129	4.8%
Amerindians adopted or raised by Canadians, who were or had been in bondage	27	1.0%
Amerindians about whom nothing specific is known, who were or had been in bondage (Panis, Foxes, Paducahs or others)	516	19.2%

Now in distinguishing between those definitely enslaved and those probably enslaved, we get the following results:

Amerindians who were slaves at one time (including any Panis)	2424	90.3%
Amerindians who were most likely slaves	259	9.7%

We are therefore definite about the condition of 90.3% of the Amerindians we chose for the purposes of this study. It would be surprising if the other 9.7% did not experience slavery: they were from nations deep in the interior of the continent, or lived with slave-owning families.

MANY PANIS

It is not easy to know exactly where these 2683 Amerindian slaves were from: the specific tribe of origin is not always indicated. For example, the Amerindian Augustin, baptized at the age of five in Sainte-Anne-de-la-Pérade in 1745, is said to be from the West.[70] The Amerindian woman Charles-Josephe belonging to Guillaume Cartier of Saint-François-du-Lac, was baptized there in 1720 at the age of three years: the priest noted she had been brought from the Ottawas. This is an intriguing detail: as allies of the French, the Ottawas were not enslaved, so she must have been captured by the Ottawas somewhere farther West. The vagueness of historical documents means we cannot definitively establish the origin of all Amerindian slaves: in fact, 16% of these slaves were of unknown origin.

Moreover, widespread use of the word "Panis" led to total confusion. The Panis nation provided a lot of slaves, and people in New France got into the habit of calling any Amerindian slave a Panis (in French "Panis" designated a male, while "Panise" designated a female). Who exactly were the Panis? In a memoir of 1757, Bougainville summed up the French perspective of the time. In writing about the post of the Western Sea, he noted, "One of the traders at this post is a Panis, from a savage nation some 12,000 strong; other nations war with them and sell us their slaves." Bougainville also wrote that the trading post beyond the Great Lakes usually produced forty to sixty "rouge" (red) or Panis slaves each year: "this nation, situated on the Missouri ... plays the same role in America that the Negroes do in Europe."[71] But he was wrong in claiming this was the only "savage nation we believe we can treat in this manner" and "this is the only post where this traffic takes place." Unless he was only referring to the year 1757. The French regime traded in slaves with many other Amerindian nations, in several other places. Whatever the case, Bougainville considered the Panis to be the Negroes of America, although they were red rather than black.

There is an additional problem with the name Panis, however, since a French family by the name of Panis settled in Quebec in the seventeenth century. This family eventually came to be known as the Janis, sometimes written Janisse, but they also owned Panis slaves, which explains that one record indicates a "Panise de Janisse" or "Panis woman belonging to the Janisse family."

Panis lived in the upper Missouri and Kansas basins, roughly in the area now occupied by the State of Nebraska.[72] They began appearing on maps and in the exploration narratives of French voyageurs of the second half of the seventeenth century, although their name was variously given (in French) as: "Pana, Panis Ricaras, Pammaha, Panis Oasa, Panis noirs and Panis blancs." Of the Arkansas River, Father Charlevoix wrote: "The river comes, it is said, from the country of certain Amerindians who are called Panis noirs; and I believe they are the same who are better known under the name Panis Ricaras. I have a slave of this nation with me."[73] Sometimes, more detail is provided, for example at Verchères in 1735, at the baptism of a white Panis, although in recording such details, priests sometimes hesitated between "Panis or Sioux" and "Panis Assiniboine."

The Panis first appeared in the historical record in 1687, whether the term meant they really belonged to the Panis nation or was applied generically to all Amerindians of whatever origin. At first, only a few turned up in New France each year, but gradually they were brought in larger numbers to the colony, twenty and thirty each year, and ultimately fifty-two in 1761, after which their annual number decreased rapidly in the 1780s, and only one was left in 1802.

The Panis are the only Amerindian nation to appear each year in slave documents with such astonishing regularity. There was a true Panis slave market, just as there was an ebony slave market.

Other Slaves from the Mississippi Basin

Apart from the Panis who came from the upper Missouri, Amerindian slaves included representatives of various tribes from the Mississippi Basin.

According to Bougainville, fifty leagues from the village of the Kansa Indians (or Kansé) lived the Aiouois (also called Aiouès or Aiyoués), known in English simply as Iowas. Two members of this tribe turn up in our lists, one aged twelve who was captured in his village, the other who had been among the Amerindians of Wabash (in modern-day Indiana) at aged eleven, before being handed over to the French.

The Missouri Indians inhabited the river basin of the same name, particularly the lower part of the basin. At least two of these Amerindians were baptized and enslaved in Quebec, one of them a female.

In this same river basin, but downstream near the Kansas River, lay the country of the Kansa Indians, two of whose members were baptized and enslaved at Montreal and Saint-François-du-Lac.

Five young Arkansas Indians came from farther to the south, on the Arkansas River: they were baptized at Lachine, Montreal, Sainte-Anne-de-la-Pérade and Quebec City.

Farther to the west, beyond Arkansas and Kansa territory, lay the Paducahs, today known as the Comanches: fifty-two members of this nation were held in slavery in Quebec, although given their proximity to the Panis nation, the two nations were often confused.

In the far south of Louisiana at the mouth of the Mississippi was found the Ouacha tribe, although only a single member – a female – was enslaved in Quebec.

Heading north along the west bank of the Mississippi was the Natchez tribe, made famous by Chateaubriand: two Natchez Indians were held slaves, and baptized at Quebec City and Detroit respectively. North of this tribe lived the Choctaws or Flatheads, six of whom feature on our list of slaves. And north of the Choctaws lived the Chickasaws, against whom two military campaigns were conducted, in 1736 and 1738: eighteen Chickasaws were slaves in Quebec, sixteen of them reaching the colony during these years of war.

On the Ohio River lived the Shawnees: this nation provided a single slave, a woman, who had a little girl by her master Jacques-François Lacelle at Detroit, in 1798. Farther up the west bank of the Mississippi lived the Cahokia tribe, one of whom was enslaved and baptized at Detroit. The neighbouring Tamaroa nation produced one eight-year-old slave. Finally, this inventory of Amerindian slaves from the Mississippi basin includes seven members of the Illinois tribe, all of whom appear in our *Dictionnaire*. These Amerindians include the Illinois man referred to above, who sold his son into slavery in order to get drunk on the proceeds of sale. More than 1700 Amerindian slaves came to Quebec from the Mississippi Basin.

A CONTINGENT OF SLAVES FROM OUT WEST

More slaves came from out West, and by "West" we mean the whole country beyond Lake Superior, known at the time as "the Post of the Western Sea." These were mainly Sioux Indians, on whom the Crees were then waging war, and the Assiniboine nation, allies of the French. In 1696, the first Sioux Indian appeared in Montreal, but in the capacity of ambassador, and was buried on February 3 that year: he is not counted here as a slave. The first Sioux slaves go back to 1712: they were initially very rare, but starting in 1733, a few came to Quebec each year at a time when Gaultier de Lavérendrye was pushing ever westward. According to the Jesuit Coquart in 1742, Gaultier de Lavérendrye's fur-trading activities suffered from the fact that Assiniboine and Cree hunters sometimes left off hunting to capture a few of these Sioux: "the number of slaves was so great that, according to the report and the expression of the savages, they occupied in their march more than four arpents."[74]

Many Sioux slaves must have come to Quebec, because Gaultier de Lavérendrye emphasized his toils provided the Crown with the benefit of "the slaves that are obtained for the country." We documented only sixty Sioux slaves, although others may well have been referred to by the generic name of Panis: indeed, the "Panis" slaves belonging to Gaultier de Lavérendrye were most likely Sioux.

Among the slaves from the West, we also documented fourteen Brochet (or Fish) Indians, who were said to come from a nation "towards the Western Sea."

Even though Gaultier de Lavérendrye was allied with the Crees and Assiniboines, some members of these nations may well have been reduced to servitude. Our list includes three Assiniboines and five Crees, although they may simply have been identified as such because the French had bought them from Crees and Assiniboines.

SLAVES FROM THE GREAT LAKES REGION

The next group of Amerindian slaves in our geographical survey were from nations in the Great Lakes region.

The Ojibwa Indians lived in the area around Sault Sainte Marie, which explains their historic French name of "Saulteux." They had long-established relations with the French, who sometimes took Ojibwa women as mistresses or wives. The most famous example of French-Ojibwa intermarriage was in the Hamelin family: both Charles and his son Louis married Ojibwa women, and had children with them. Despite these relationships, our list of Amerindian slaves includes seven Ojibwa, unless these were Amerindian slaves whom the French had bought from the Ojibwa.

The Fox Indians meanwhile – also known as the Outagamis – lived between the western shores of Lake Michigan and the Mississippi. They had long fought the French and their allies. Lamothe-Cadillac invited them to settle near Detroit, as a means of pacifying them: about forty families accepted the invitation but, in 1712, the Hurons and Ottawa could no longer put up with Fox arrogance and attacked them. Although some managed to escape, most of the women and children were enslaved and sold to the French.

War broke out again between the Fox nation and the French. In 1716, the Fox Indians faced the full onslaught of a French military expedition, were defeated and had to provide hostages. Fighting resumed and they sent ambassadors, but the king ordered them all to be arrested and transported to the Caribbean for sale as slaves. Fox slaves started reaching Quebec in 1712: we documented sixty-four from 1712 to 1719, and thirty-one more from 1730 to 1734. The total number of documented Fox slaves was 134, of whom nine were born in Quebec to slave parents.

The Menominees lived in the Green Bay region: six members of this nation were slaves in Quebec. The Mascouten Indians lived in the same region, west of Lake Michigan, between the Fox and Illinois nations: only three Mascoutens were held in bondage. South of Lake Michigan lived the Potawatomis, six of whom turn up in historical records as slaves. The Ottawas were traditional allies of the French: two members of this tribe were slaves.

South of Lake Ontario lived the Iroquois Confederacy. For an entire century, the French considered the Iroquois Five Nations to be the scourge of God: if there was any single group of enemy Amerindians the French wanted to reduce to slavery it was the Iroquois nations, the most aggressive of which were the Mohawks. Once Amerindian slavery was established in the mid-seventeenth century, the French began considering enslaving the Iroquois. In 1687, Governor Brisay de Denonville sent Iroquois prisoners to France where they toiled as galley slaves. Louis XIV found these slave imports profitable and encouraged the governor to capture the greatest possible number of Iroquois "robust and accustomed to the task," so they could serve on galleys. But on second thoughts, a wiser policy seemed to lie in granting them their freedom: they were sent back to Canada, where Governor Buade de Frontenac received them at his table before sending them home to Iroquois territory. It was hoped that good treatment would help them forget "whatever distress they had known during their slavery."[75] The Peace of Montreal was concluded in 1701, at a time when Amerindian slavery was becoming more widespread, although under terms of the treaty, the French could no longer hold Iroquois slaves.

To the south of Iroquois territory, near the Ohio River, lived the Wolf tribe, allies of the Iroquois: three members of this tribe were held in slavery. The tribe was sometimes confused with another tribe living south of Iroquois territory, variously called Mohicans, Mahigan, Maraingans and Moraingans. French colonial documents describe them as English Amerindians or on the English side. Between 1748 and 1760, five members of this tribe were in New France, during the final years of the colonial struggle between Great Britain and France.

SLAVES FROM NORTHERN NATIONS
The historical record also indicates that slaves were taken from an aboriginal nation called "Gens des terres," "Têtes de boules" or Montagnais. Bougainville used the expression "Gens des terres" and "Têtes de boules." According to the engineer Franquet, the Montagnais "wandered, without any fixed abode" between the Saint Lawrence River and Hudson Bay, and were commonly referred to as "Gens des terres." We understand this group included Amerindians

from the backcountry, among them the Papinachois and Naskapis.

Two Amerindians from the "Gens des terres" nation were held as slaves. In addition, two "Têtes de boules" were referred to as Panis, which under terms of the ordinance of 1709 meant they were slaves, even if "Têtes de boules" from the upper Saint Maurice River came down to Trois-Rivières to trade in furs. A single Papinachois and a single Naskapi are identified in the historical record as slaves.

We documented twenty-five Montagnais slaves, although it is not clear whether these were members of the Montagnais nation which Franquet loosely equated with these northern nations, or whether these were Amerindians from the Montagnais nation allied to the French from the very beginning of the colony and who could therefore not be held in slavery.

Finally, we documented twelve Inuit slaves. The French had long tried to establish friendly relations with the Inuit nation, but all of these overtures had failed. According to Bougainville's memoir of 1757, the Eskimos were "the most intractable and cruel" natives of North America, whereas the engineer Franquet claimed in 1752 that these Eskimos could not be made more human since they were treacherous cannibals.[76] Inuit slaves did not live long: seven of these twelve Inuit died at an average age of 17.6 years.

THE ADVANTAGE OF TAKING SLAVES FROM FAR-AWAY TERRITORIES
Native slaves can be broken down by geographic origin, as follows:

Mississippi Valley	1782	66.9%
Western territories (beyond Lake Superior)	83	3.1%
Great Lakes Region	167	6.3%
Northern Nations	43	1.6%
Of unknown origin	588	22.1%

Of the 588 Amerindian slaves whose geographic origin is unknown, 28 were Métis whose parents were Amerindian slaves and Canadians: we have counted them among the slaves, since the children of a slave mother were slaves just like their mother, irrespective of their father's condition. Such children could only be considered free if they had been formally emancipated.

Overall, these Amerindian slaves generally came from deep in the interior of the continent. Over three-quarters of them were from the Great Lakes region and the territory beyond Lake Superior and the Mississippi River. Buying slaves as far as possible from French territory offered an advantage: it was much harder for slaves to return home.

At Least 1443 Blacks

Establishing an inventory of black slaves proved just as difficult as putting together the one on Amerindian slaves. We first had to be careful not to assume that members of the Nègre or Noir families were black slaves, just as we had to be careful not to take Canadians named Sauvage for Amerindians; in 1752, the Hôtel-Dieu de Québec patient registry shows a Calvinist named Joseph Nègre *dit* Latreille, from the diocese of Riez; in other records, we found Jean-Baptiste Nègre *dit* Saint-Jean, and also the Noir *dit* Rolland family. It was fairly easy to avoid falling into these traps.

Precise identification of black slaves posed the same problems as that of Amerindian slaves. Many blacks appear anonymously in the civil registry, their age variously reported as young or old depending on who was making the entry, and their owner's name often missing, even though it would have helped us to identify them.

We included 1443 blacks in our *Dictionnaire.* The formal abolition of slavery dates from 1834 but blacks who were considered slaves or who belonged to an owner actually disappear from the historical record in the first years of the nineteenth century. After 1800, we could only document seven black slaves and former slaves: two of them in 1802, one in 1806, four more starting in 1822 (one in 1822, two in 1825 and one more in 1831): these last four may not have been slaves at the time, although they were certainly former slaves.

As we saw earlier with Amerindians in bondage, 324 of these 1443 blacks are not explicitly identified in historical records as slaves (324 blacks fall in this category). They were either called slaves, were the subject of a commercial transaction, or had been formally emancipated. We know other blacks were slaves, since the record shows they belonged to a master: this group includes 575 individuals. Still others are described as servants or domestics: this group includes fifty-nine individuals, all of whom were likely slaves. Finally, twenty-seven blacks "residing with" a Canadian were or likely were slaves. Historical records indicate twelve "free" blacks, and "free" means they had to have been held in bondage before that. A last group comprises 446 blacks about whom no additional information is provided: in our *Dictionnaire* we count them as slaves, given that all blacks at the time were or had been slaves. These groups can be summarized as follows:

Blacks said to be slaves	324
Black said to belong to a master	575
Black said to be servants or domestics	59
Black said to be residing with a Canadian	27
Blacks said to be free	12
No details	446

Apart from Couillart's black slave between 1632 and 1654, the 1443 blacks we have documented appear in the colony on a fairly regular basis from 1686 to 1831.

Starting in 1783, the number of black slaves in Quebec increased significantly. That year marked the arrival of the Loyalists with their slaves: they settled particularly in the Missisquoi region. Coincidentally, that year also marked roughly the end of the Amerindian slave trade. But then the number of black slave arrivals declined after 1800, when the slave market was less active, and judges refused to convict runaway slaves. Slave-owning activities ceased altogether when slavery was officially abolished in 1834. Many blacks came to Canada after 1834, but mainly to escape their masters in the United States: they secretly crossed the border, using the so-called Underground Railway, in search of liberty.

1632-1654	1	1761-1770	65
1686	1	1771-1780	195
1691-1700	5	1781-1790	337
1701-1710	6	1791-1800	254
1711-1720	16	1801-1810	3
1721-1730	20	1811-1820	–
1731-1740	43	1821-1830	3
1741-1750	121	1831-1834	1
1751-1760	95	Date unknown	277

There had been petitions in New France calling for shiploads of black slaves, but nothing of the sort ever took place. Instead, black slaves were obtained in the Thirteen Colonies as war booty or through smuggling. Starting in 1692, the fur trader Jacques Leber had in his service a black taken from the English. In 1700, an English black was baptized at Pointe-Lévy: he had been captured by Abenakis and sold to a Canadian. A document from 1700 mentions another black prisoner: Titus Jones, a native of New England. In 1718, the officer Pierre You d'Youville de Ladécouverte traded in furs at Albany and returned to New France with a black. In 1731, the Crown attorney Louis Poulin de Courval baptized a New York-raised black he had bought. The black Charles-Joseph fled New England, taking refuge with Governor Beauharnois in 1732: the governor donated him to the Hôpital-Général de Québec.[77]

The war in 1745 gave Canadians an opportunity to acquire a few blacks. In November about a hundred people were taken prisoner at Lake Champlain, "men, women, children and Negroes who were partly dispersed among the Amerindians who had captured them, while others were cast in prison in Quebec City."[78]

Among these blacks were the parents of a one-year-old girl named Étiennette: they became the property of the officer Luc Saint-Luc. The merchant Joseph-Jacques Gamelin then bought the baby for the sum of 500 livres. This batch of prisoners also included a pregnant black woman acquired by the officer Michel Maray de

Lachauvignerie: on December 26, she gave birth to a black infant who was baptized the next day. While the fort was being attacked, another black woman witnessed her husband's death. She was taken prisoner and offered to the officer Daniel Hyacinthe Liénard de Beaujeu; she was pregnant and gave birth on May 2. Another black woman, Diane, was captured by the Amerindians with her daughter: mother and daughter ended up as the personal property of the merchant Pierre Guy.

Booty was also seized during naval battles: for example, while sailing from France to Quebec, the master of a vessel seized a black named Jeannot from the English, although on arrival in the colony this black was admitted to the Hôpital-Général, where he died.

The war continued, and blacks from the Thirteen Colonies continued to turn up in Canadian historical records. In November 1747, four blacks taken from the British ran away: they were recaptured and then shipped off to Martinique, where they were sold. Another prisoner was the Negro Thomas who stayed at the Hôtel-Dieu de Québec in that same autumn of 1747. The following July, Niverville de Montizambert brought a black back to Montreal. War came to an end, but blacks captured as booty stayed on.[79]

In peacetime as in wartime, Amerindians raided the British Colonies, spiriting prisoners away to New France. For example, the British wanted to get back the black Samuel Frement, but Governor Beauharnois allowed Lacorne Saint-Luc to keep him. With the resumption of hostilities, more blacks from the British Colonies turn up in historical records. When the French army marched on Fort Oswego in 1756, a black man captured from the British went over to the enemy. At the capture of Fort William Henry, blacks were killed or captured.[80]

Under French rule several blacks were acquired from the Thirteen Colonies, but documents only occasionally give their origin. The British Colonies were the nearest and sometimes the least expensive market, since ebony slaves could be seized there in times of war.

An additional source of slaves was Louisiana, which like Canada was part of New France and could be reached by waterway through Illinois Country or by sea. In Louisiana there were many slaves, some of whom could boost Canada's black population. In one of the rare documents to indicate a black slave's origins, we find Marie-Françoise who in 1759 married the black Joseph *dit* Neptune, slave of Governor Vaudreuil-Cavagnial: her parents were from New Orleans. It would be surprising if she were the only slave to have come north to Canada from Louisiana.

Some slaves came from even farther afield than Louisiana: Canadian merchants trading in the Caribbean sometimes brought blacks on the return voyage north. The merchant Renaud brought the black Pierre-Louis from Martinique to Quebec City, baptizing him there in 1724. The bourgeois François Aubert de Lachesnaie bought a black woman, Marie-Louise, in Saint-Domingue (modern-day Haiti), placing her at the Hôtel-Dieu de Québec in July 1728, shortly after her arrival.

Other blacks came from the Caribbean, although we cannot tell for certain whether their masters went in person to fetch them. Intendant Hocquart had a black woman from the Caribbean. In 1742 the State bought the black Angélique-Denise in the Islands of French America: she was destined to be married to the black executioner of Quebec.[81]

Even farther still was the slave-rich coast of Guinea. Did anyone leave New France for Guinea, with a view to bring back slaves? We know of at least one owner—the merchant Joseph Fleury Deschambault de Lagorgendière—who went to Guinea and bought the black boy Joseph-Marie, admitted to the Hôtel-Dieu de Québec in February 1728, at the age of seven. When historical records indicate the presence of other blacks from Guinea, we wonder if they had also been directly brought over by Canadians. The navigator Michel Salaberry, the merchant Pierre Lestage, the navigator François Lemaître-Jugon, and the merchant Joseph Dufy-Charest may well have acquired their slaves in an African trading post.[82]

NEARLY 4200 SLAVES IN QUEBEC
Bringing together all the Amerindian and black slaves we have identified from the mid-seventeenth century until the abolition of

slavery in 1834 gives us a total of 4185 slaves, who can be divided into three groups, as follows:

Amerindians	2683
Black	1443
Amerindian or black (origin not specified)	59

The number of new slaves appearing in the historical record only begins to be significant after 1709, the year in which Intendant Raudot legalized slavery. Then, in the last two decades of French rule, the total number of slaves reached 400 and 500, due to the importance of the fur trade, which made it easier to acquire Amerindian slaves. With the decline of the fur trade, the number of Amerindian slaves then quickly fell off, whereas the number of blacks rose suddenly to well over 600 as Loyalists fleeing the American Revolution brought their black slaves up to Canada. Subsequently, after 1800 but well before the formal abolition of slavery in Canada, blacks continued arriving in Quebec, but the documents indicate almost no slaves— indeed, slavery was already gradually disappearing, and judges were unwilling to punish fugitive slaves.

GRAPH I
BREAKDOWN OF 4185 SLAVES, BY RACE

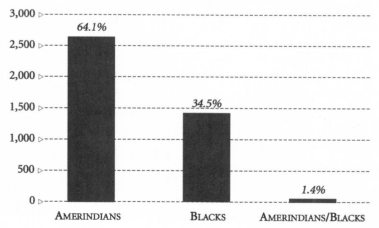

Of this grand total of 4185 slaves, 2683 Amerindians make up 65.1% or two-thirds of the 4124 slaves whose origins are known, whereas 1443 blacks account for 34.9% or just over a third.

We are convinced that our seventeenth- and eighteenth-century Canadian ancestors had more slaves than the 4185 identified in the *Dictionnaire*. We say this because, from the early eighteenth century onwards, owners complained how hard it was to hold onto their Amerindian slaves; moreover, given that Amerindian slaves were often baptized late in life, either because their religious education took time or because they were in no hurry to be baptized, it follows that many of these slaves died before being baptized and therefore do not appear in the civil registry. If no documented trace can be found of their sale, then such slaves simply do not turn up in the record: could there have been a hundred, two hundred, three hundred or more of these "undocumented" persons?

To this slave population of nearly 4200 we could add all those whose existence is not documented in surviving records: yet 4200 is still a ridiculously low number, compared to the number of slaves in other colonies. What are 4200 slaves spread over two centuries, compared to New York's 2000 black slaves over just twenty years? In 1749 alone, New York had 10,500 blacks; in 1710, Maryland had 8000; in 1721, South Carolina had 12,000; in 1746, Louisiana had 5000; around 1744, the French West Indies had 250,000. Canadians were relatively modest slaveholders. Perhaps that is why slaves were so rarely mentioned here...

In lobbying for black slaves, Canadians emphasized particularly the need to cultivate the land; we should therefore examine the geographical breakdown of the slave population, to determine whether slaves lived in the countryside or the city.

In the following pages, we list the places where slaves were held, but only when it is known that these slaves were Amerindians or blacks. This inventory by region is based on administrative regions called "gouvernements" under the French regime, given that the gouvernements of Quebec, Trois-Rivières and Montreal correspond roughly to regions in the age of slavery.

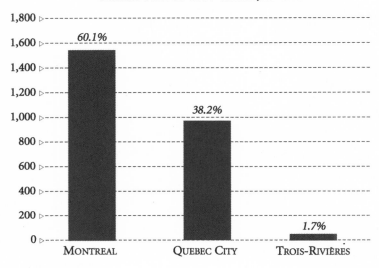

GRAPH II
BREAKDOWN OF 2537 SLAVES, BY CITY

60.1%

38.2%

1.7%

MONTREAL   QUEBEC CITY   TROIS-RIVIÈRES

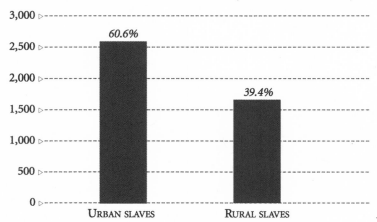

GRAPH III
URBAN SLAVES AND RURAL SLAVES (OUT OF 4185 SLAVES)

60.6%

39.4%

URBAN SLAVES   RURAL SLAVES

In the administrative region of Quebec, we include additional territories coming under it, where slaves were found: Acadia (Cape Sable and Louisbourg); Lake Champlain until 1763; the Ontario region under the French regime and then from 1774 to 1791; Detroit, Michilimackinac and Fort Duquesne were officially part of Quebec until 1783 and, in fact, until 1796; and finally, on the Mississippi River at Kaskaskia, the Sainte-Famille mission was administered by the Séminaire de Québec whereas the mother house of the Jesuits was also in Quebec.

	Amerindians	Blacks	Total
I. Acadia			
Cape Sable		1	1
Louisbourg		1	1
II. Quebec			
1.Quebec region			
North Shore:			
Tadoussac			
Île d'Orléans			
Saint-François	1	1	2
Saint-Jean		1	1
Saint-Laurent	2	2	
Saint-Pierre	3		3
Sainte-Famille		1	1
Château-Richer	1	1	
Beauport	7	4	11
Charlesbourg		2	2
Lorette		2	2
L'Ancienne-Lorette	1	1	
Quebec City	400	570	970
Sainte-Foy	1	1	2

	Amerindians	Blacks	Total
Neuville	3	1	4
Les Écureuils	2		2
Cap-Santé	2		2
Deschambault		1	1
Grondines	15		15
South Shore:			
Lotbinière	1		1
Pointe-Lévy	3	7	10
Saint-François-de-Beauce	6	1	7
Beaumont	4		4
Saint-Vallier		1	1
Saint-Thomas-de-Montmagny	4		4
Cap-Saint-Ignace	5	1	6
Saint-Jean-Port-Joly	1	1	2
Sainte-Anne-de-la-Pocatière		2	2
Kamouraska		2	2
New-Richmond		1	1
2. Trois-Rivières region		.	
North Shore			
Sainte-Anne-de-la-Pérade	38	2	40
Batiscan	15	1	16
Sainte-Geneviève-de-Batiscan	1		1
Champlain	6		6

	Amerindians	Blacks	Total
Cap-de-la-Madeleine	1		1
Trois-Rivières	35	7	42
Yamachiche	2		2
Rivière-du-Loup-en-Haut (Louiseville)	2		2
South Shore:			
Saint-Pierre-les-Becquets	1		1
Saint-François-du-Lac	3	1	4
3. Montreal region			
North Shore:			
Berthier-en-Haut	8	9	17
Saint-Cuthbert	1		1
Île-Dupas	1		1
Lanoraie	1		1
Lavaltrie	5		5
Saint-Sulpice	2		2
L'Assomption	8	3	11
Repentigny	1		1
Lachenaie	5	7	12
Terrebonne	7	3	10
Oka	1		1
Saint-François-des-Sales (Rivière-des-Prairies)	8		8
Saint-Vincent-de-Paul	2		2
Sault-au-Récollet	6	1	7

	Amerindians	Blacks	Total
Pointe-aux-Trembles	6	1	7
Saint-Laurent	4	1	5
Longue-Pointe	7	5	12
Montreal	1007	518	1525
Lachine	90	31	121
Pointe-Claire	18	2	20
Sainte-Anne-du-Bout-de-l'Île	18	3	21
Île-Perrot	2		2
Vaudreuil	5	7	12
Rigaud		8	8
Les Cèdres (Soulanges)	17	4	21
South Shore:			
Sorel	9	9	18
Verchères	10	1	11
Varennes	41	3	44
Boucherville	47	15	62
Longueuil	17	1	18
Laprairie	66	2	68
Saint-Constant	1		1
Saint-Philippe-de-Laprairie	3		3
4. Richelieu valley region			
Saint-Antoine-sur-Richelieu	1	5	6

	Amerindians	Blacks	Total
Saint-Mathias		1	1
Chambly	9	3	12
5. Lake Champlain region			
Saint-Armand (Philipsburg)	13		13
Fort Saint-Frédéric	5	3	8
6. Great Lakes region			
Fort Frontenac	2		2
York-Toronto		8	8
Detroit	523	127	650
Michilimackinac	135	25	160
Fort Saint-Joseph des Miamis	15		15
Fort Duquesne	1		1
7. Mississippi region			
Kaskaskias (Sainte-Famille)	12	12	24

Accordingly, these 4087 Amerindian and black slaves can be broken down geographically as follows:

Acadia	2
Canada (French regime)	3264
Lake Champlain region	21
Great Lakes region	874
Mississippi region	24

The abundance of slaves in the Great Lakes region – especially Amerindian slaves – should not come as a surprise, since the main towns in the region, Detroit and Michilimackinac, were in the middle of "Indian country." Of these regions, the one with the highest prevalence of slavery was Canada under the French regime, in other words on the North and South Shores of the Saint Lawrence river.

There was practically an equal number of male and female slaves: males represented 1973 slaves (47.8%), while females represented 2151 slaves (52.2%). However, if we break down each of these two groups separately, the result is not so evenly matched. There were more women than men among Amerindian slaves (1543 or 57.5% were women), whereas there were fewer women than men among black slaves (608 or 42.2% were women). Several travelers noted that Canadian men were attracted to "savage" women, and it is tempting to see the high proportion of enslaved Amerindian women as a reflection of this tendency, although it is likely that the real reason was simply that it was easy to obtain female slaves from Amerindian nations.

On the banks of the Saint Lawrence, 3264 slaves were found overwhelmingly in two regions: Montreal led the way with 2077 slaves (63.6%), many of whom were acquired from Amerindian nations through the fur trade, Montreal's economic lifeblood. The Quebec region followed with 1063 individuals (32.6%), and it is interesting to note the larger proportion of black slaves in Quebec. The geographically small and sparsely populated region of Trois-Rivières had only a modest iron industry, and no more than 115 slaves (3.5% of 3264).

The administrative authorities of New France sought slaves mainly for the cultivation of land. The king agreed to this request, but no slave ship ever reached the colony, which meant that the colonists had to acquire slaves by other means. However, slaves did not end up where we would most expect them: they were found in towns rather than in the countryside. Quebec, the capital of the colony, had 970 slaves, 460 of them Amerindians and 570 blacks; Montreal had yet more slaves – a total of 1525, 1007 of of them Amerindians and 518 blacks. In other words, 2495 slaves lived in towns – over three-quarters of the total number in New France and subsequently in colonial Quebec under the British regime. Slavery here was an urban phenomenon.

CHAPTER FOUR

The Slave Market

O n June 15, 1709, Madeleine Just, wife of Pierre You d'Youville Ladécoverte, sold a Panis to Pierre-Thomas Tarieu de Lapérade, husband of Madeleine Jarret de Verchères; then on October 19, Jacques Nepveu sold the Panis Marie to his own brother. In September 1796, Louis Payet, parish priest of Saint-Antoine-sur-Richelieu, sold a black woman, Rose, to Thomas Lee; and Jean-Baptiste Routhier sold his mulatto to Louis-Charles Foucher.[83] These examples constitute the first two slave sales in Quebec, in 1709 and, then the very last two such sales, in 1796. Buyers and sellers were French-speaking Canadians in each case.

SLAVES AS PERSONAL PROPERTY

On April 13, 1709, Intendant Raudot issued an ordinance making it legal to buy and sell slaves: "All Panis and Negroes who have been and who shall hereafter be bought, belong in full ownership to those who purchased them as slaves." According to the 1685 edition of the *Code Noir* (but also the 1724 edition specially drafted for Louisiana, another part of New France), slaves were likened to personal property.[84] The *Code Noir* never came into force in the St. Lawrence Valley, but slaves were considered to be personal property here as elsewhere, and Canadians treated them as such.

By "personal property" we mean that slaves were owned in just the same way as livestock. When the notary Raimbault drew up an inventory of the property of the late François-Madeleine You d'Youville, whose wife came to be known as Mother d'Youville, he simply wrote at the end:

A Panis by birth, around ten or eleven years old, value about 150 livres. A second-calf cow, red undercoat, value about thirty livres.[85]

The only difference between the slave and the cow was that the slave was worth five times as much as the cow.

The same mercantile approach was taken to slaves under the British regime. In a 1783 advertisement the printer William Brown offered an eighteen-year-old black woman for sale, adding "We also have a lovely bay mare available." An English-speaking resident of Quebec City offered a thirteen-year-old black boy for sale, as well as a black woman aged twenty-six, along with a horse, cart and harness.[86] Slaves could be offered for sale along with animals, and could be exchanged for animals. This for example was the case of John Turner, a Montreal merchant, who struck a deal with a Bostonian to trade the black Josiah Cutan, about twenty-two years old, for a grey horse and thirty-one pounds ten shillings.

Since slaves were treated as personal property, they could serve as security for debts. In 1784, Elizabeth Chautler, wife of Alexander Bissett, master of languages, was a creditor of the inn-keeper Paterson of Sorel; Paterson owed forty pounds, Quebec currency (160 dollars in the eighteenth century). The Patersons handed a twelve-year-old black girl over to the Bissetts as security, but if the Patersons paid off the loan they would get their slave back.[87]

A similar case arose in 1797. The former lieutenant George West-phal borrowed the sum of twenty pounds Quebec currency, from Richard Dillon, owner of the Montreal Hotel; the loan contract stipulated that he would repay the capital over eighteen months, with 6% interest. As security, Westphal provided his mulatto woman Sedy, who would work for Dillon as a domestic servant until the loan was fully paid; however, the services she rendered to Dillon meant that fifteen shillings (two dollars) would be deducted from the debt each month; if Westphal did not pay down the loan in the agreed time, then the mulatto would become Dillon's property, which would in turn extinguish the debt (Lukin registry, November 22, 1797).

Even a Baptized Person Could Become Personal Property

Could a baptized slave be treated as personal property, just like an animal? How could such a practice be reconciled with the fact that the charter of 1627 automatically granted full citizenship to the baptized person?

The problem arose in the Court of Montreal in 1733. A Paducah belonging to Philippe You d'Youville de Ladécouverte was seized and then sold. But this slave was a baptized Catholic. Youville de Ladécouverte sought, on the grounds of baptism, to have the Conseil supérieur void the sale, and also reprimand the judge who had ordered the sale. The Conseil handed the problem over to the intendant, who upheld the court's decision. When the king was apprised of the situation, he refused to give his opinion on Amerindian slavery, and replied instead that customary practice should be followed.[88] This meant that baptized Amerindians could be sold as slaves.

This problem reappeared during a trial in 1740. The Panis Marie-Marguerite, whom Chevalier Dormicourt was on the point of transporting to the Caribbean, used every possible argument in court to avoid being sent into exile; in a brief drawn up by a legal practitioner, she pleaded that as a baptized Catholic she should be allowed to regain her liberty. This argument was not admitted, however, and she lost her trial.

As a result of this case in 1740 and Intendant Hocquart's ruling in 1733, slaves could be sold even if they were baptized Catholics. We found at least five Amerindian slaves who fit this description.

This problem did not arise for blacks, however: they could not cite Article 17 of the Charter of the Compagnie des Cent-Associés. As a result, no legal objections were raised when baptized blacks were sold.

When a slave changed masters, whether by sale or otherwise, steps were taken to ensure that religion was not affected. Missionaries in Detroit continually sought to maintain slaves in the Catholic faith. For example, when the Récollet Bonaventure Léonard baptized Louis Campeau's two young blacks in Detroit in 1739, he wrote in the register that Campeau "undertook to raise and educate them as if they were his own children and if he was forced to sell them, he would only sell them to Roman Catholics, otherwise I would not have baptized them." As the word "otherwise" indicates, the missionary had set an ultimatum...[89] When Cuillerier baptized his slave's child in Detroit in October 1736, he promised he would only hand the child over to Christians or to its mother, so the child could be raised in the Catholic faith. Pierre Chesne-Labutte and Pierre Saint-Cosme made the same commitment to baptize a newborn slave in Detroit in 1737, and Guillaume Dagneau-Douville de Lamothe made the same promise in 1752.

Where the new owner of a Catholic slave was Protestant, he took a solemn pledge: Louis-François de Lacorne sold a Catholic Amerindian woman to the Protestant merchant Connolly, who promised he would not force her to convert to his religion; and he evidently kept his promise because in Michilimackinac in May 1763 this slave's child was baptized according to the Catholic rite.

Various Opportunities to Acquire Slaves

Since deliveries of slaves were generally slow and scattered, it is safe to assume that potential buyers found it hard to secure supplies of Amerindian and ebony slaves. They had to wait for the opportunity to buy slaves.

The luckiest masters were the ones who had received a slave as a gift. Around 1754, some Amerindians gave Saint-Ours Deschaillons a Panis woman to compensate him for the accidental death of one of his men; in another case, a slave woman who had just delivered a baby gave the newborn to one Leduc-Persil.

Inheriting a slave was a profitable option. The most interesting example of slaves being inherited was when Charles Lemoyne, first Baron de Longueuil, left his two sons a legacy of seven black slaves: one of the baron's sons inherited the father and mother with three children, while the other son inherited two other children but as a way of making the distribution more equitable he also obtained a Panis man and woman from his brother.

Where slaves could not be inherited, they could be bought. Slave purchases sometimes took place in unusual circumstances. For example, in Detroit in 1769 two slave owners joined forces to buy a young Panis who was gravely ill (his master had bothered neither to treat nor to baptize him); they had the young slave baptized and he died three days later.[90] Another owner, John Askin, was motivated by the same sense of charity, in buying a young slave from Charles Paterson of Montreal; the slave belonging to Paterson had suffered at the hands of the Ottawas, and Askin offered to trade an Amerindian woman for him.[91]

Another unusual slave purchase took place when a buyer sought to acquire a Sioux woman in order to marry her. This was not the latest instalment of some romance, but rather a way of stifling a scandal. The Sioux woman, Marie-Marguerite-Caroline, belonging to Claude Landry *dit* Saint-André, had five illegitimate children with Firmin Landry *dit* Charlot; to put an end to this cohabitation, the priest in Detroit noted, the Sioux woman's owner undertook to sell her to Landry *dit* Charlot on the express condition that he marry her, which he did on July 17, 1771 (Register of Sainte-Anne-du-Détroit).[92]

An even more interesting case occurred when the black Louis-Antoine, who had been freed from bondage at a very young age, fell in love with the merchant Dominique Gaudet's eighteen-year-old black slave Marie-Catherine Baraca. Gaudet had no objection to marriage, but he did not want to lose his slave by letting her marry. He was prepared to accept that the two marry as long as Louis-Antoine voluntarily became his slave. This presented no problem for Louis-Antoine who sold himself before a notary to Gaudet; the deed of sale specified that the master would dispose as he saw fit of Louis-Antoine, the woman and their future children. The following week, Louis-Antoine married his beloved. He would only recover his liberty on Gaudet's death, in 1769 (Panet registry). Motivated by love, this voluntary slavery lasted eight years.

The black woman Mary Bulkley also volunteered to become a slave, but in her case it was in order to free herself of "considerable" debt. On November 28, 1785, she undertook to serve Elias Hall "in the condition of a slave for a period of thirty years," and Hall could sell her as he saw fit. He actually did sell her; Mary Bulkley would have four other masters during the thirty-year term of her contract. When she was acquired by the last of these masters, in 1797, by contract she still had eighteen years of bondage to go. But her new owner was concerned about talk of abolishing slavery, so he got her to commit to a new thirty-year contract, as a domestic servant (according to the registries of notaries Bathélemy Faribault and Maurice-Louis de Glandons).

Acquiring slaves as gifts, inheriting them, or having individuals become slaves of their free will did not change the fact that supply still fell short of demand. Anyone wanting to purchase a slave had to accept that trading in slaves followed a routine of sorts, and often started with ascertaining whether a master was willing to sell one of his slaves. The merchant John Askin, for example, wanted to acquire two young Panis girls, and let it be known he was willing to part with a mulatto woman.[93] In 1766, when William Brown, the printer of the *Quebec Gazette*, faced a desperate shortage of labour, he was told the only solution was to buy slaves: he finally decided to acquire a young black man through a friend in Philadelphia, who sent the slave to Quebec by sea, but only after taking the precaution of insuring the merchandise.[94]

The Public Slave Market and Sales by Auction

Was there a public slave market in Canada the way there was in the Thirteen Colonies and the Caribbean? And if there was such a market, was it in continuous operation, or only occasionally? The historical record does not enable us to provide a satisfactory answer to these questions. In 1733, when You d'Youville de Ladécouverte claimed in court to be shocked that a baptized Amerindian was sold at auction, he referred to a slave sold in a public market just like animals. Was he referring to an actual slave market in Montreal or was this merely a colourful figure of speech designed to impress the judge? Benjamin Sulte stated categorically, "No Negro or Panis was ever sold in Canada at public auction."[95] But Sulte was wrong about this.

Public sales of slaves at auction definitely occurred in Canada. We only know of one such case under the French regime, when in 1733 the merchant Charles Nolan de Lamarque bought a Paducah on the market square, who had previously been seized from You d'Youville de Ladécouverte. Several more public slave sales took place under the British regime. In Quebec City in 1778, Captain Thomas Venture offered his mulatto slave Isabella at auction, and the butcher Hipps made the highest bid.[96]

According to the *Quebec Gazette*, there was to be a sale on October 5, 1782 of a young black by auctioneers "in their public showroom" in rue Notre-Dame in Quebec City. John Brooks of Quebec offered a black for sale, specifying that the slave could be inspected in his home until May 20, after which he would be offered in a public sale.[97] In 1765, two public slave sales took place: William Ward of Vermont sold a black man and woman and a black boy to William Campbell of Montreal, and the following month, Campbell resold the three slaves to Doctor Charles Blake (J.-G. Beck registry). In 1791, the auctioneer put a young black up for auction.[98]

Moreover, these public sales and auctions were regularly advertised in newspapers. Between 1767, when the first slave sale ad appeared, and 1798, when the last such ad came out, there were at least 137 advertisements for thirty different slaves; only one of these thirty slaves was an Amerindian – a Panis woman whom the merchants Melvin Wills and Burns offered for sale in July 1782 in the *Quebec Gazette*.

One ad featured a young black man who was trained in domestic service, and knew how to shave and style hair. Prospective buyers who preferred a black woman could read in another ad of a slave who had belonged to Governor Murray and had now become (what a let-down!) the slave of Prenties the tavern keeper; she was a good servant who knew how to milk cows and made butter to perfection. Another ad offered both an eighteen-year-old black man and "a beautiful mare"; interested parties were advised to contact the newspaper for particulars.

The slave put up for sale for the longest period was Joe, an unruly black man belonging to the printer William Brown: the master had punished him many times and even had him whipped by the executioner, for stealing and running away. Nothing could be done to change his ways. From 1779 to 1784, Brown tried unsuccessfully to sell the slave, who still belonged to his master in 1789.[99]

It is clear that slaves were indeed put up for auction in Quebec and Montreal, and sold to the highest bidder. Slavery was legal in Canada, so why would slaves not have been sold at auction here, as they were in other colonies?

We know of an oral tradition concerning the slave market. In his memoirs, the Oblate missionary Damase Dandurand wrote: "I can state quite definitely that in my early childhood, a full-fledged slave market existed in Montreal." Since Father Dandurand was born in 1819, his early childhood coincided with the first quarter of the nineteenth century, well before the official abolition of slavery in the British Empire. He said he had come to Montreal with his mother, and they both walked by this market where a sick old black man begged Madame Dandurand to buy him.[100] Father Dandurand lived to the age of 102: he wrote his memoirs long after the fact, and the word-for-word dialogue he sketched in, between the black man and his mother, was probably inaccurate. But the memory itself – of a public market and a slave for sale – seems authentic enough. In fact, in a small colony featuring over 4200 slaves, it would have been astonishing if there had been no slave market in Montreal, where almost half of all Quebec slaves lived.

A SLUGGISH MARKET

Despite regular slave ads and the labour shortage, the slave market does not seem to have been particularly active. Apart from cases of inheritance, it was extremely unusual for a single slave to change hands and even rarer for the same slave to pass repeatedly from one master to another. In 1785, William Ward sold three blacks to

William Campbell, who resold them the following month to Doctor Charles Blake. Some slaves had four successive owners, such as the mulatto Isabella who belonged to Lieutenant-Governor Cramahé among other masters. Three slaves had five successive owners: the black woman Marie Bulkley, the black woman Cynda (who had five owners in just two years), the black woman Rose, who belonged for one year to the parish priest in Saint-Antoine-sur-Richelieu. Two slaves had six successive owners: the Panis Jacques under the French regime, and the black Josiah Cutin, who had six owners in six years, and finished on the gallows.

Our documentation of slaves in Canada indicates that slaves usually remained the property of a single master, which may have meant that slavery had less of a commercial and more of a humane nature.

In the rare event slaves were sold by the batch, the batch was small. On September 25, 1743, the merchant Charles Réaume of Île Jesus sold a group of five slaves to the bourgeois Louis Cureux *dit* Saint-Germain of Quebec City for 3000 livres: the group included two black men and three black women.[101] In 1785, William Campbell bought and immediately resold three blacks (including a young Negro, six months old) for 425 dollars.[102] In 1787, Jacques Lafrenière bought four blacks on behalf of the "Département des Sauvages" or "Indian Department": these slaves were destined to serve Amerindian masters.[103]

All in all, slave sales were infrequent: we counted 120 sales, forty-one of them involving Amerindians, even though most slaves were Amerindians. It is probable that some sales by mutual agreement escaped our attention.

In Search of Healthy Merchandise

Canadians were inveterate horse-dealers, intent on outwitting and outmanoeuvring their opponents, and this approach must also have been taken when prospective buyers and sellers got together to deal in slaves.

Advice was always available for slave trading:

[Do not accept] subjects below four and a half feet in height, depending on their gender. According to Van Alstein, it is advisable to have surgeons examine the subjects. They should examine the eyes, mouth, noble parts, get the slaves to walk, run, and cough loudly with their hands placed on the groin, in order to detect hernias. An anonymous directive from 1769 urges buyers to avoid wrinkled old men, with dangling and shrivelled testicles. No big skinny Negroes, with narrow chests, wild eyes, or the look of an imbecile which is a harbinger of epilepsy. [Similarly for women], no propped up [i.e. false] breasts, no flabby bosom; an appearance of promptitude and cleanliness.[104]

Were slaves scrupulously examined from head to foot in Canada, according to the recommendations of specialists in "Negroes"? Since slaves were bought and sold here just like domestic animals, slaves must have been examined with just as much care as anywhere else.

It would have been very foolish to buy a slave without first inspecting the merchandise. In 1737, when Joseph Chavigny de Lachevrotière de Latesserie bought a thirteen- or fourteen-year old Fox girl from Jacques-Hugues Péan de Livaudière, he declared that, having "met her in person, he recognizes she is healthy and not in any way crippled." In 1779, the merchant James Finlay sold a black woman to the Jewish fur trader and seigneur Aaron Hart, specifying in the deed of sale that she was "sound and free of all Sickness and disorders whatsoever." In 1786, James Bloodgood made the same statement when selling another black woman to Aaron Hart.[105] Most deeds of sale specified that the slave had already had syphilis or chickenpox, which amounted to immunity.

We can learn some physical details about black slaves from sales contracts, reports of fugitive slaves and other documents of this kind. They were generally tall: in 1796, the mulatto Jean-Louis stood five feet ten inches tall; a black slave belonging to Pinguet de Vaucour was five and a half to six feet tall.

Historical documents provide further details about these slaves. Jean Orillat's twenty-two-year-old black slave: "is well built, seems very gentle, with a slightly elongated face, a small scar on the left side of his neck, next to the jaw, resulting from a gland which has not yet healed." Crofton's mulatto Andrew, twenty-three years of age: of average height, with an exceptionally large mouth, thick lips, crooked fingers, and a very lively and alert disposition. Christie's black slave Bruce, thirty-five years old: "is tall and well built," with "an upturned nose and a quite dark complexion," and "speaks in a somewhat hesitant manner." Turner's black slave Ismael, thirty-six years of age, "has something remarkably sad in his expression, and skin of a colour between black and swarthy; his hair is short, thick and curly, his face extremely pockmarked, he has lost some of his upper front teeth as well as the first joint of the fourth finger of his left hand, and he also has a fresh scar in the middle of the right leg, where a horse kicked him, an injury from which he has recently recovered"; Ismael spoke with the characteristic accent of his native New England. This was surely a slave with little commercial value; but as a deserter, he was not for sale, and his master wanted to recover him.[106]

Young Merchandise

According to slave traders, a good, marketable "Negro" (also known as a *pièce d'Inde*) should not be over thirty years of age, since black slaves over this age quickly lost their value. Prospective owners therefore had to buy slaves as young as possible.

Of the twenty-five blacks whose age is indicated in the deed of sale, twelve were under twenty years of age, ten were under thirty, and three were over thirty. However, these last three do not appear to have been bargains, since Sullivan in buying a thirty-three-year-old black slave ended up with a lot of grief, as we shall see. The average age of these twenty-five blacks was just 18.8 years.

Prospective buyers of Amerindian slaves were also concerned about age, since they wanted to keep their slaves in bondage as long as possible. There was the added challenge of Amerindians being tempted to return to their native ways in the forest: masters thus took Amerindian slaves at as young an age as possible, in order to familiarize them with the values of French civilization and make them less likely to run away as adults. Civil registries tell us more than deeds of sale about the age of Amerindian slaves. We know that the average Amerindian slave died at 17.7 years of age (this was an eyeball estimate), which means slaves were generally acquired during adolescence and especially childhood. Based on deeds of sale alone, Amerindians were sold into slavery between the ages of five and twenty-five years, and on the average at the age of 14.1 years, which gives an indication of just how young Amerindian slaves were.

BLACK SLAVES COST MORE THAN RED ONES

In 1720, Intendant Bégon wrote to the Regent that communities and residents of Canada were prepared to buy black slaves for 600 livres apiece, but he was careful to add "or by mutual agreement in Quebec" with the masters of slave ships. The intendant was wise not to insist on 600 livres and to mention the prospect of mutual agreements, since slave traders would not have found this price very attractive: at the time, a black already cost the supplier more than that, as was indicated by the prices a merchant of La Rochelle offered the inhabitants of Louisiana in 1737, prices they accepted in principle: Negro children of ten to fifteen years, 650 livres; black women sixteen to thirty years, 750 livres; black men of the same age, 850 livres. The French West Indies were much closer to sources of supply than Canada, and average prices there were as follows: in 1728, 800 livres; in 1750, 1160 livres; in 1776, 1825 livres. Slave valuations naturally fluctuated depending on conditions such as age, physical appearance, health, skills and the country of origin.

For the years 1737-1797, we have a list of forty-four slave prices, varying from 200 to 2400 livres. A black slave who only cost 200 livres must have been fairly poor merchandise, since a high-quality slave could fetch up to 2000 livres. In Quebec City in 1768, two black men between seventeen and twenty years of age sold for an average of 2400 livres. Of the forty-four prices on our list, sixteen blacks brought 600 livres or less, eleven brought 700 to 1000 livres apiece, while seventeen cost over 1000 livres. This list contains the only specific pricing information we were able to obtain. On this basis, the average black slave was sold for 900 livres, or already 300 livres more than Intendant Bégon's estimate.

What did it cost to buy an Amerindian slave? We only located eighteen examples, which do not provide absolutely conclusive information, since many details could affect the price of Amerindian as well as black slaves. These examples range from 1709 to 1792, and nevertheless provide an approximation.

The Amerindian slave could fetch 120 livres and we did not find any single Amerindian slave worth more than 750 livres: five Amerindians were sold for less than 300 livres, ten cost between 300 and 600 livres. In no case did the maximum price paid for an Amerindian slave reach the average price paid for a black one. The average Amerindian cost only 400 livres, whereas the average black cost 900. Another way of putting this is to say a black slave was worth twice as much as an Amerindian slave. This should come as no surprise, since New France was close to the market in "savages," but far from the market in black ebony, and the additional cost of acquiring black slaves was passed on to the purchaser.

The price paid for a slave, whether black or Amerindian, usually included clothing, because slaves were not sold naked. In 1753, the Panis woman Catiche was sold "with the clothes and linen on her back"; in 1778, the mulatto Isabella was sold to Lieutenant Governor Cramahé "with the clothes and linens on her back, which the said Purchaser acknowledges having received in his house"; in 1748, when Widow Philibert sold her black man to the explorer Gaultier de Lavérendrye, she undertook to deliver him "with the clothes on his back at the time of delivery as well as three shirts."[107] In short, the slave only reached his new master with what he had on his back, or a small bundle under his arm.

Going into Debt to Buy Slaves

Slaves were luxury items, so it was normal that wealthy people should be the ones acquiring them. In January 1787, Louis Payet, parish priest of Saint-Antoine-sur-Richelieu, bought a ten-year-old black boy from the bourgeois Samuel Mix for the sum of twenty-three pounds, Quebec currency, or 552 French livres, this payment being made in gold and cash (Leguay registry). But prospective buyers did not always have ready cash for such purchases. Sometimes slaves were bartered rather than sold for cash: Joseph Chavigny de Lachevrotière de Latesserie bought a twenty-two-year-old Panis woman from the merchant Jean-Baptiste Auger for the sum of 400 livres; but instead of paying cash, he undertook to import the equivalent from Martinique in pepper and coffee; in 1732, the merchant Pierre Guy bought a Paducah, ten to twelve years of age, from Louis Chappeau for the sum of 200 livres: he made payment in beaver and other pelts; in 1790, Pierre-Charles Boucher de Labruère bought a black boy aged eight and a half years in exchange for ninety minots of wheat (the old French dry measure of minot was slightly more than a bushel). On another occasion, the above-mentioned Latesserie bought a ten-year-old Paducah slave for cash and barter, providing 250 livres in card money and two barrels of molasses, or the equivalent of 550 livres.

Prospective buyers with neither cash nor goods to barter could take out loans. On June 15, 1709 the officer and Seigneur Pierre Thomas Tarieu de Lapérade, husband of Madeleine Jarret de Verchères, took out a loan to buy a fourteen-year-old Panis boy for 120 livres, which involved obtaining an advance on the salary he would receive for June and July. On May 4, 1757, the merchant and goldsmith Ignace-François Delzenne only had 600 livres in hand to buy a black slave at the cost of 1192 livres: he undertook to pay the remainder in fifteen days, which involved mortgaging his property, and he managed to pay off this debt two months later. In 1797, the tavern keeper Thomas John Sullivan bought a thirty-three-year-old black man for thirty-six pounds, Quebec currency, or the equivalent of 864 French livres: he mortgaged his property, planning to pay for this black slave at the rate of seventy-two livres per month.[108] It took him just one year to pay for a "Negro" although this was a "Negro" aged thirty-three!

Some Deals Worked Out Badly

Transactions have their perils, and slave transactions were no exception. Ownership was not always clearly established, which led to disputes, for example between Doctor Timothée Sylvain and Widow d'Youville – Marie-Marguerite Dufrost de Lajemmerais – later known as Mother d'Youville. Sylvain claimed ownership of the Panis held by Widow d'Youville, and he accused her in court of having seized this slave from him during the night.[109] In 1762, one Falson had a Panis woman in his household whom he claimed to have bought from a ship surgeon; the Jewish merchant Eléazar Lévy maintained in court that he was the real owner, since he had bought the slave from Joseph Lorrain. Lévy won his case.

One had to be wary of transactions where the seller wanted to get rid of poor merchandise while seeking an inflated price. Jean-Baptiste Barthe entrusted his brother-in-law, the merchant John Askin, with the sale of his Panis slave. Askin was an able businessman, and knew the Panis had limited value since he was "too stupid to make a sailor or to be any good whatever."[110] Askin nonetheless managed to obtain 750 livres for the slave – the highest price paid for an Amerindian slave, according to the documents we consulted. Things did not work out well for the buyer.

The buyer sometimes accepted huge risks, by legally acquiring a slave who had disappeared. In May 1724, Jean Gaultier de Landreville of Île Sainte-Therese, sold a Panis to Seigneur Louis-Hector Piot de Langloiserie, whereas this Panis had not been seen anywhere for six months. The buyer took it upon himself to locate the Amerindian, and by agreement, even if his efforts were to fail, the seller would still be paid. This was a risky business! Piot de Langloiserie hoped this transaction would enable him to recover 200 livres Gaultier de Landreville owed him. Whether or not Piot de Langloiserie laid his hands on the Panis slave, the debt was extinguished.

In 1751, the merchant Louis Dunière took the same risk. He paid the butcher Jacques Damien 500 livres in cash for a black slave. But when the black slave learned on what day he was to be sold, he disappeared the day before, and no one had seen him. Even so, the buyer had assumed all risks by contract, and concluded the transaction was still valid.

In 1785, Mary Jacobs bought two black women from Mr. and Mrs. Fisher for the cash sum of fifty pounds, Quebec currency, the equivalent of 1200 French livres, then waited for her two "Negro wenches" to show up. Time went by, and still no delivery of slaves took place. Mary Jacobs thought things would speed up if she served the Fishers with a summons, but they did not respond. Finally, three years later, she filed a complaint in court, claiming either her black slaves or a compensatory sum of 2400 livres. The Fishers did not even bother to turn up in court. They were ordered to restitute the slaves or pay her 1200 livres. The buyer received no compensation for the time spent waiting.[111]

A Montreal man named Mogé also cut a bad deal, in paying 500 livres for an Amerindian slave brought back from the Thirteen Colonies by the Iroquois of Sault-Saint-Louis. Then the English turned up, demanding to have their Amerindian back. Mogé was willing to restitute the slave as long as he was refunded his 500 livres, which the English refused to do, on the grounds that the Amerindian was a prisoner of war. In order to avoid any delay in the exchange of prisoners, Governor La Jonquière ordered Mogé to hand the Amerindian over, offering the meagre consolation that the latter could eventually ask the Court for compensation.[112]

Just as startling was the case of a prospective owner buying a black man, only to discover he claimed to be free. In August 1797, the tavern keeper Thomas John Sullivan bought a black man for 864 livres and agreed to free the slave after five years of bondage. This was not much of a deal for Sullivan, who paid 864 livres on credit for a thirty-three-year-old slave in 1797 at a time when the anti-slavery campaign was underway. Sullivan expected to have this black man in his service for at least five years: yet shortly after, the man claimed to be free, and ran away. Sullivan was desperate because he still owed 720 livres for the black man. Then in March 1798, Mr. and Mrs. Turner intervened, demanding the slave as compensation for the amount Sullivan owed them. Sullivan defended himself by accusing the Turners of having sold him a free black man. Justice William Osgoode did not recognize slavery, and ruled that the Turners had failed to prove their rights to the slave, ordering them to refund what Sullivan had already paid them. The black man, meanwhile, seems to have established his free condition as a result. Another reason for going to trial was when someone sold a slave he did not actually own. Around 1754, Amerindians accidentally killed a man named Petit *dit* Rossignol in the St. Joseph River region, south of Lake Michigan. In order to console his mother, the Amerindians decided to "cover" the death by offering a Panis woman and a few strings of wampum (the Amerindian equivalent of currency). Following established practice, she would benefit from having this Panis in her service. But the commander of the post, Pierre-Roch Saint-Ours Deschaillons, decided that the Panis woman belonged to him instead, and he sold her for 500 livres and kept the proceeds of sale. At the end of 1763, the Petit *dit* Rossignol family took the case to court in Montreal, and the judge ordered Saint-Ours Deschaillons to pay the 500 livres to the family.[113]

CHAPTER FIVE

Owners at All Levels of Society

Colonial Canada's population of legal slaves was made up of native Amerindians and blacks bought and sold in private transactions or auctioned off to the highest bidder in a public market. We should examine whether slave ownership was restricted to the most powerful members of society, and whether any particular group of society, such as the clergy, refused on principle to enslave other human beings.

FRENCH-SPEAKING SLAVE OWNERS

In reviewing historical records, it is clear that not all Amerindians and blacks who lived in slavery in Quebec were actually slaves at the time the documents record their presence: some had regained their liberty some time after entering the country as slaves, and the documents do not always tell us who their owners were. Even in cases where documents identified individuals as slaves at the time of writing, the names of owners were not always indicated.

It is therefore impossible to make an exhaustive study of slave ownership, and we can only come up with approximations, both of owners and of slaves themselves. Of the approximately 4200 slaves in our *Dictionnaire*, 3200 (or 76.2%) had clearly identified owners. It has not always proven straight-forward to identify these owners, given that the first and last names of just 1137 owners are recorded. Moreover, it should be noted that ownership was not always confined to individuals: the state, religious communities and merchant associations could hold slaves in collective ownership. We will leave aside collective owners for the moment, to focus on individual owners.

Our history of slavery can conveniently be divided into two traditional periods, the French regime and the British regime. In this respect, the influential nineteenth-century nationalist historian François-Xavier Garneau claimed that slavery in Quebec was largely a British institution. Was this really the case? Were slave owners of French or of British origin? Before 1760, they were necessarily all or almost all of French origin, whereas after the Conquest a certain number of British slave owners settled in Quebec. Actually, of 1535 individual owners, we found that 1312 (85.5%) were of French origin, whereas 223 (just 14.5%) were of British origin.

Our study of Quebec slavery from 1632 to 1834 has enabled us to establish that owners of French origin were the leading slave owners, given that they accounted for 2858 or 86.8% of all known owners. Even more significant is the fact that these slave owners of French origin owned 79.1% of all Amerindian slaves. Evidently, once the British settled in Quebec following the Conquest, it was much harder for them to acquire Amerindian slaves than it had been for the French prior to 1760, given the rapid decline of the fur trade.

GRAPH IV
BREAKDOWN OF 1,574 OWNERS

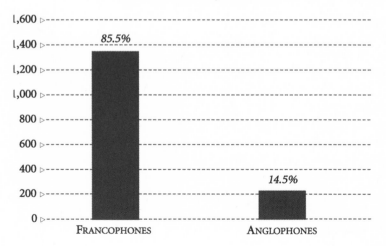

During the colonial period, French-speaking owners held almost all the Amerindian slaves we have identified in official records, and they even held 596 black slaves, far outnumbering the 301 black slaves held by English-speaking owners.

OFFICIALS UNDER THE FRENCH REGIME

Slave ownership in our society was not something like great wealth or honours – it was not restricted to a handful of people. We have only identified about 4200 slaves in Quebec, but since owners tended to hold a few slaves, the number of slave owners was proportionately greater as a result. We have identified 1574 slave owners. One of the most interesting aspects of the history of slavery here is that 965 surnames turn up among slave owners, and only 197 of these surnames were British. Readers who would find it intriguing … or horrifying … to find out whether they are descended from slave owners should consult the *Dictionnaire*.

This list of surnames does not give an idea of the relative importance of these families in terms of slave ownership. Some families had more slaves than others, and the same family name was shared by several distinct slave-owning families, such as the Bourassa, Campeau, Côté, Cardinal, Hubert-Lacroix and Leduc families, each of which owned several slaves.

What social standing did slave owners enjoy, and how could they afford the luxury of slave ownership? Historical records are incomplete, and we cannot determine the profession or occupation for 690 (or 43.8%) of the 1574 known slave owners.

Slavery was a formally established institution, and as such the highest authorities in the colony, both secular and religious, owned slaves. Under the French regime, at least four governors general owned slaves. In 1679, Buade de Frontenac entrusted the Convent of the Ursulines of Quebec with the education of an Amerindian girl considered a slave, and in 1674 he seems to have been the recipient of a young slave boy that Louis Jolliet brought back from the Mississippi and who drowned before arriving. In 1671, Rémy de Courcelle received two Potawatomi slaves from the Iroquois.

Rigaud de Vaudreull, governor from 1703 to 1725, had eleven slaves, including four blacks. The Marquis La Boische de Beauharnois, governor from 1726 to 1746, had twenty-seven slaves; Vaudreuil-Cavagnial, son of the first Vaudreuil, governor from 1755 to 1760, had sixteen slaves, thirteen of whom were blacks and three more were Amerindians, including the Panis Marie-Louise whom he had received from his father.

At least two intendants, Hocquart and Francois Bigot, had slaves – Bigot only had three, whereas Hocquart, New France's longest-serving intendant, had six.

In addition to these governors general and intendants, we also find governors of Trois-Rivières and Montreal among slave owners: Charles Lemoyne de Longueuil and his sons Charles and Paul-Joseph Le Moyne de Longueuil; Jean Bouillet de Lachassaigne, Boisberthelot de Beaucour, Vaudreuil-Cavagnial and his brother François-Pierre Rigaud de Vaudreuil, and Claude de Ramezay. We should also mention two king's lieutenants (serving as deputies to a particular governor): François Galliffet and Louis Laporte de Louvigny.

The Conseil supérieur was the highest Court of Justice in New France. Sixteen of its members, including six judges and four procureurs du roi (Crown attorneys) owned a total of forty-three slaves. Senior officials of the colonial administration also held slaves: a commissary (alternate intendant in Montreal), a treasurer of the Marine, a director of the Compagnie des Indes, an assistant commissary of provisions, a port captain, and three storekeepers. In other words, a total of forty-seven of the most senior administrative officials in New France owned 260 slaves.

SENIOR BRITISH OFFICIALS

Senior British officials also held slaves. Governor General Murray had at least one black woman slave whom he transferred to the tavern keeper Miles Prenties in 1766; he seems to have been the only governor of the British regime who owned a slave. In November 1768, Lieutenant Governor Hector-Theophilus Cramahé bought a fifteen-year-old mulatto girl, selling her off again the following

April. A lieutenant governor of Detroit (from the time when Detroit was part of Quebec), and husband of Marie-Julie Réaume, had a few slaves.

Twenty-three members of the Executive and Legislative Councils were slaveholders, and of these twenty-three, ten were francophones although they owned more slaves than the other thirteen anglophone members of these councils. This confirms what we already knew, namely that even after the Conquest, French Canadians had more slaves than the British of Canada did.

Among other senior officials under the British regime who owned slaves, we may note eight judges (including two francophones) and a solicitor general: this group held seventeen slaves.

Seventeen members of the House of Assembly, including ten francophones, owned a total of forty-two slaves. In 1792 alone, the year of an abortive parliamentary attempt to abolish slavery (we will return to this subject later), thirteen of fifty-one members of the House of Assembly were slave owners. In addition, the Receiver of Customs, Thomas Ainslie, owned three black slaves.

Merchants Were Leading Slave Owners

It cost an average of 900 livres to buy a black slave, and 400 livres to buy an Amerindian one. Merchants engaging in trade in the *pays d'en haut* around the Great Lakes could acquire Amerindian slaves at better prices. In any case, merchants had ready cash, they traded with the Amerindians, or they maintained commercial relations (sometimes secretly) with the Thirteen Colonies: they were thus the best-placed people to acquire slaves.

Merchants were leading slave owners as a result. We identified 316 slave owners in historical records who were described as merchants, traders, entrepreneurs or bourgeois. They represented the colony's leading commercial interests, whether under the French or British regimes. This group included the merchant-bourgeois Pierre Guy, with eight slaves; the merchant Dominique Gaudet, who had seventeen; and the Chaboillez, Courault *dit* Lacoste, Cuillerier, Decouagne, Douaire de Bondy, Gamelin, Hubert-Lacroix, Lestage,

Lecompte-Dupré, and Trottier-Desaulniers merchant families, all of whom had several slaves. A total of 314 merchants, traders and bourgeois owned 832 slaves.

To this group should be added thirty-six slave owners described simply as trading families, such as the Blot, Campeau, Gouin, Trutaut and You d'Youville families. The single most prominent of the slave-owning traders was Jacques-François Lacelle, who is known to have held sixteen slaves.

Some historical documents specify the business activity of these slave owners: among them were nine butchers including the celebrated Joseph-Michel Cadet; eleven tavern keepers, innkeepers or publicans, the merchant and goldsmith Ignace-François Delzenne; and voyageurs who were not just employed paddling canoes but were actually fur traders in their own right. This group of 419 slave-owning business people can be broken down as follows:

	Owners	Slaves
Merchants, traders, bourgeois	314	832
Fur traders	35	112
Starchmakers, gunsmiths	5	8
Butchers	9	13
Bakers	6	11
Hotel keepers, tavern keepers, publicans	11	18
Goldsmith	1	1
"Voyageurs"	38	73
Total	419	1068

Four hundred nine of these merchants were slaveholders, or fully 51.2% of owners whose occupation was recorded. This group owned a quarter (1068 individuals) of all slaves. Since members of this merchant class included both francophones and anglophones, the question naturally arises which group held the most slaves under British rule. Of 157 slave-owning merchants after 1760, eighty-seven were francophones, holding 234 slaves, while seventy were anglophones holding just 168 slaves. In other words, 55.4% of merchants after 1760 were French and they owned 58.2% of the slaves in this period.

AMONG PROFESSIONALS

Merchants formed the largest group here, but other professions were also well represented among slave owners.

Coming immediately after merchants were military officers, who also played a key role in the fur trade: they controlled trading posts and forts, which also served in the fur trade. We already mentioned several governors and king's lieutenants who owned slaves. In addition, 164 other military officers (20% of owners whose profession was recorded) owned a total of 431 slaves. In this group of officers, we should note General de Lévis who had a black slave in 1759; Bissot de Vincennes (father and son) with eight slaves; the Céloron de Blainville, Chaussegros de Léry and Coulon de Villiers (including the celebrated Coulon de Jumonville) families; the various Dailleboust families (Argenteuil, Cuisy, Cerry, Périgny and Manthet), the Denys de Laronde and Duplessis-Fabert families; the Fleurimont de Noyelle (father and son); the Hertel (Beaubassin de Lafresnière, de Rouville) families; the Jarret de Verchères, Joncaire de Chabert, Juchereau-Duchesnay, Leber de Senneville, and the Legardeur families (Repentigny, Courtemanche, de Saint-Pierre, de Croisille, de Montesson, de Beauvais); the Marin (de Laperrière, de Lamalgue), Péan de Livaudière, Pécaudy de Contrecoeur and Picoté de Belestre families.

Three names stand out among military families owning slaves: Lavérendrye, Lacorne and Lapérade.

We already noted that the explorer Pierre Gaultier de Lavérendrye counted as one of three major advantages of explorations "the slaves procured thereby for the country," but it seems he only had three slaves. His sons had at least six: for example, in 1749 Chevalier Louis-Joseph de Lavérendrye gave an Amerindian boy about six years old to the Jesuit mission of Michilimackinac.

The five Lacorne brothers had a total of forty-four slaves: Antoine Lacorne de Lacolombière had just one black woman and François-Josué Lacorne-Dubreuil just four Amerindians, but Louis Lacorne the elder and Chevalier Louis-François Lacorne each had eight slaves, while Luc Lacorne Saint-Luc had twenty-four.

The Tarieu de Lapérade family were among the wealthiest slave owners. Pierre-Thomas Tarieu de Lanaudière de Lapérade, husband of Madeleine Verchères, had thirteen slaves, all of them Amerindians, whereas his son and grandson each owned four slaves.

In addition to these well-known officers, some lesser known military men turn up in historical records, such as a sergeant by the name of Sansquartier, who had a fourteen-year-old Amerindian girl slave. Actually, all ranks profited from slavery.

Twenty-two physicians and surgeons (only five of whom were anglophones) counted a total of forty-six slaves among their personal property. The surgeon Ferdinand Feltz led this group with a stunning ten slaves.

Notaries also practiced slavery. We know of twenty such notaries, all of them francophones. Leading this group was Jean-Baptiste Campeau of the famous fur-trading family, who owned seven slaves. However, care should be taken not to count some notaries twice if they practised two professions: the notaries François-Pierre Cherrier and Robert Navarre were also merchants; Marien Tailhandier was both notary and surgeon, and Pierre Mézière and Simon Sanguinet practised both as notaries and lawyers. Even so, twenty notaries appear in our catalogue, and they owned a total of thirty-eight slaves.

Other professions were less well represented. We found just two surveyors, Claude Gouin with eleven slaves and Paul-François Lemaître-Lamorille with five. The master sculptor Dominique Jourdain-Labrosse was comfortable enough to own a Panis woman, and when she gave birth to a son, he ended up owning two slaves. In 1784, a "master of languages" in Sorel, Alexander Bissett, paid 960 livres for a black girl twelve years of age, but this was only a way of recovering a loan he had made, and once his debtor paid up, Bissett was to give the slave back. Five interpreters had one slave each.

Printers also owned slaves. The first printers operating in Quebec were William Brown and Thomas Gilmore, who printed the *Quebec Gazette*: they owned black slaves, at least from 1767. Their partnership was dissolved in 1773, after which Brown owned the blacks working in the printing shop, the most notorious of whom was assuredly Joe, whose escapes and mischief were well known. When John Neilson took over the publication from Brown, he had a black woman and a mulatto man in his service. Fleury Mesplet had at least one black slave when he published the *Gazette de Montréal* (now the *Montreal Gazette*). When Edward Edwards took over this publication, he had two black women and a mulatto man. Finally, William Moore, printer of the *Quebec Herald*, had a black man.

Three entrepreneurs had two slaves each. Twenty-five navigators had a combined total of thirty-one slaves. These navigators – all francophones – included ten ship captains, among them Michel de Salaberry, ancestor of the celebrated Salaberry family.

Finally, tradesmen also had slaves. The master carpenter Nicolas Morand had six Panis; the carpenter Charles Payan had a black woman in 1792. Nine blacksmiths had a combined total of twenty-five mostly black slaves: the most important of these blacksmiths was Louis Cureux *dit* St-Germain of Quebec City, who bought five black slaves in 1743 – two of them men, and three women. Four masons owned five slaves each. A woodworker, an anglophone saddler and a toolmaker held one slave each. Three tanners had six slaves working for them. Eight tailors, two of them anglophones, owned a combined total of ten slaves.

Many of these slave owners, whether tradesmen, businessmen, professionals or senior officials, had one thing in common: they were seigneurs. Indeed, 146 owned a seigneurie as well as a combined total of 467 slaves:

	Number	Slaves
French-speaking seigneurs	136	442
English-speaking seigneurs	10	25

Given that there were about 300 seigneuries in what is now Quebec, and even though some slave owners succeeded one another as seigneurs, we can say conclusively that half of all seigneurs owned slaves. The Lemoyne de Longueuil, Tarieu de Lapérade and Rigaud de Vaudreuil families owned several slaves at a time; other seigneurial families consistently owned one or two slaves: for example, the Aubert de Lachesnaie, Boucher de Niverville, Juchereau-Duchesnay, Rimbault de Simblin, Ramezay and Trottier-Desruisseaux families. This means that many seigneurial manors had just a single slave working for them (if the seigneur lived modestly), whereas several slaves could be found in the larger seigneuries of Longueuil or Sainte-Anne-de-la-Pérade.

Bishops, Priests, Nuns ... and Slaves

We already mentioned the nineteenth-century historian François-Xavier Garneau, who flattered the Church with the following statement (perhaps as a way of excusing himself for his previous attacks): "the government and Canadian clergy should be honoured for consistently opposing the introduction of Blacks into Canada." Actually, we could not find any single instance where the clergy opposed introducing blacks into Canada. Individual clergymen may have stood against slavery, for example during a 1740 trial involving a Panis slave, when Chevalier Dormicourt testified he was "astonished to see priests and monks secretly arming against him without prior warning, in order to snatch away his slave, and to see clergymen groundlessly attacking the reputation of an honest man, while treating a rascally wench and a libertine gently and with all consideration." But were these priests and monks intervening on behalf of the Panis because she was treated as a slave, or were they defending an Amerindian woman who claimed to be the daughter of a Canadian officer? And even if it turned out that these clergy "secretly armed against" Dormicourt because they were opposed to slavery, that does not change the fact that bishops, priests and religious communities all owned slaves. In a society where slavery was sanctioned by law, practiced by the most prominent people, and widely accepted as a social fact, we do not see why the clergy would have acted differently from the rest of society: the Church, after all, had the same property rights. Four bishops were slave owners: in 1690, Bishop Saint-Vallier sought treatment at the Hôtel-Dieu de Québec for the young Amerindian Bernard, who belonged to him; in 1734, Bishop Dosquet arrived in Quebec with a black man in his service; in April 1754, Bishop Pontbriand owned the Panis Joseph who was admitted to the Hotel-Dieu de Québec; during his European travels in 1819-1820, Bishop Plessis was accompanied by a black slave.

Two Sulpicians feature in our catalogue of slave owners: in 1753, François Picquet who went to France with his black Charles; and on September 28, 1760, Pierre-Paul-François Delagarde buried his eleven-year-old Panis Anselme in Montreal.

Four other secular priests also feature in the catalogue. In 1751, Gaspard Dunière, priest of St-Augustin, had a black slave, Daniel-Télémaque, who was admitted to the Hôtel-Dieu de Québec. On July 28, 1779, Henri-Nicolas Catin, priest of St-Cuthbert, baptized his seventeen-year-old black Pierre-Antoine in Montreal. On June 13, 1794, Pierre Fréchette, a priest of Detroit (which was still part of Quebec), baptized his Panis Marianne. But the most famous priest to own slaves was Louis Payet, a priest of Detroit, and subsequently of Saint-Antoine-sur-Richelieu, who owned a total of five slaves: an Amerindian boy twelve years old; two black males, ten and thirty-one years old; two black women, one twenty years old who lived with him in Detroit and the other thirty-one years old whom he bought once he became priest of Saint-Antoine-sur-Richelieu and whom he sold again in September 1796.

Indeed Father Payet seems always to have had one or two slaves in his presbytery from at least 1785 onwards. He lost his black slave François, so he took on another ten-year-old black slave, Jean-Baptiste-Pompée, on a temporary basis; in January 1787, he bought this latter slave; in Saint-Antoine on September 13, 1789, Payet baptized his two slaves in style – the black as Jean-Baptiste-Pompée and the Amerindian Antoine *dit* César. In March 1785 he bought the thirty-one-year old black woman Rose, at a time of rising agitation against slavery; but in September 1796, when

Payet's bishop ruled it unsuitable for this slave woman to cohabit with him in the presbytery, the priest sold her off by proxy. In fact, this slave sale undertaken by Father Payet was among the latest slave transactions in Quebec. All of which means that his contemporary, the historian Garneau, was completely misinformed.

The Séminaire de Québec was a community of secular priests, and owned slaves the same way individual secular priests did. Not in Quebec, it seems, but in the far-distant mission of Sainte-Famille, at Kaskaskia on the Mississippi. We know from a deed of sale from 1763 that the seminary owned thirty black and Amerindian slaves there. Once France ceded Canada to Great Britain, Father Forget du Verger, member of the Seminary and vicar general of the bishop of Quebec, decided to return to France in November that year: he sold a dozen black slaves for 20,000 livres, gave two slaves to the Récollet Father Luc Collet and freed the rest.[114]

The Jesuits also owned slaves. At the Michilimackinac mission, the Jesuits held four slaves, among them a black man; one of the Amerindians had been given to them by Chevalier de Lavérendrye. At Pointe-de-Montréal (across from Detroit), they had a Panis slave (described as such in the civil registry). At Sault St-Louis they owned the Panis Alexis, who was buried in Montreal in 1723. Joseph Aubery and Marin-Louis Lefranc, missionaries at Saint-François-du-Lac, had a Sioux woman named Françoise serving them (the Sioux were reduced to slavery); according to Franquet, she was "quite pretty, she has a sweet and seductive voice." Jesuits based in Quebec City had a recently-freed Paducah who had been baptized in 1730; one of their Panis and two Illinois Amerindians were admitted to the Hôtel-Dieu: these latter three were described as domestic servants, but given that they originated from the Midwest, we believe they were or had been slaves. Finally, the Jesuits had thirty-four black slaves in the Kaskaskia region of the Mississippi mission, where the Séminaire de Québec also had a mission.[115]

We should add a Récollet Father to this catalogue of slave owners: the Récollet Bonaventure Léonard, missionary in Detroit, owned three Amerindians, a Paducah, a Fox woman and her son. Since Récollet Fathers could not in principle own property, either individually or collectively, these slaves probably came from donations to the Church's treasures.

The Brothers of Charity, active at Louisbourg, owned the black man Baptiste, but lost him in circumstances unknown to us, although the commissary of Île Royale had the slave returned to them, an action which received the official endorsement of the president of the Conseil de la Marine.[116]

Did nuns own slaves? The Hôpital-Général de Québec had a black slave, a deserter from the Thirteen Colonies, who had been donated to them by the governor general; he was baptized in 1733. Six years later, a Panis sought treatment at the Hôtel-Dieu de Québec. The Hôtel-Dieu de Montréal seems to have owned three Amerindian women and one black woman (civil status registries for 1720, 1733, 1737 and1798). The Sisters of the Congregation of Notre Dame had a Fox girl in bondage, Tonton, who died at the Hôtel-Dieu de Québec in April 1733; they also had a black male in bondage, baptized in Montreal in 1771 and buried two years later.

The Hôpital-Général de Montréal had more slaves than any other women's religious community. In 1763, a female member of the Jarret de Verchères family who was the widow of a member of the Raimbault de Simblin family, donated a teenaged Panis to the hospital. Before heading back to France the following year, the merchant André Grasset de Saint-Sauveur gave the hospital his eleven-year-old Panis girl, who was baptized in 1772. The same institution had a Sioux who was baptized in 1774 in Châteauguay.

Mother d'Youville, superior of this community, accepted gifts of slaves from Widow Simblin and Monsieur Grasset de Saint-Sauveur. But this was not the community's first experience of slavery. Mother d'Youville personally owned slaves. In 1731, a notary drew up an inventory of the estate of her deceased husband, François-Madeleine You d'Youville, noting a Panis slave who became his widow's property. Mother d'Youville had other slaves, for example a Sioux woman baptized in 1739 and buried in 1742; in Lachine in 1766, another Panis woman belonging to Mother d'Youville was baptized without the usual rites. In other words, this founder of the Sisters of Charity practiced slavery the same way as other members of Canadian religious congregations, in particular, and the society of New France in general.

We did not find any documented trace of slaves among the Ursulines of Quebec. Did this community abstain from slave ownership on principle or out of indifference? It would be interesting to consult the memorandum submitted by Intendant Bégon to the Regent, although we were not able to track it down. We do not believe it would be fair to assume that the Ursulines decided on principle against slave ownership. Louisiana was after all part of the diocese of Quebec, and therefore subject to the same church discipline: the Ursulines of New Orleans acquired a batch of "twenty-four Negroes" in 1746, at a cost of 30,000 livres.[117]

The following table summarizes slave ownership by bishops, priests, nuns and religious communities:

	Slaves		Slaves
Four bishops	4	Hôpital-Général de Québec	1
Jesuits	46	Hôtel-Dieu de Québec	1
Récollets	4	Hôtel-Dieu de Montréal	4
Séminaire de Québec	31	Congrégation de Notre-Dame	2
Séminaire de Montréal	2	Hôpital-Général de Montréal	3
Four secular priests	8	Mother d'Youville	3 or 4
Brothers of Charity	1		

Bishops, priests, nuns and members of religious communities thus owned a hundred slaves – a relatively small number, although what counts in this case is not the overall numbers of slaves but the fact that religious owned slaves at all.

Our discussion of slave ownership would be incomplete were we to leave out the state. In New France, the state received some slaves as gifts from Amerindians attending councils prior to fur trade negotiations. The state also needed slaves to perform certain unpleasant tasks such as public executioner. The king, in other words the state, became a slave owner in various different circumstances.

We identified twenty-eight state-owned slaves in historical records: three blacks and twenty-five Amerindians. The three blacks were from Quebec: Mathieu Léveillé was public executioner from at least 1734 until his death in 1743; Angéline-Denise was a twenty-four-year-old black woman brought by authorities from the French West Indies to serve as the executioner's wife; in 1752 the black Étienne was assigned to work at the shipyard. Of the twenty-five above-mentioned Amerindians, two Fox slaves were transported to Martinique for sale in 1734, while the remainder served in Montreal – twelve Panis males, eight Panis females and three more Amerindian slaves of unknown origin, all of whom ranged in age from five to forty years.

As owners of more than a quarter of all Canadian slaves, merchants were the leading slave-owning group, while public officials were a distant second, and military officers well behind in third place. The rest of society accounted for only 7.9% of all slave ownership.

There is nothing absolute about these data, since the owners of 600 slaves are unknown to us, and we were only able to identify the profession of 819 of 1574 slave owners overall. It is conceivable that of the 755 slave owners whose profession is unknown to us, some may have been simple *habitants* – farmers tilling the land.

WHO WERE THE LEADING OWNERS?

The slave population in colonial Canada was small, compared to what could be found in the Thirteen Colonies and the Caribbean. An analysis of more than 1574 owners indicates that few owners here had many slaves, although the concept "many" is relative, since even the leading slave owners in Canada would have seemed small-scale owners in other countries where slavery existed.

Slave Owner	Slaves
Askin, John, merchant	23
Beauharnois, Charles, Governor	27
Beuffait, Louis, merchant	10
Boisberthelot de Beaucour, Josué, Governor	11
Cabassié, Joseph, bourgeois	14
Campbell, John, officer	17
Louis Campeau, fur trader	11
Campeau, Simon	10
Chesne-Labutte, Pierre, shopkeeper	15
Cicotte, Zacharie, bourgeois	16
Duperron-Bâby, Jacques, merchant	18
Feltz, Ferdinand, surgeon	10
Fleurimont de Noyes, Nicolas-Joseph, officer	12
Fleury Deschambault de Lagorgendière, Joseph, merchant	15
Gaudet, Dominique merchant	17
Gouin, Claude, surveyor	11
Grant, Alexander, officer	10
Jesuits	46
Lacelle, Jacques-François, fur trader	16
Lacorne Saint-Luc, Luc, officer	24
Lemoyne de Longueuil, Charles, Governor	10
Lemoyne de Longueuil, Paul Joseph, Governor	23
Meloche, Jean-Baptiste	10
Péan de Livaudière, Michel-Jean-Hugues, officer	10
Pelletier, Jacques	11
Poulin de Francheville, François, merchant	10
Rigaud de Vaudreuil, Philippe, Governor	11
Rigaud de Vaudreuil-Cavagnial, Pierre, Governor	16
Séminaire de Québec	31
Tarieu de Lanaudière, Pierre-Thomas, officer	13

The previous table provides thirty names of slave owners who held at least ten slaves each.

The list contains only thirty of some 1574 owners, yet only two of the people on this list had more than thirty slaves. Slave ownership in Quebec was not at all on the same scale as slave ownership in colonies to the south...

In fact, slavery in Quebec was not some economic imperative, but rather a form of public extravagance which conferred prestige on to members of high society but also on to all other levels of society indulging in it. Among the second rank of important slave owners and well ahead of the nobility were the "little people" – the Campeau family, engaged in the fur trade.

CHAPTER SIX

The Living Conditions of Slaves

When owners purchased a slave in a notarized sale, or had the slave baptized, they generally promised to treat the slave humanely; but was this a promise to meet standards of treatment set by the authorities, or was it a voluntary commitment on the owners' part, reflecting their intention to treat the slave as a human being? In other words, did owners have to comply with a code defining the respective duties of owners and slaves? Were slaves treated humanely? Did they enjoy certain rights?

SLAVE LEGISLATION AND PROTECTION IN CANADA

In March 1685, Louis XIV responded to requests from colonial authorities by issuing an edict comprising sixty articles, known as the *Code Noir*, to settle "issues dealing with the condition and quality of slaves."[118]

The *Code Noir* stipulates that slaves are personal property, they can be seized as movable property, but husband, wife and prepubescent children cannot be taken and sold separately; these slaves can have nothing which does not belong to their master, and whatever they earn through their own industry or generosity belongs to their master; they are "incapable of disposing or contracting on their own behalf"; they cannot exercise any public office, and their statements in court are to be treated as briefs from which "neither presumption nor conjecture can be drawn."

The *Code Noir* also states that all slaves shall be baptized and instructed in the Catholic faith, they cannot publicly practise any other religion, and any masters allowing their slaves to practise any non-Catholic faith shall be severely punished; slaves shall observe

Sundays and no slave markets shall be held on Sundays. All baptized slaves shall be buried in holy ground, and on dying, any non-baptized slave shall be buried "by night in a field near the place" of death.

The *Code Noir* stipulates that whites are prohibited from concubinage with "Negresses", and the free man having children with such a concubine shall be fined two thousand pounds of sugar, together with the master who accepted it; and where the master himself lives in concubinage, the black woman and children shall be confiscated and awarded to the Hôpital-Général without being emancipated, unless the master (where celibate) marries his concubine slave, in which case the slave woman is emancipated by the very fact of marriage and children are both freed and legitimized. The *Code* authorizes black slaves to marry, but under certain conditions: the slave does not require the consent of his own father and mother, but he must obtain the consent of his master; furthermore, the master is not allowed to marry slaves against their will; children born from marriages between slaves shall be slaves, and if the father is free and the mother a slave, the children shall also be slaves; if a male slave has married a free woman, their children, either male or female, shall be free like their mother.

The *Code Noir* specifies the minimum food and clothing a master must provide to his slaves, although slaves are prohibited from drinking alcoholic spirits. If a master does not meet this minimum standard, the slave may lodge a complaint with a Crown attorney who shall prosecute the party concerned. Moreover, the slaves who are infirm due to age, illness or otherwise, shall be cared for by their masters, failing which they shall be cared for by the Hôpital-Général at their masters' expense.

Masters may free their slaves; these freed slaves shall not need letters of naturalization to enjoy the benefits of natural subjects, "even when they are born in foreign countries," and freed slaves are granted the same rights, privileges and immunities enjoyed by freeborn persons.

The *Code Noir* also specifies slave punishments. It stipulates various penalties for the slave who carries an offensive weapon or "large stick," who gathers in a crowd; the slave who has drawn the blood of his master, mistress or their children, shall be punished by death; slaves who assault free persons, and also some cases of robbery, shall be subject to severe penalties or even the death penalty. The fugitive slave shall have his ears cut off, and shall be branded with a fleur de lys on the shoulder; if he commits the same infraction a second time, he shall have his hamstring cut; the third time, he shall be put to death. When masters wish to punish their slaves, they may chain them and have them beaten with rods, although they are forbidden from torturing them or mutilating any limb; officers of justice may prosecute masters who have killed a slave under their control.

Such were the provisions of the *Code Noir*. France was the first country to define relations between masters and slaves with such precision. There was a trace of humanity in the *Code Noir*. Since slaves were guaranteed minimum living conditions: they had to be instructed in the Catholic faith; no master had the right to abandon slaves who had grown old; father, mother and children could not be sold separately; by marrying a white male, the female slave became free; in general the freed slave enjoyed the same rights as the natural subject without needing letters of naturalization. In other words, the slave was considered a human being, who could eventually enter white society and enjoy the same rights and privileges as whites. However, the *Code Noir* also acknowledged that the slave was dangerous, and it therefore protected the white person by imposing strict measures against the slave who plundered, revolted or fled.

The preamble to the *Code Noir* of 1685 states that it only applied to the Islands of French America (in the Caribbean). In 1724, the King of France issued another *Code Noir* to settle the condition of blacks in Louisiana.[119] The Louisiana *Code Noir* comprises fifty-four articles, thirty-one of which were drawn directly from the previous *Code Noir*; the new articles consist of minor changes, except in the case of marriage: whites of both sexes are prohibited "from contracting marriage with blacks, under penalty of punishment and arbitrary fines" and priests are prohibited from celebrating such marriages. Apart from the absolute prohibition of marriage between whites and blacks, the Louisana *Code Noir* did not cover much new ground, although it showed that a *Code Noir* published in one French colony was not necessarily valid in another colony.

Given the small number of slaves in New France, there did not seem to be any need for a distinct *Code Noir*, or rather *Code Rouge*, since Amerindian slaves (called "rouges" or redskins) outnumbered black slaves. New France did not even get a freshly-printed edition of the *Codes* of either the Caribbean or Louisiana. We could find no specific rules on how to treat slaves in Canada, whether in the royal edicts and ordinances issued for Canada, the transcription of acts in public registries by the Conseil supérieur, or Intendant Raudot's ordinance legalizing the purchase and possession of Panis and black slaves. As a result, we do not need to ask whether a slave owner was complying with a law of Canada, in granting a particular privilege to his slave, or in imposing a condition: in fact, no such law existed in Canada. It is interesting to note however that slave owners generally complied with provisions of the *Code Noir* of the Caribbean or of Louisiana, even when not required to do so.

Were Slaves Treated as Adopted Children?

Benjamin Sulte claimed "slaves were merely servants who made up part of their master's family," although he did not investigate slavery as thoroughly as we did.[120] Sulte should have qualified this statement, which nonetheless gives an idea of the character of slavery in New France. By law or through custom, Panis and Amerindians from several other nations were handed over to servitude, and presented as adopted children. When the Panis Charlotte was buried on April 13, 1777 in Terrebonne at the age of five years, she belonged by adoption to Hyacinthe Janis; when the Fox Michel-Louis, aged six, was baptized on September 29; 1718 he was recorded as having been adopted by Lanoullier; when the Fox Jean-Baptiste was baptized on November 26, 1715 he was adopted by Jacques Hubert-Lacroix; the same could be said for the Missouri Joseph-Nicolas, aged nine years, whose July 18, 1731 act of baptism stated that he had previously been adopted by the late Joseph Legris; the Panis Pierre, aged six, was adopted by Pierre Garault *dit* Saint-Onge when he was baptized on October 7, 1713. Sometimes, civil registries simply indicate "adopted child." This was the case for the Panis Claude, adopted son of Pierre Beigné in 1742; of the Panis Élisabeth, adopted daughter of Louis Leroux *dit* Lachaussée in 1713; of the Panis Jean-Baptiste, adopted son of Jean Cardinal in 1722; of the Panis Marie-Françoise, adopted daughter of Jean-François Chorel Dorvilliers in 1713. These Amerindians were sometimes later identified in records as the property of their masters, but the fact they were characterized as adopted children gives a whole different flavour to slavery in New France, as compared to the French West Indies.

Whether the master treated his slave as an adopted child or not, the slave received special care. For example, a newborn slave was sometimes put out to nurse: was this an indication of the master's paternal concern or simply of his desire to maintain the quality of livestock? He could have had both motivations. When Pierre Raimbault's unnamed Panis slave gave birth to a son Joseph in 1723, the master put the child out to nurse in the household of a parishioner of Rivière-des-Prairies, Nicolas Benoist, husband of Catherine Thibault: the child died there, aged six weeks, and was buried on June 1, 1723. When the Fox Marie, belonging to the widow of Georges Regnard-Duplessis, gave birth in December 1727 to an illegitimate daughter she had with Le Verrier the younger, the child was sent to Ancienne-Lorette, a place where people in Quebec often put their children out to nurse: the illegitimate infant girl, Marie-Françoise, was buried there on January 25, 1728. Marie-Anne-Victoire, a black slave belonging to Governor General Vaudreuil-Cavagnial, gave birth to a son in November 1757, who was baptized in Montreal the same day – the governor immediately put the infant out to nurse with Widow Janot-Lachapelle at Pointe-aux-Trembles, although the child was buried there on December 1, at the age of six days. We also know of the case of Marie-Charlotte, legitimate daughter of Jacques and Marie, a black couple belonging to Luc Lacorne Saint-Luc: she was born January 23, 1759 and baptized two days later in Montreal, then immediately put out to nurse with

Widow Lapistole, of Longueuil, but the child died there in August, aged eight months. There are not many historical records of wet-nursing, but it seems that the children of slaves actually received the same care as the owner's own children.

READING AND WRITING AMONG SLAVES

The young slaves grew up alongside other children, but did they get a basic education? What did slaves receive besides religious instruction, a subject we discuss elsewhere in this book? We would first of all have to establish what children of average families got in the way of education, although the lack of specialized studies in this area means we have to content ourselves with guesswork. Canadians under the French regime and after the British Conquest often signed their names with a cross: did this mean they were illiterate? Or did they sign their names with a cross, as some authors have claimed, because they were afraid to affix their signature? Very little is known about illiteracy in New France and colonial Canada, so we will focus solely on the education of slaves.

Slaves were usually illiterate. Several times, slaves or freedmen were called upon to sign civil registries or other official documents, and they almost always replied they could not sign. Some slaves ventured to sign documents with a cross or mark. For example, as we said above, Guillaume Couillart's black slave gave evidence in court, in 1638: he drew a cross at the bottom of the document, even though he was enrolled in the Jesuit school of Father Le Jeune. His master Guillaume Couillart was no more knowledgeable, however: he signed with a drawing of a man lying on his back.

It is interesting for a historical researcher to discover slaves signing with a cross, but it still more interesting to discover actual signatures. We only found one such signature among Amerindian slaves: the Fox Michel-Louis, identified as a Panis and called Michel Ouysconsin.

There were far fewer black than Amerindian slaves, yet we found five signatures among black slaves: Pierre-Dominique Lafleur, Joseph Lafricain, Marie-Louise Williams, Joseph Pierson and Nancy Bradshaw. Of these five slaves able to sign their names, only one lived under the French regime; the others lived after 1800, and were either slaves or freedmen.

Signing one's name was not necessarily proof of having been educated: did some slaves get beyond the point of signing their names? In July 1779, the merchant John Turner Sr. announced that his black Ismael, aged about thirty-five years, had fled; according to the description given in the *Quebec Gazette*, this slave read English fairly well. Dollier de Casson mentioned a female Potawatomi slave who (thanks to a dowry) was educated by the Sisters of the Congregation, learned French and was in condition to marry: her education had to be roughly like that of the young girls of the Congregation. A former slave reportedly studied at the Collège de Montréal: Charles Mouet de Langlade, son of Charles Mouet de Langlade, was born before 1754 to an Amerindian slave, and according to the custom of the time, was therefore a slave like his mother; but he was fortunate enough to be recognized legally by his father, who took pains to raise him and send him to the Collège de Montréal.[121] These were exceptional cases.

LEARNING A TRADE

Did Amerindians and blacks have qualifications for particular types of employment, at least during the time they were held in bondage? Few Amerindians seem to have had technical skills: they generally fell into the somewhat vague category of domestic service. When Amerindian slaves belonging to Governor Beauharnois were admitted to the Hôtel-Dieu-de-Québec, they were described as lackeys or footmen: in 1733, the Fox François, aged 11; the Fox Louis, aged 10, the two Eskimos Charles Coli and Charles-Hilarion; in 1736, the Paducah Joseph. The title they were given possibly did not accurately reflect their duties, but whatever the case, the position of footman provided some security since footmen were so rare. While she was held in bondage, one Amerindian woman worked as a servant outside of her master's home: the Panis Catherine belonged to the wife of Louis Maray de Lachauvignerie, and worked as a servant for the surgeon Benoist;[122] the Lachauvignerie family probably did not need a Panis idling in their home, so they put her to work elsewhere. Another case was the Panis Charlot, of Detroit, who seems to have become the parish beadle. At a time when few slaves served as witnesses at church ceremonies, he attended forty-three burials, most of them burials of children.

Some Amerindian slaves worked as weavers. We know that Madame Legardeur de Repentigny, née Agathe Saint-Père, operated a small factory in Montreal; in 1705, Canadian authorities wrote that "the public derives a benefit from Madame de Repentigny's factory, which manufactures large covers of coarse linen thread out of tree bark, and a kind of drugget made of coarse wool from the colony, which is a great help to poor people unable to buy costlier goods from France." Madame de Repentigny spent a lot of money "buying materials from the English Indians who knew this trade" and "took Canadians in, to train them."[123] She procured workmen who knew weaving from the English, to get her factory up and running. We do not know the names of the slaves who kept this short-lived Montreal factory going.

It is particularly interesting to note that several Amerindian slaves got their master's permission to serve as boatmen and voyageurs in the *pays d'en haut*. This meant masters had to make sure they did not lose their slaves in the wilderness! We found eight names of Amerindian slaves working in the fur trade.

They served in the fur trade between 1719 and 1766, but in five cases, the master himself signed the employment agreement on the slave's behalf, and in two more cases a notary specified that the master had authorized his slave to serve in this capacity. The Panis François and Pierre handed half their earnings to their master: according to the *Code Noir* for the Islands of French America, everything the slave earned went to the slave owner, whereas in this case, the master settled for half of his slave's earnings. Two of these Amerindians had a special task to perform: the Brochet Louis, belonging to the French merchant Jolliet, was hired as a guide, while the Panis slave Louis-Josephs, belonging to Farly, served as helmsman.[124]

Amerindian slaves only worked as servants or boatmen, but the *Gazette de Montréal* and the *Quebec Herald* reveal that black slaves practiced a range of trades, from barber to hairdresser, printing pressman, cooper, sailor, soldier and executioner.

Blacks often had several different skills, and owners putting their slaves up for sale never failed to list their many talents: Samuel Morin's mulatto slave was good in the kitchen, knew how to keep a house in order, did needlework and cared for children; when Moore the printer put his black slave up for sale in 1790, he described her as "suitable for almost all kinds of work, a good cook and maid; she knows how to milk cows and how to make butter." If we are to believe the classified ads in newspapers, all these black people – male and female alike – were very good cooks. It seems that the mulatto Rosalie, who first belonged to Duperron-Bâby, then to Charles-Eusèbe Casgrain, was an expert chef: "Rose knew the culinary arts just as well as her mother did," wrote P. B. Casgrain. "She excelled in pastry and confectionery. We still talk about her baked piglets and roast snipe."[125] In reading Casgrain, one is tempted to cry out "Long live slavery!"

Like Amerindian slaves, blacks held in bondage sometimes worked in the fur trade with the permission or on the initiative of their master, or to make the voyage to the Illinois Country, working as a sailor. In the latter case, the slave received food, a jug of alcoholic spirits each month and tobacco.[126] He may have preferred this to a straight money wage.

DRESS

How did slaves dress? The *Code Noir* of the French West Indies required the owner to provide his slave with two coats of linen or four ells of cloth. Masters obviously needed to provide more clothing in Canada, although they did not need to go as far as Ruette d'Auteuil's proposal of dressing black slaves in beaver fur. We are working here on the basis of fragmentary information.

Details of Amerindian slave dress are extremely scarce. During a trial in 1727, the Panis Catherine, belonging to Maray de

Lachauvignerie, sued the surgeon Joseph Benoist with whom she was in service. The Panis complained that her belongings had been confiscated by the surgeon. For the previous three weeks, she had been deprived of the only clothes "she owned, whereas she had none other to change into." These clothes were as follows:

A cotton apron
Three hemp shirts
Eight caps (five large and three muslin)
A mantelet
A pair of gloves
Three skeins of yarn
An old pair of stockings
A pair of moccasins
A flannel petticoat
A stitched cap

Aside from the clothes on Catherine's back, this represented the Panis slave's entire wardrobe, so she was suing to retrieve them. The Court ruled in her favour, and the surgeon was ordered to return her clothes...[127]

The description of a runaway Panis provides us with a few more details of Amerindian slave dress. On June 14, 1778, the Panis Françoise, aged about thirty-five years, ran away from her owner, the widow of Thomas-Ignace Trottier-Dufy-Desaulniers: the slave was said to be of "ordinary height and medium build" and simply dressed in striped cotton. On July 14, 1783, the *Quebec Gazette* announced that the Panis Jacob, aged about twenty, had run away from Daniell and Dalton, wearing "a blue bonnet, a white feathered hat, a ruffled shirt, English shoes and silver buckles, and a bundle of clothes with a greyish coat of fine cloth tied up with a handkerchief." This was evidently a well-dressed slave: with English shoes and silver buckles, a cuffed shirt, his coat of fine cloth and a white feathered hat, the Panis Jacob must have cut a fine figure.

There is far more information about the dress of black slaves. We have, for example, the account books of the printer William

Brown, which enable us to track the various expenses the printer incurred to dress his black slave Joe (excluding, of course, the cost of having Joe whipped).

From the list of expenses in these account books, we conclude that providing Joe with shoes was costly: he often needed new moccasins – three times in 1779, and three more in 1785; in February 1787, the printer gave him five shillings for shoes,[128] but laid out more money for shoes in April and then again in June and September! One wonders whether Joe was reselling all these shoes on the sly.

Newspapers provide interesting details about the dress of fugitive black male slaves:

> Black man belonging to Jean Orillat, of Montreal, about twenty-two years old: on running away on August 20, 1775, he wore a short coat, grey, made of English drugget [coarse wool fabric].

> Black man belonging to Lévy Solomons, of Montreal, about thirteen years old: on running away on April 24, 1788, he wore a stocking cap, large blue breeches [trousers for men, ending above the knee] and a round hat.

> Caleb, a black man belonging to Mathew and John McNider, from twenty-six to twenty-seven years old: he ran away on Sunday, April 13, 1788, wearing "A dark blue frock coat, a coat and a grey jacket, dark blue breeches, white stockings and a round hat."

> Charles, a black man belonging to Pierre-Guillaume Guérout, about twenty years old: he ran away on July 31, 1783, wearing "a grey stocking cap, and large cloth breeches."

> Cuff, a black man belonging to Elisabeth McNeill, of Quebec City, about thirty-eight years old: he ran away on May 28 or

29, 1785, wearing "a white shirt, a grey jacket, the sleeves of old stockings, a blue frock coat, a round hat with band and buckle, green leggings, black buckles on his shoes."

Drummond, a black man belonging to John McCord, of Quebec City: he ran away on the morning of June 25, 1765, wearing a dark cloth coat and leather breeches.

Fortune, a black man belonging to McMurray, about twenty-five years old: he ran away from Carleton Island on July 18, 1780, wearing a large shirt and large cloth breeches.

Ismael, a black man belonging to John Turner, of Montreal, about thirty-five years old: in July 1779, he ran away, wearing a "hat painted white, a smock and large breeches of Osnaburg cloth, a plaid cloth shirt and moccasins." He ran away again on March 7, 1784, wearing "a round pointed hat, with a blue ribbon surrounding the shape of the hat, a plush red jacket, a pair of Amerindian leggings and blue Bergen-op-Zoom breeches, a pair of shoes with metal buckles." On running away a third time, in 1788, he wore a round hat, a blue sailor's waistcoat, a white vest, large blue breeches, but was barefoot.

Jack, a black man belonging to Finlay and Gregory, of Montreal, ran away in the night of Saturday, May 10, 1778, wearing a red coat, trimmed with green, a pair of breeches, a buffalo-skin jacket and an old cap.

Jack, a black man belonging to William Grant, of Quebec City: he ran away in 1792, wearing a stocking cap of thick blue cloth lined with white flannel, a waistcoat of the same color, large breeches of coarse brown cloth.

Jacob, a mulatto belonging to Miles Prenties, of Quebec City, about eighteen years old: he ran away on Friday evening, July 10, 1778, wearing a short coat of light brown fustian and white cloth breeches, a round hat.

Joe, a black man belonging to William Brown, of Quebec City: he ran away on November 22, 1777, wearing a green-coloured soft hat, an old coat of sky blue broadcloth, an old coat of grey cloth, leather breeches, Amerindian leggings and moccasins. He next ran away on January 25, 1778, wearing a green-coloured soft hat, a blue coat with matching vest and breeches, a pair of grey woollen stockings and moccasins. He then ran away on December 22, 1778, wearing an old green-coloured soft hat, a coat of grey-brown cloth and a side-buttoned jacket and fall front trousers of the same cloth with yellow buttons, a pair of black Manchester velvet breeches, grey wool stockings and a pair of Amerindian moccasins. Joe ran away a fourth time on September 16, 1779, wearing "a coat of grey-brown cloth, torn under the arm, and a side-buttoned jacket and fall front trousers of the same cloth with yellow buttons, a pair of leather breeches, old yarn stockings, and a pair of moccasins." He escaped from prison on February 18, 1786, wearing "a blue frock coat, a red stocking cap, a white waistcoat, and a round hat." Finally, he ran away in August 1789, wearing "a red bonnet, a pair of large striped cotton breeches."

Lowcanes, a black man belonging to William Gill, of Quebec City, about twenty-five years old, ran away on November 18, 1775, wearing a short white coat with a red cap, jacket and breeches.

Nemo, a black man belonging to Hugh Ritchie, of Quebec City, about eighteen years old, ran away on October 24, 1779, wearing "a striped flannel side-buttoned waistcoat, old wool stockings and a pair of English shoes."

Nero, a black youth belonging to John Mittleberger, of Montreal, about fourteen years old: he ran away wearing "a blue short coat, lined with red baize, a grey short coat, a ditto [a coat] coloured green, a green cross-stitched stocking cap, a ditto and a large twill breeches, a pair of breeches and a jacket of fustian"; this fourteen-year-old black slave lifted a good supply of clothes before running away from his master, the tailor Mittleberger.

Pompey, a black man belonging to the merchants Johnson and Purss: on August 12, 1771, "when he cleared off," he wore a brown vest and breeches.

Richard, a black man belonging to the merchant Rosseter Hoyle, twenty-five or twenty-seven years old: he ran away in 1790, wearing a brownish-black stocking cap and large breeches.

Robin, a black man belonging to James Fraser: on August 12, 1798, he ran away, wearing "a shirt and large breeches of course cloth, a light coloured jacket, a wool hat and old shoes."

Thompson, John, a black man working on board the ship *Susannah*: he ran away on September 27, 1779, wearing a brown jacket with a flannel stocking cap and black knit breeches, without stockings.

Welden, Elber, a mulatto and apprentice cobbler, about nineteen years old: he ran away on October 7, 1792, wearing a brown coat, a coat of twill, gaiters, a pair of boots and a new hat.

As for runaway black femaile slaves, they are described as follows:

Black woman belonging to Isaac Werden, of Quebec City, about twenty-four years old: she ran away on August 22, 1766, wearing "a black dress and a red callimanco petticoat."

Bett, a black woman belonging to Johnson and Purss, about eighteen years old: this rather short black woman ran away on March 5, 1787, wearing a blue jersey skirt, a brown striped cotton bonnet and an Amerindian shawl worn around the neck.

Cash, a black woman belonging to Hugh Ritchie, of Quebec City, about twenty-six years old: she ran away on October 24, 1779, in the company of the black man Nemo, taking a lot of cloth and personal effects with her, and a big pack of clothing which may include "a mantle of black satin, caps, bonnets, ruffles, ribbons, six seven skirts, an old corsage."

Isabella, a mulatress belonging to George Hipps, of Quebec City, about fifteen years old: she ran away on August 18, 1778, wearing "a striped woollen jacket and petticoat, without stockings or shoes". She ran away again on October 29, 1778, wearing "a striped cotton dress and skirt, a fashionable cap and a black silk handkerchief."

Lydia, a black woman belonging to James Fraser, of Montreal: she ran away on August 12, 1798, wearing "a short blue and white striped dress with a blue drugget skirt and a black silk cap: she [the runaway female slave] is fat and well proportioned."

Given these fragments of information, it is hard to know for certain what slaves wore, although they did not likely wear uniforms. They do not seem to have worn livery, with the possible exception of the Panis Jacob, the slave of Daniell and Dalton, who wore a white feathered hat, clothes of fine cloth, a ruffled shirt, and English shoes with silver buckles; or the black slave Jack, belonging to the merchant William Grant, who wore a thick blue cloth stocking cap lined with white flannel, a waistcoat of the same colour, breeches of coarse brown cloth; or again a black slave belonging to Prentiess put up for sale by the printers of the *Quebec Gazette*: according to an advertisement in March and April 1769, he cut a fine figure, dressed in livery.

In general, slave clothes seem to have been somewhat incongruous, even though black slaves evidently went for the round hat, coarse cloth and English shoes. The mulatto Andrew, slave of the innkeeper James Crofton, ran away in May 1767: according to the *Gazette*, he could be picked out from other mulattos because he made a point of dressing well. Other slaves, however, were shabbily dressed, either through carelessness or because they had nothing better to wear: the merchant John Turner's black slave wore a hat painted white and moccasins; James Fraser's black slave Robin ran away wearing old shoes; and in 1773 the mulatto Isabella, belonging to the butcher Hipps, ran away wearing neither shoes nor stockings. Yet the owners of these slaves were all comfortable bourgeois.

SLAVES AT THE HOSPITAL

The *Code Noir* of the French West Indies (and also of Louisiana) provided that if sick or disabled slaves were not kept in the master's home, they should be admitted to the hospital, where they would be maintained at their master's expense. The *Code Noir* was never actually implemented in Canada, so it is worth asking whether Canadian owners unable to keep their slaves any longer took pains to ensure they got proper care at the hospital. The Hôpital-Général de Montréal as well as the Hôpital-Général and Hôtel-Dieu de Quebec conserved their patient and death records, so we can track the time slaves spent in these hospitals. Unfortunately, records at the Hôtel-Dieu de Montréal did not survive: we only know that eighty slaves died at this hospital because the burial records at Notre-Dame-de-Montréal recorded their place of death.

In any case, we found a high rate of hospitalization among slaves. Between 1690 to 1800 – that is, over a century – 525 slaves were hospitalized in Quebec, Montreal and even in Detroit (although in the latter case, just one slave was admitted):

Hôtel-Dieu de Québec	301 slaves, including 204 Amerindians
Hôpital-Général de Montréal	121 slaves, including 101 Amerindians
Hôtel-Dieu de Montréal	80 slaves, including 64 Amerindians
Hôpital-Général de Québec	19 slaves, including 10 Amerindians
Hôpital de Détroit	1 Amerindian

In statistical terms, far more slaves were admitted to the Hôtel-Dieu de Québec than other hospitals, although we would get a different picture of slave hospitalization if records had survived at the Hôtel-Dieu de Montréal. The first two slaves, both Amerindians, were admitted to the Hôtel-Dieu de Québec in 1690. Of 301 slaves admitted to the Hôtel-Dieu de Québec, 207 stayed there on one occasion, fifty-one were admitted twice, nineteen stayed on three separate occasions, and others were admitted more often than that. The Eskimo Coli and the black Thomas-Louis both stayed at the hospital eight times, whereas the Fox Gilles-Hyacinthe, belonging to the Intendant Hocquart, was admitted to the Hôtel-Dieu on no less than ten different occasions, and does not seem to have died there, despite these repeated visits.

According to statistics on slave admissions, the Hôpital-Général de Montréal ranks second, but it is important to note that slaves were discharged from the Hôtel-Dieu de Québec as soon as they got better, whereas slaves stayed much longer at the Hôpital-Général de Montréal since this latter hospital actually served as a refuge, a final resting place: slaves who were disabled or could no longer be maintained in private homes were admitted to the Hôpital-Général de Montréal, where they remained until their deaths. The family they had served most often sent them to the hospital: for example, the Fox Catherine belonging to the merchant Guillet, entered the Hôpital-Général on October 25, 1754 at the Guillet family's expense (whose accounts books have come down to us); she died on October 7, 1768 at the age of sixty. The Hôpital-Général also opened its doors to abandoned slaves: such was the case, for example, of the poor black slave Catherine, wife of the black Antoine Lamour, who died there in August 1811, at the age of seventy.

Slaves Died Young

The King of France consented to the request of Canadians for black slaves, although he warned them "that Negroes may die in Canada because of the difference of the climate there," resulting in the waste of large expenditures.[129] These fears were justified. The most surprising feature of Amerindian and black slavery in Canada is that slaves died young: of the 4087 slaves whose age at death has been established, 38.8% lived to an average age of 19.3 years! If Amerindian and black slaves are treated separately, however, it comes as a surprise to discover that black slaves lived much longer than Amerindian ones; the average age at death of black slaves was 25.2 years, whereas the average age at death of Amerindian slaves was just 17.7 years. It would seem that blacks were better suited for living among the whites of Canada than Amerindians were. We cite these averages of 25.2 and 17.7 years as if we had worked them out with great precision. Actually, except in the case of children born in New France, the age given in burial records was only an eyeball estimate, which could in turn affect the average. Moreover, we only know the ages of 1239 out of 2683 Amerindian slaves (46.2%) and of 348 black slaves out of 1443 (24.1%). Given the fragmentary information we are working with, we are offering this average age of death at 19.3 years as a reasonable approximation.

Amerindian slaves reached the colony in large numbers earlier than black slaves did: records of a few deaths turn up in the 1680s, and then from 1700 onwards the greater number of deaths means we can establish average lifespan for each decade. In the case of black slaves, we can only estimate average lifespan starting in the 1730s.

Likewise, it is impossible to calculate average lifespan for Amerindian slaves after 1800, whereas we can estimate average lifespan for black slaves up till 1820. In other words, the first slaves in Quebec were Amerindians, while the last slaves were blacks.

The average age at death for Amerindians was 15, 16 or 17 years, and this average rose suddenly in the years 1791-1800, while the average age at death of blacks reached a high of 46.9 during the years 1811-1820: this rise can be attributed to the few slaves who lived to an unusually advanced age, and died at the time.

Starting in 1731, the number of deaths of Amerindian slaves per decade was above one hundred, and stayed there until 1790: this might at first make it seem that the first Amerindians to arrive in the colony reached the natural limit of their life expectancy. But this was not the case, since the average age at death remained below 17 years, right up to 1760.

However, the averages per decade do not tell the whole story, because they give the impression of a fairly constant death rate, whereas there were surprising fluctuations in the total number of deaths from year to year. In fact, the peak years with the highest number of deaths correspond to certain epidemics. The single year with the highest number of deaths was 1733: in that exceptional year, sixty-one slaves (including fifty-eight Amerindians) died.

In 1733, a smallpox epidemic raged across all of New France, including Detroit, lasting a full five months in Montreal: fifty-eight Amerindian slaves died during this epidemic, at an average age of just 16.8 years. Other epidemics followed, carrying off Canadians and Amerindian slaves alike. In Fall 1755, during another outbreak of smallpox, fifty-six Amerindian slaves died at an average age of 15.8 years. In 1757, new diseases reached New France by sea, in addition to which smallpox broke out again in Quebec, carrying off fifty-one Amerindian slaves at an average age of just 12.1 years. The years 1759, 1769 and 1761 also mark the peaks in the number of deaths, whether caused by fever, smallpox, deprivation or perhaps all of these factors together. If we compare the number of deaths among Amerindian slaves for these same years with those among black slaves (even bearing in mind there were three times more Amerindians than blacks), it is surprising to note the low mortality of blacks: in 1733, fifty-eight Amerindians and two blacks died; in 1755, fifty-six Amerindians and six blacks died; in 1757, fifty-one Amerindians and four blacks died, and so on. Evidently, Amerindian slaves had far less resistance to epidemics than black slaves. This fact was frequently mentioned by writers observing the Amerindians; they had no defences against the most benign diseases from Europe.

Experience showed that the black slave was worth more than the Amerindian slave, since the black more easily resisted common diseases. Indeed, the highest peak year for deaths among blacks was 1776, when just ten deaths were recorded. The other side of the coin is that the infant mortality rate among blacks was higher than among Amerindians. Of 336 children of Amerindian slaves, 84 died before the age of one year (which is already a high proportion of 25%), whereas of 238 children of black slaves, 93 died before reaching the age of one year (39.1%). It is true that this percentage is not valid from a scientific point of view, since the figure should have been drawn from a sample of 1000, but we could not manage otherwise, given the small size of the slave population. In our view, the fact that 93 of 238 children died before reaching the age of one year constituted a very serious problem for the black population. Were these infant deaths due to the climate, as Louis XIV had feared? Were owners negligent in caring for Negro infants? We should not forget that the infant mortality rate was high even among whites: in the eighteenth century, for every 1000 live births in Canadian families, fully one quarter of infants died before their first birthday[130]. The infant mortality rate was thus roughly the same among Amerindian slaves and Canadians, whereas among black slaves it took on simply disastrous proportions.

Accidents could also abruptly bring slave lives to an end. On July 10, 1753, the twelve-year-old Panis Jean-Baptiste Bourdon *dit* Content drowned at Saint-Augustin and was buried the next day. The black girl Françoise-Charlotte, daughter of the slave Sylvie belonging to Seigneur Jean-Baptiste Boucher de Niverville, died at the age of seventeen years, "having unfortunately drowned in the rapids," and was buried at Chambly on July 21, 1776. The eighteen-year-old black slave Jean, belonging to the merchant Robert Lester, drowned and was buried in Quebec City on May 20, 1783. Then, in June 1792, the four-year-old Panis André-Gabriel, belonging to MacLeod, drowned as well, at Lachine, and was buried fifteen days later in Montreal, on July 9, 1792. The black Caesar Brown, a sailor aboard the *Sappho*, drowned on September 2, 1804, and received an Anglican burial five days later in Quebec City. The seventy-year-old black Jean-Baptiste, who had been a freeman for several years, died in a fire on December 13, 1791, at the mill just outside of the Récollets Gate in Montreal. Fire broke out, probably started by ash falling from the old Negro's pipe, and within "five quarters of an hour" the mill was consumed by fire and Jean-Baptiste had perished, part of his body being recovered from the embers and his burial taking place the next day in Montreal.[131]

FEW SLAVES LIVED PAST THE AGE OF SEVENTY
Based on the averages we calculated, slaves were almost twenty years old at death, so slaves reaching middle age were rare. Of 1239 Amerindian slaves whose age at death is known to us, only sixty-eight (most of them women) died between forty and fifty years of age, while of 348 blacks, only forty (most of them men) died in this range.[132] A smaller number of slaves died between the ages of sixty and seventy: only thirty-seven, of whom twenty-one were Amerindians (one of them a man) and sixteen were blacks (six of them women).

Twenty-five slaves lived into their seventies, of whom sixteen were blacks (four of them women) and nine Amerindians: at this point, we can only speak of Amerindian women, since no Amerindian male slave reached seventy. Almost as many slaves – twenty-three – lived into their eighties, of whom eight were Amerindian women and fifteen were blacks (six of them women).

Of these twenty-three octogenarians, three lived almost to their ninetieth birthday: the black Marie-Rose lived to eighty-six, the Panis Marie-Louise lived to eighty-seven and the black Marie-

Élisabeth lived to eighty-eight. Two blacks reached the age of ninety years: Cicona, buried on October 3, 1820, and Jenny, buried on October 6, 1832, both of them in Detroit.

One Amerindian and one black slave reached lived a full century. The Panis Marie-Joseph died at the age of 100, while the black Mary Young lived longer than any other slave, dying at the age of 106 years; she had been alive during the reign of Louis XIV, and now passed away at the end of the reign of Napoleon.

Among Amerindian slaves, no men reached old age, none for example living to their seventieth year. Amerindian women, meanwhile, tended to live much longer. Among black slaves, more men than women lived into their seventies, but then almost three times more women than men reached the milestone of eighty years. What is even more important to note is that a greater proportion of black men than Amerindian men lived past forty years: of 1239 Amerindians whose age at death is known, only 107 lived past the age of forty – a tiny proportion of 8.6% - whereas of 348 Negro men whose age at death is known, ninety-two lived past forty – a proportion of 26.4%. Blacks lived much longer than Amerindians and if their infant mortality rate had not been so high, the average age of black slaves at death would have been much higher. On the one hand, the Amerindian typically lived just a few years once enslaved by the French, and on the other hand, infant mortality was very high among black slaves: for these reasons, slaves died on average before their twentieth birthday.

SLAVE BURIALS
Were slaves buried more hastily than free people? Even if the slave was the personal property of an owner, like cattle, did the owner ensure the slave was buried as a human being?

The slave burial sometimes took place on the day of death. For example, the Amerindian Jean-Baptiste, belonging to Noël Pelletier, was baptized and buried on October 17, 1755 in Neuville; an unnamed thirteen-year-old Panis girl, belonging to François Campeau, died on November 10, 1757 around five o'clock in the morning, and was buried the same day in Montreal; an unnamed twenty-year-old Amerindian woman, the slave of Pierre Chesne-Labutte, died on February 9, 1759 and was buried the same day in Detroit. To know whether these burials were hasty affairs or not, we need first to determine the cause of death. For example, burials were accelerated when people died of a contagious disease.

Most often, slaves were buried the day after death. If we consented ourselves with reading the burial act, we could end up with the impression that the owner wanted to dispatch the corpse as quickly as possible. Yet we should remember that under the French regime and even in the nineteenth century, it was customary to bury a deceased person, whatever his condition, immediately after death. Embalming was a costly business, and was therefore generally avoided. The deceased were not exposed very long. We know, however, of four slaves buried the day after they died. These were exceptional cases, made possible by the time of year when death occurred.

The burial act of the slave was no different in form from that of the free person: the same simple and uncluttered ritual formula was used, and the act was signed by just one person, the officiating priest. We have seen that baptisms and weddings took up more or less space in parish registries, depending on the social rank of the people involved, and the largest possible number of people signed as witnesses. But this was not the case with the burial act – whether nobleman or commoner, Governor General or simple slave, the same stark formula was used in the burial register: "And so were lost the names of these masters of the earth," according to Malherbe. We should note, however, that in general the slave maintained his or her condition of slave even in the burial act, and this can actually be seen as fortuitous, since it means more slave names can be added to our inventory. We should also note the priest did not always bother to name the slave being buried: we found 450 anonymous slave burials, 365 of them Amerindians and forty blacks.

The burial had to take place in the presence of witnesses. The burial of the deceased slave was sometimes witnessed by fellow slaves, which comes as a surprise since the slaves were considered minors in the eyes of the law. Between 1742 and 1752, the Panis Charlot, who may have served as church beadle, served as witness at forty-three burials in Detroit. Black slaves were most likely to serve as witnesses at the burials of fellow black slaves, to the point that we can speak of a generalized custom, many examples of which can be given. In fact, some blacks made a point of attending the burials of fellow blacks – Paul Cramer Polydore, Robert Jackson, Francis Smith and his wife Dorothy Hutchins attended all funerals of black people.

Slave owners only attended slave burials on five occasions. Such cases were uncommon, and in each case the slave owner was French Canadian. We sought such cases in English society in vain; English slave owners simply did not attend the burial of their slaves.

Details are scarce about the actual burial ceremony; the ritual observed was not differerent from any other burials. In officiating at the burial of an unnamed young black in October 1736, the Récollet Daniel, a missionary in Detroit, took the trouble to add the following lines to the burial act: "I buried him the way I bury Christians, according to the rite of the diocese." The ritual must have been the same for everyone, but were some ceremonies more elaborate than others?

On this point, burial acts are obviously short on details. One of them reveals that on December 14, 1755, the funeral of the Fox Madeleine in Les Écureuils took place in the presence of "a great concourse of people." Another burial act provided more generous details: the Jesuit Pierre Laure incorporated a long note in Latin in the *Miscellaneorum Liber* to describe the burial of the Montagnais Marie-Louise, who had been the slave of Fleury Deschambault de Lagorgendière and who was buried at the Hôtel-Dieu de Québec on November 25, 1732: "*Cum Monialium Solatio defuncta est a me in Petro Laure in coemeterio, companis Sonantibus, Sequentibus puellulis magnifice Sepulta fuit.*" This slave was given a magnificent burial. She died at the age of twelve, after having received the care of nuns, and was laid to rest to the sound of bells and a procession of children. We do not know of other such cases, but we believe this single case gives an idea of the relatively humane character of slavery in New France.

What did slave funerals cost? We have no idea, and have not turned up even a single document in this regard. Civil registries contain two references to burial fees, however: on August 31, 1759, Nicolas Lefebvre had to pay five livres for his fifteen-day-old black infant Marie-Angelique, who was buried in Montreal; meanwhile, adult burials were evidently more expensive, because on July 15, 1740, Commissaire-ordonnateur (financial administrator) Michel, who represented the intendant in Montreal, paid a burial fee of ten livres for his twenty-two-year-old black slave François.

The *Code Noir* of the Caribbean and of Louisiana stipulated that "all baptized slaves shall be buried in holy ground." There were no specific rules for the burial of Catholic slaves in New France. Catholic slave owners naturally acted the way Catholics were expected to act. In Montreal, slaves were usually buried in the paupers' cemetery, outside the city, and this often happened in Quebec City as well. This should not necessarily be considered an indication that owners did not care about the burial of their slaves: leading members of the colony, from rich merchants to senior officials, often humbly asked to be buried in the paupers' cemetery! At least one slave, the Amerindian Marie-Athanase, belonging to the merchant Charles Hamelin, died at Michilimackinac in January 1748, and received the unusual distinction of being buried next to her master's late wife, in the church itself, as if the slave had really been part of the family.

DEVOTION TO MASTERS
Obviously not all slaves enjoyed such special privileges, nor did all slaves feel like members of their master's family. Some slaves were harshly treated – how often is impossible to say. For example, the Panis Jacques swore in an official statement in 1734 that he had fled because his master, the officer Tarieu de Lanaudière de Lapérade, used to beat him: did this husband of Madeleine de Verchères regularly beat slaves or had the Panis Jacques done something to deserve beating? We do not know. Many slaves deserted under the British regime and we do not know whether they ran away after

abusive treatment or because they wanted to live their lives as they saw fit. This problem is very complex. For example, the black slave Joe belonged to William Brown, publisher of the *Quebec Gazette*: Brown was forced several times to clap Joe in prison and have him whipped by the hangman because the slave had run away or had stolen property; but in examining Brown's very detailed accounts, it seems the slave had nothing to complain about—his master fed him well, gave him clothes over and over again, with disconcerting patience. At the New Year, Brown was in the habit of giving Joe money, and starting in 1788 he gave him a weekly allowance.[133]

Although other slaves were sincerely devoted to their master, we cannot come to any general conclusion about the sentimental relations between owners and slaves on the basis of the few examples known to us. We already mentioned Pompée, a black slave belonging to Doctor Antony, who died from a stab wound in 1776 while defending his master from an attacking Ojibwa. This courageous slave provides one example of devotion. In June 1736, a female Sioux slave also saved the life of her master: when Sioux Amerindians captured the Jesuit Father Aulneau's canoe and tied Bourassa, the lead paddler, to the stake to burn him, the Sioux woman successfully pleaded for Bourassa's life.[134]

Black slave women caring for the master's children sometimes loved these children as their own. In his family mémoirs, Father Henri-Raymond Casgrain remembers the story of the mulatto Thérèse who lived with the Duperron-Bâby family of Toronto:

Our mother still laughs with all her heart, when she recalls a funny incident she caused on arriving in Toronto. As she entered the avenue leading up to the residence of the Honourable Mr. Bâby, a terrified black woman came running up to her, gesticulating and babbling frenetically. At first, our mother was taken by fear, and thought she was dealing with a mad woman; but Mr. Bâby and his son reassured her, laughing uproariously. The woman was his father's old slave, whom he had inherited from his mother, and she was expressing her joy at seeing the master's daughter, by performing a "Negro" dance, accompanied by an African chant.

Father Casgrain's brother evokes happy memories of another slave in the Bâby family, the mulatto Rose Lontin, known as Rosalie: "Wonderful Rose often lulled me in her arms and had a singular attachment to me. The most extraordinary thing happened in 1851, when I knocked on her door in Amherstburg. I was now a man, yet she had not seen me since my childhood. On opening the door, she recognized me at once and hugged me, kissing me and showing her amazement and joy." And he ends the anecdote with a spontaneous detail that seems to give an accurate idea of relations between masters and slaves: "With the naivety of a true child of her race, [Rose] did not hesitate to listen to the conversation of her masters, and came squatting on her heels at the door of the dining room, relishing in their presence and the pleasure of hearing them talk."[135]

Philippe Aubert de Gaspé relates an actual scene of his own family life in the romance *Canadians of Old*:

At last Archie [wandered about the manor] in search of the servants and found Lisette, the coloured cook, busy in the kitchen making dinner. Lisette had been a second mother to Jules. Unable to speak for tears, she threw her arms around Archie's neck as she used to in the days when he came to spend his holidays at the manor with his friend. With all her faults, this mulatress, whom the captain [Ignace-Philippe Aubert de Gaspé] had purchased when she was four years old, was very attached to the whole family. She held the master of the house in some slight awe. But no one else. The mistress she obeyed only when she felt like it, on the principle that she, Lisette, had been in the household longer than Madame d'Haberville. Blanche and her brother were the only ones whose gentle treatment could make Lisette do their bidding, and although Jules very often teased her, she only laughed at his mischievous ways and was always ready

145

to cover up his misdeeds and take his part when his parents were wont to scold… This same indomitable woman had nevertheless taken her masters' misfortunes to heart like a true daughter of the family.[136]

The example of the Fox slave Geneviève, belonging to Seigneur Couillart de Lespinay, provides another indication of the tone of slavery here. She entered Couillart's service at the age of twelve years, and according to Aubert de Gaspé, "she developed a tender and maternal devotion for the lovable child [the son of Seigneur Couillart] who was hers to amuse. She called him her 'son' as soon as she learned to prattle in French." When swimming in the bay, she delighted in taking him on her shoulders. "Poor Grosse! She would frequently tell us in her patois, as she looked across the fine reach of the Saint-Thomas bay at high tide, 'Cross bay many times with my son on back, va! But not now. Me six-foot Seigneur Couillart.' [...] One day he wrote to his wife from Quebec that a slight indisposition prevented him from coming to the seigneury for several days. The Fox woman "died of anxiety and a broken heart at Saint-Thomas, repeating incessantly 'My son is going to die!' About three days later, the excellent Monsieur Couillart expired in my arms in Quebec City, in the street that bears his name. He was very fond of the gentle Indian, and we had been careful not to tell him of her death. [...] They left this earth to meet in heaven."[137] Aubert de Gaspé's written account strays from the truth: the Fox woman actually died not three days but rather two and a half months before Couillart. Yet the fact remains that he lived close to the era of slavery, and gives a sense of the mutual affection of masters and slaves.

CHAPTER SEVEN

Slaves and the Sacraments

No explicit state law or church regulation obliged Canadian slave owners to raise their slaves in the Catholic faith.[138] Admittedly, Catholicism was the state religion in New France, and in principle the colony could only be inhabited by Catholics, so one could imagine that slave owners would naturally have been inclined to baptize slaves and to ensure they were raised as Christians. It remains to be seen if the facts fit this theory.

MASTERS WERE SLOW TO BAPTIZE THEIR SLAVES

Actually, slave owners did not baptize their slaves as quickly as one might think. For example, three unbaptized slaves were sold by their owners. On September 14, 1737, Jacques-Hugues Péan de Livaudière sold the thirteen- or fourteen-year-old Fox slave Thérèse to Joseph Chavigny de Lachevrotière de Latesserie: the deed of sale states that this Fox Amerindian had not been baptized, and there is no way of knowing whether her new owner had her baptized. On October 1 the same year, Augustin Bailly de Messein sold his ten-year-old Paducah slave to the same Latesserie: this was another pagan slave and it is impossible to ascertain how long Bailly de Messein held him; Latesserie had him baptized the following October 20. The Panis Fanchon, aged ten to eleven years, had belonged for an indeterminate period to the Montreal merchant Jacques-François Daguille, before she was sold to Mathieu-Théodore de Vitré, on November 4, 1751, by which time she had still not been baptized.

Some slave owners put off baptizing their slaves, or possibly did not even bother with baptism at all. It seems to have been a fairly common practice to wait one, two or even three years. In hindsight, some delays seem utterly astounding. Most black slaves were acquired before they reached thirty years of age, and most Amerindian slaves in their twenties and sometimes as very young children. So if they were ultimately baptized at forty, fifty or even sixty years, something must have held up their Christian education. For example, the Panis Marie had been living from a young age in the household of Philippe Vinet-Préville and it was only on April 29, 1775, the day of her death at the age of fifty-five, that she was finally baptized in Longue-Pointe and received Communion for the first time. In Laprairie on January 15, 1739, Clément Laplante-Lérigé baptized his Amerindian female slave, then sixty years old and on the point of death!

In March 1776, the black slave Thomas, who belonged to Desmoulins, was sixty years old when finally baptized on his death-bed at the Hôpital-Général de Montréal. On October 7, 1815, a seventy-year-old black slave, Margaret Cuff Morocco, was baptized at the Presbyterian Church of Montreal. Catholic slave owners were just as slow in baptizing their slaves. On September 2, 1771, the black Étienne-Paul – described in documents as belonging to the Sisters of the Congregation – was baptized in Montreal at the age of seventy. But the record for late baptisms was held by the black slave Jean-Baptiste, who belonged to William Park and his Catholic wife Thérèse Gouin: he was baptized on his deathbed, on March 20, 1808, at the age of eighty.

A way of measuring the frequency of these delays is to track the number of slaves who were baptized on their deathbed. We identified 198 of these slaves in Catholic registers, which represents 12.1% of the 1636 slaves whose baptismal records have survived to this day. This figure does not tell the whole story, since many Catholic owners simply did not baptize their slaves on taking possession.

The question is, why? Why, for example, did the Panis slave Marianne, who definitely belonged for several years to the priest Pierre Fréchette of Detroit, only get baptized on June 13, 1794, at the age of forty? Why did the black slave belonging to the Sisters of the Congregation only get baptized at seventy? Why did the Panis belonging to Mother d'Youville, Superior of the Hôpital-Général de Montréal, only get baptized on October 23, 1766, by which time, at the age of twenty-four, she had contracted a dangerous disease? These masters can hardly have been indifferent to the Christian education of their native Amerindian and black slaves!

The answer is doubtless that slave owners in general, whether priests, religious or lay people, could face various obstacles in their efforts to convert their slaves to Christianity. A first obstacle was language: a slave coming from the Upper Missouri (the region producing most Amerindian slaves) had to learn the rudiments of catechism, and some slaves may have stubbornly resisted any such indoctrination, or have been unable to understand and remember anything. Around 1746, an Abenaki sold the Fox Marie-Geneviève to Jean-Baptiste Couillart de Lespinay, but she was only baptized fifteen years later, in 1761. Philippe Aubert de Gaspé attributed this delay to a lack of intelligence: : "La Grosse (I never knew her by any other name) had in fact a very limited intelligence, although she was by no means an imbecile. She spoke haltingly, using a patois of her own invention."[139]

EIGHTY PERCENT OF SLAVES WERE BAPTIZED

Whether months or years elapsed between a slave's purchase and baptism, what really mattered is that the slave was eventually baptized. In general, slaves were baptized. Historical records indicate this to have been the case for 80% of all slaves. The year of baptism is not always known; we only found the dates for 1620 slave baptisms, seventy-one of which were in Protestant churches. In other cases, we resorted to indirect but solid evidence, such as confirmations, Communion, church weddings and burials in holy ground, all of which presupposed a solemn or private baptism.

It was perfectly natural for Catholics to baptize their slaves, but even Huguenots (French Protestants) had their slaves baptized in Catholic churches. On May 20, 1741, in the Catholic church in Quebec City, the Huguenot merchant François Havy baptized his black slave, Joseph-François, aged about twelve; likewise on March 8, 1744, in

Quebec, his fellow Huguenot and business partner, Jean Lefebvre, baptized their black slave, François-Joseph, aged about twenty-seven. Was no Huguenot minister available? Or were these Huguenot slave owners trying to make it easier to transport black slaves to the French West Indies where the *Code Noir* stipulated that all "Negro" slaves be Catholic?

Roughly the same situation prevailed under the British regime. Protestant slave owners baptized their slaves in the Catholic faith. These owners were Protestants who had married Canadian Catholics. In the case of mixed marriages, boys were raised in the Protestant faith because of British inheritance laws, whereas girls received a Catholic education. For slaves, the problem of inheritance did not arise, since Protestant owners generally let their own Catholic wives choose the faith of their slaves. We say "generally" because out of thirty-four Protestant slave owners who had married a Canadian Catholic woman, there was a single exception – in 1762, the merchant Acklom Rickaby Bondfield married Marie-Madeleine-Françoise Martel de Brouague, and baptized his slaves in the Anglican faith.

Under the French regime, there were no Protestant slaves; under British rule, the slave followed his master's religion, unless the master had married a Canadian Catholic. Overall, given that most slave owners were French Canadians, it is not surprising that 2748 of 4185 slaves, or at least two-thirds of the slave population, were Catholic.

Amerindian slaves were baptized starting in 1681 and up to 1799 (with the exception of one case in 1802 and another in 1809). We know of only four Amerindian slaves who were baptized in a Protestant church: the first in 1770, the second in 1774 and two more in 1779. All other Amerindian slaves were Catholics. As for blacks, they only started to appear on a continuous basis in 1713, and turned up in records until 1828.

BAPTISMS WERE SOCIAL EVENTS

For many slaves the baptismal ceremony was so rushed that they were not even given a name, but for other slaves baptism was an important event bringing together the most influential members of society. On August 15, 1727, Mgr. Saint-Vallier himself baptized the twenty-three-year-old black slave Thomas-Louis who belonged to François-Étienne Cugnet, general agent of the Compagnie d'Occident: Intendant Dupuy served as sponsor (or godfather) at this solemn baptism. On August 27, 1745, a bishop presided over another slave baptism at Quebec when Mgr. Pontbriand baptized the Natchez Victor, aged thirty-three, with Jean-Victor Varin de Lamarre, a member of the Conseil supérieur, acting as sponsor along with the wife of Charles Tarieu de Lanaudière. Another important social gathering took place in Quebec on May 24, 1738, at the baptism of the Fox Indian Gilles-Hyacinthe, aged twenty-two, who belonged to Intendant Hocquart. The intendant himself served as godfather; the godmother was the wife of the king's lieutenant Saint-Ours Deschaillons, and the priest wrote in the margin of the baptismal register: "Grosse cloche" (Big shot). Evidently, the godfather did things in style.

The importance of a baptismal ceremony can be judged by the number of signatures in the register – the same goes for marriage contracts. There was keen competition to sign as witnesses at some slave baptisms. On August 9, 1735, Louise-Claire, an Amerindian girl from Anticosti Island aged three and a half, belonging to the merchant Joseph Fleury Deschambault de Lagorgendière, was baptized in Quebec City; her godfather was the master's son-in-law, Pierre François Rigaud de Vaudreuil; seven people signed as witnesses. When the black slave François-Denis was baptized in Quebec City on March 31, 1739, seven people signed as witnesses, although the name of the master was not recorded.

In other cases, even more people signed the baptismal act. On June 2, 1732, when the Fox Amerindian Madeleine-Gilles belonging to Intendant Hocquart was baptized, the intendant served as sponsor, and ten more people signed as witnesses. And when the ten-year-old black slave Pierre-Louis-Scipion was baptized in Quebec City on August 11, 1717, a record thirteen people signed as witnesses at the baptism.

Slaves were prestigious luxury items, which sometimes turned slave baptisms into glittering social gatherings. It was all-important to get the right sponsor at a slave baptism. Sometimes governors served as sponsors. For example, on April 17, 1732, at Quebec, the Governor of New France Charles de Beauharnois de la Boische served as godfather to his Eskimo slave Charles Hilarion; the Governor of Trois-Rivières François-Pierre Rigaud de Vaudreuil was sponsor at the baptism of the Amerindian Marie-Claire, aged fourteen to fifteen, who belonged to the officer Hubert Coutrot. Two intendants served as godfathers: Claude-Thomas Dupuy at the baptism of the black slave Thomas-Louis, who belonged to the general agent of the Compagnie d'Occident, and Gilles Hocquart at the 1732 baptism of his Fox Madeleine-Gilles and the 1738 baptism of another slave, Gilles-Hyacinthe.

When governors and intendants were absent, other prominent people were called on to serve as godparents. On August 9, 1739, at Fort Saint-Frédéric, the fort's commander Lemoyne de Longueuil served as godfather to the Panis slave Joseph-Gaspard who belonged to the merchant Charles Nolan de Lamarque.

Other senior officials were called on to serve as sponsors, such as a member of the Conseil supérieur, an engineer, an explorer, a governor general, the wife of an intendant. Lemoyne de Longueuil, Ramezay and other members of high society should be mentioned for serving as godparents to slaves.

Clergymen also acted as sponsors at slave baptisms. Here are a few examples. In 1728 in Sainte-Anne-de-la-Pérade, the priest Gervais Lefebvre served as godfather to the Amerindian girl Marie-Joseph Cordulle, aged six to seven, who belonged to Louis Gastineau-Duplessis. In 1742 at Michilimackinac, the Jesuit Jean-Baptiste Lamorinie served as sponsor to the Panis Jean-Baptiste-François, the slave of Louis-Jean-Baptiste Céloron de Blainville. In 1747, the curate of Beauport, Louis Chardon, acted as godfather to the Assiniboine Louis-Antoine, who belonged to Antoine Juchereau-Duchesnay. In 1777 in Chateauguay, Henri-François Grave, priest of the Seminary of Quebec, and Sister Thérèse Pépin, superior of the Sisters of Charity (the Grey Nuns), served as godparents to a twenty-one-year-old Sioux belonging to the Hôpital-Général de

Montréal: the Sioux slave was given the name Henri-Thérèse in honour of his godparents.

When a slave owner did not call on some important person or family friend to stand in as godparent, then the owner likely played this role himself. In many instances, the owner, his wife or some other family member turns up in the baptismal registry as a godparent. If the priests recording baptismal acts had taken the trouble to clearly indicate the names of slave owners and of sponsors, it would be easier to track how many slave owners were present at the baptism of their slaves. Here, in any case, are the numbers we found:

Master or mistress serves as godparent	164 baptisms
Both master and mistress serve as godparents	27 baptisms
A member of the slave owner's family serves as a godparent	67 baptisms
Total	258 baptisms

It was a Catholic and French custom for owners to serve as godparents to their own slaves. Of 258 Catholic baptisms, the owner or a family member served as a godparent, while this was the case with only one Protestant, the merchant Acklom Rickby Bondfield, of Sillery. In 1770, his son was godfather of a Panis woman baptized in the Anglican faith; in 1774, the merchant and his wife served as godparents to this Panis woman's child. The Bondfields were the only English slave owners in Canada who bestowed this honour on their slaves, and we believe this is attributable to the influence of Madame Bondfield, who was a French Canadian.

SOME SLAVES SERVED AS GODPARENTS

Another feature makes slavery in Canada seem more humane compared to other colonies – Panis and blacks served as godfathers and godmothers in Catholic and Protestant ceremonies.

This was a very rare occurrence under the French regime, probably because the honour was reserved to the slave owner or a friend, and it only happened twice. The baptism of the black Marie-Charlotte occurred on August 30, 1748 in Montreal. She was the daughter of blacks belonging to the merchant Pierre-Jean-Baptiste Hervieux. The blacks Joseph and Charlotte served as godparents. On October 17, 1749, in Sainte-Anne-du-Bout-de-l'Île, the Panis Jean-Baptiste served as godfather to Jean-Baptiste Lalonde, the legitimate son of Louis Lalonde and Marie-Louise Picard, while Marie-Élisabeth Duclos served as godmother; this Panis gave his name to his godson. It was extremely unusual that a Panis should serve as godfather to a white person of a free condition: we have reason to believe that this Panis had been emancipated by then.

It was far more common under the British regime that slaves served as godparents to fellow slaves. There were few Amerindian slaves by then. We just mentioned the case of the Panis Jean-Baptiste in 1749. It was not until May 29, 1788 in Detroit that another Amerindian served as godparent. The Panis Charles, belonging to Girardin, and the Panis Geneviève, belonging to Duperron-Bâby, served as godparents of the daughter of Caldwell's Panis, while the third and final such case occurred in Detroit on March 9, 1794, when the Panis Charles served as godfather to the black Pierre, son of one "Malome."

On the other hand, slave sponsorship at slave baptisms was a well-entrenched habit under the British regime. The records indicate forty-eight slave baptisms at which blacks or Amerindians served as sponsors, although it is impossible to say whether they were all slaves at the time of sponsorship. These forty-six baptisms break down as follows:

| Baptisms with black godparents | 43 |
| Baptisms with Amerindian godparents | 3 |

Of these forty-six baptisms, only six took place in a Catholic church. This demonstrates not only that black or Amerindian sponsorship was a rarity under French rule, but also that it was a rarity among Catholics, probably because the function of sponsor was reserved to the master or friends of the master's family. In any event, black sponsorship was typically a characteristic of the British regime.

The following table presents this information another way:

Under the French regime	Black sponsorship	1
	Amerindian sponsorship	1
Under the British regime	Black sponsorship	42
	Amerindian sponsorship	2

THE MOST COMMON FIRST NAMES

The 4185 slaves we catalogued cannot all be identified by a first name: 930 of them, including 680 Amerindians – 22.2 % – remain completely anonymous. They received no name at baptism, whether because they were on the point of death or the priest did not bother to enter a name in the registry. In such cases, priests wrote "We, the undersigned priest, baptized the Panis belonging to" a particular person. This proved an even more common occurrence in burial registries. Distinct cultural habits grew alongside slavery.

Slaves received a wide variety of single and compound first names, and these names were generally of the kind borne by people of a free condition. Slaves were often named after their godparents or, as in the case of 239 slaves, their masters. Confusion could arise when a slave received not just the same first name but also the same surname as his master: in 1712 Jacques Cardinal the elder baptized an Outagamie slave who also received the name Jacques Cardinal.

The most popular first name was Marie, followed by Joseph, Jean-Baptiste and Pierre. Among other common first names were Marie-Anne, Marguerite, Charles, Jacques, Louis and Catherine. These names also proved popular in the civil registries.

There were exceptions however. Throughout the slave world there existed a tradition of using names from classical Antiquity: a few Canadian slaves received classical names: thirteen were called César (Caesar), eight Pompée (Pompey), three Néron (Nero), two Scipion

(Scipio) and one Caton (Cato). The names of classical gods were even rarer: five were called Phoebe, one Neptune and another Jupiter.

Some slaves had a nickname of obscure origin: Governor Vaudreuil-Cavagnial had a black slave named Canon; Charles Héry had a black slave Damoiseau; Ramezay had a Panis named La Diligence (was it because he was fast or because he was lazy?); Lusignan had a Panis named Religionnaire (Religionary); Boutin's black slave was named Boncoeur. In 1795, Dumoulin's mulatto slave was called Prince; Lacorne's Amerindian slave had the enchanting name of Rossignol (Nightingale). Jean-Baptiste Gourdon *dit* Lachasse had a slave named "Dontguichaut," whom we are tempted to see as Don Quixote – and why not? Sanschagrin's Panis answered to the name of Sarasto (Saratoga), perhaps because he had been captured there. In 1807, a black decided simply to take the name of Montreal. In 1749, Vergor's black slave had the dazzling name of Versailles. We even found a slave named Louis XIV. On January 1, 1773, in Saint-Vallier, the parish priest buried the black slave Louis Quatorze, aged seventy-two: this man had been born a slave in the era of the Sun King, and continued radiating that royal sunlight, whether of his own will or because it had been decided to call him Louis Quatorze.

THE SACRAMENT OF CONFIRMATION

Baptism sealed the individual slave with the spiritual mark of faith, but what was done to strengthen that faith by confirmation, the Church's second sacrament of initiation? Providing a satisfactory answer to this question would involve consulting a large number of lists of confirmands, but only a few such lists have been preserved for Quebec City, Montreal, La Prairie and Lachine, to mention only the more interesting ones.

This fragmentary documentation has only enabled us to ascertain that forty-eight slaves, including sixteen blacks, ever received the sacrament of confirmation. Lestage confirmed two Panis the same day; Joseph Cureux *dit* Saint-Germain confirmed three blacks in the same ceremony. On February 28, 1767, Montreal witnessed an imposing procession of confirmands (there was no bishop from 1760 to 1766), including nine female Panis and one male Panis.

While Cureux *dit* Saint-Germain's three blacks were confirmed immediately after their baptism, there was generally a considerable lapse of time between the two sacraments.

The confirmation lists provide scant information, but they nonetheless make it possible to establish that slaves had access to the sacrament of confirmation: some lists placed slaves at the very end, below all other names, while other lists mingled slave names with those of free persons, without distinction, suggesting a form of integration.

COMMUNION

First Communion lists do not provide much more detail, but by combining them with other strands of evidence we can establish the slave was on the same footing as the free person. Slaves who did not take Communion were cause for concern. When the curate of Quebec visited a parish in 1792, he reported a black woman living at 24 rue du Sault-au-Matelot in the household of the carpenter Charles Payan, who was married to a Protestant. The priest wrote in the margin: "She claims to be Catholic but has never been to Communion, nor likely to confession." In May 1730, when Gervais' black servant Pierre, aged seventeen, was buried, the missionary in Pointe-aux-Trembles (near Montreal) was concerned that this black person had not received his First Communion.

We identified twenty individuals, slaves and former slaves, who had made their First Communion: sixteen of them were Amerindians and four were blacks. It should be remembered that once a baptized Catholic reached the age of reason, taking Communion was an obligation at Easter (the so-called Easter duty). So of 2971 baptized slaves, there had to be many more than just twenty individuals receiving their First Communion. The information available is quite fragmentary. A few scattered First Communion lists have been preserved, but we did not manage to locate those precious records where some priests entered the names of Catholics fulfilling their Easter duty.

In this list of twenty slaves who made their First Communion, the advanced age of some slaves comes as a surprise: thirty-one, forty-two, fifty and even fifty-five years.

It is true that under French rule and long afterwards, First Communion came late. According to Mgr. Saint-Vallier's *Grand Catéchisme*, a Catholic "must take Communion once he has a just discernment of the Lord's Body, around the age of twelve years." We therefore cannot expect to find slaves, any more than people of a free condition, taking Communion before the age of twelve. The age of the slave on arrival in the colony should also be taken into account, and we know that slaves generally arrived at a very young age, and were not bought beyond the age of thirty. Thus, the slave taking First Communion past the age of thirty was a slave whose religious education had been neglected, or who had not managed to integrate much religious knowledge. This may have been the case for the Panis Marie who spent her youth in the Vinet-Préville household in Longue-Pointe, and who only made her First Communion at the age of fifty-five, and also for the black Jacques-César, slave of Ignace Gamelin, who was baptized in 1730 at the age of nineteen, but only made his First Communion twenty-six years later.

THE OTHER SACRAMENTS

We have very little information about the sacraments of penance or extreme unction: the only record of them is in those burial acts, where the priest took the trouble to record no more than the burial. The Panis Daniel-Clément, in service to the merchant Antoine Pascaud, fell gravely ill at the age of about twelve: according to the burial act, written August 13, 1704 in Montreal, he was able to receive the sacraments of "baptism, penance and extreme unction before his death." The black Philippe, who died in the house of Antoine Canac, received the last rites, according to the burial act of May 5, 1715, in Sainte-Famille on the Île d'Orléans. The Panis Marie-Victoire, servant of François Daine, also received the last rites before dying in October 1748, at the age of about nineteen.

But circumstances did not always enable the dying slave to enjoy these final privileges. The Panis René Duchesne, aged twelve to thirteen, fell ill in Pointe-aux-Trembles in April 1718; he was not fit to receive the last rites, so the priest merely had him "perform" the acts of faith, hope and charity. An old Fox woman belonging to Seigneur Couillart de Lespinay died suddenly in October 1808 without receiving the last rites, but the priest of Saint-Thomas noted that a few days earlier she had been to confession. The Chickasaw slave Jean-Baptiste-Christophe died just as suddenly. He probably belonged to Jean-Baptiste Dusault, seigneur of Les Écureuils. When the Chickasaw became dangerously ill, he was conditionally baptized on April 20, 1743 in the seigneur's manor, then rallied, but suddenly passed away on May 11 "without anyone noticing." In the burial act the next day, the priest said the Chickasaw had not received the last rites "because he had rallied from the disease, then had died suddenly."

What about the sacrament of Holy Orders? Could a slave aspire to become a priest if he had received the necessary instruction? Did any of Canada's 4185 slaves become clergymen? Saint-Vallier's *Rituel* had specified that slaves could not enter the priesthood. In listing the canonical impediments preventing men from becoming priests, the bishop had noted "those born out of lawful wedlock or who are slaves." Slaves were ineligible for the priesthood, but was this also the case once slaves had been formally emancipated? The *Rituel* did not address this question. In any case, we know of no slave who became a priest or even tried to become one.

Slaves had many descendants, so it is interesting to consider whether their sons or grandsons might have gone into Holy Orders. Assuming that all prisoners captured by Amerindians became slaves (that was, after all, the reason they were captured), we could characterize Father Amable-Simon Raizenne as the son of a slave. A man named Rising was taken by Amerindians during the raid on Deerfield and brought to the mission of the Lake of Two Mountains, where he fell in love with a lady prisoner, who was also English. He married her, changing his last name to the French-sounding "Raizenne." His eldest son was ordained in 1744. This seems, however, to have been a case of accidental and temporary slavery, and the case of Father Raizenne, son of a man taken prisoner by the Amerindians, does not offer as much interest as if he had been the son of a real slave.

Slaves were able to take part in the sacrament of marriage, whether between Amerindian slaves, or even between whites and Amerindians, or between whites and blacks. We will return to this interesting subject in a later chapter.

CHAPTER EIGHT

Crime and Punishment

B lack and Amerindian slaves unwillingly found themselves in a society whose standards were foreign to them. Did they behave in ways that led to punishment? Were slaves punished more harshly than persons of a free condition? Was the very presence of slaves a threat for society?

In colonies with a high proportion of slaves, stringent measures were taken to protect masters. Under the *Code Noir*, slaves were forbidden from carrying any offensive weapons or large sticks at the risk of being whipped; they were also forbidden from congregating, risking the same punishment, while repeat offenders could be punished with death; once recaptured, runaway slaves would have their ears cut off and the fleur de lys branded on one shoulder; runaways recaptured a second time would have their hamstring cut and be branded with a fleur de lys on the other shoulder; runaways recaptured a third time would be put to death. A slave who struck his master in the face or drew blood would be put to death; a slave caught stealing could be subject to public humiliation and even put to death; masters could chain slaves and have them beaten with rods or straps, but masters were forbidden from torturing slaves or mutilating any limb, since mutilation and the death penalty were the prerogative of royal justice alone.

There seems to have been very little humanity in these repressive measures, which were adopted at the time in the French West Indies, with a view to protecting the tiny population of white slave owners from the surrounding mass of black slaves. In New France, meanwhile, the *Code Noir* never came into force. How did masters keep their slaves working, and how did they punish them?

Rebellious Slaves

The criminal records of slaves contain some mild offences that were simply ignored or lightly punished. In 1712, a Panis was involved in a smuggling case. The Panis Joseph belonged to the fur trader François Lamoureux *dit* Saint-Germain. The slave accompanied his master, along with Pierre and Nicolas Sarrazin, on a journey north of the island of Montreal to trade in prohibited goods. The four were arrested, and Saint-Germain and the Sarrazins were found guilty. Although the Panis was interrogated, his name appears neither in the guilty verdict nor in a later appeal to the Conseil supérieur.[140] The authorities may have considered that the Panis, as a slave, could not be held responsible for actions which he had not freely committed; no historical record suggests he received any punishment.

Guillaume Couillart's black slave also got off lightly, even though the offence he had committed – slander – could lead to serious consequences. During the first English occupation of Quebec from 1629 to 1632, Nicolas Marsolet entered the service of the Kirke brothers. Then in 1638, at a time when Marsolet had every interest in showing complete loyalty to France, which had regained possession of Quebec, the black slave Olivier claimed that Marsolet had received a message from a traitor named Le Baillif, the very man who had donated the slave to Guillaume Couillart. After a summary investigation, the black man admitted in the presence of Guillaume Couillart and Guillaume Hébert that he could not back up his statements; he was condemned to ask forgiveness and "to spend four hours in irons,"[141] that is, with his feet in chains.

The Panis Charles was so rebellious that he actually raised an insurrection, and was deported to the Caribbean in 1730. While in service at Fort Niagara, he incited part of the garrison to revolt, either to avenge harsh punishments meted out by Nicolas-Blaise Bergères de Rigauville or because of the food; the rebels planned to get rid of the commander and break out in revolt on July 26. Rigauville got wind of the plot in time, and sent a messenger to Montreal for help; Governor Beauharnois dispatched a detachment; the rebels including the Panis were arrested, sent to Montreal and put in irons. At the court martial the Panis was sentenced to be deported and the other rebels sentenced to execution by hanging, although they managed to escape with the connivance of the Récollet brothers; the Panis meanwhile was placed on board the *Saint-Antoine* and transported to Martinique, there to remain in servitude.[142] It is worth noting that in this case of sedition, the slave got off with a lighter sentence than the soldiers. Were there extenuating circumstances? We do not know.

William Brown, printer of the *Quebec Gazette*, had all sorts of trouble with his black slave Joe, and could not get the upper hand. In August 1774, the printer put his slave (here mentioned for the first time) in prison: Joe had apparently stolen 4 pounds 15 shillings 3¾ pence from his master, a large sum at the time (one British pound, Quebec currency was worth four dollars at the time, and was made up of twenty shillings, each shilling being worth twelve pence); moreover, the master had to pay two shillings six pence to lock his slave up, then two pounds ten pence for his board in prison. In other words, the master was first robbed, and then had to defray the costs of his slave's punishment.

Once Joe returned home William Brown taught him the craft of pressman, but in April 1777, the slave ran away and it cost Brown seventeen shillings nine pence to find him. Joe escaped again in November that year: Brown paid a man named Davis two shillings nine pence to find Joe and the jailer Couture two pounds five shillings to lock him up, while the slave's board in prison cost the master another thirteen shillings four pence. On January 25, 1778, Joe fled again, and Brown offered ten shillings to whomever managed to bring the fugitive back. On December 22 of the same year, Joe escaped again: Brown had him jailed and whipped by the hangman, at a cost of one pound eight shillings ten pence. On April 30, Joe stole one pound three shillings four pence, and ran away; Brown paid five shillings to have the black man brought back. On September 16, 1779, Joe escaped his master again. He was found on board the ship *Empress of Russia* and the printer paid out an additional one pound thirteen shillings four pence. On October 13, 1781, Joe was sent to jail, where he remained until May 8, 1782: Brown paid two pounds ten shillings, and tried unsuccessfully to sell him to someone about to leave for the Caribbean. At the end of 1785, Joe ran away again, and it cost Brown ten shillings to track him down; he was sent to prison, but on February 18, 1786, he bolted at dawn with the criminal John Peters. The sheriff offered a reward first of five pounds for each fugitive, then of two; Brown offered a reward of three guineas (about four pounds) to whomever brought back his "printing pressman" – a reward that was still being offered in June 1786. Joe eventually returned home and even turned over a new leaf, because on New Year's Day 1788, Brown made him a gift of six shillings five pence.

This situation could not last. On February 12, 1788, Joe laid his hands on a pitcher of brandy, which had cost his owner two shillings; on March 20, Brown paid four shillings to saw wood, owing to Joe's negligence; finally, the slave's behaviour improved and beginning in May 1788 his master gave him pocket money each week. Joe then became the property of Samuel Neilson, and ran away again in August 1789, before disappearing from the historical record altogether.

Here was a slave who caused his master a lot of grief. According to our calculations, between 1774 and 1789 Brown had suffered losses and paid out rewards and fees of nineteen pounds three shillings eleven and a half pence, for Joe's robberies and escapes, his board in prison and the hangman's expenses. If we remember that a "Negro" at the time was worth forty or fifty pounds, it is clear that Joe's insubordination came at a heavy cost. Brown sought to protect his investment by tracking Joe down and applying a combination of kindness and cruelty to reform him. If Joe had been subjected to the *Code Noir*, Brown could have had his hamstring cut after the second escape, and have him hanged after the third. (For more information on Brown's difficulties with Joe, see the article "Joe, nègre de Brown" in the *Dictionnaire*.)

Brown's contemporary, Seigneur Chartier de Lotbinière, spent far less in dealing with the misconduct of his Negro Michel-Henri: he simply booted him out the door.[143]

Sending Thieves to the Gallows

During the seventeenth and eighteenth centuries, criminal justice for thieves was extremely harsh: no matter what the value of goods stolen, once a theft was committed or even attempted at night, the thief warranted execution; with unlit streets and no night watch, residents were vulnerable, so the death penalty was liberally handed out in cases of breaking and entering.

In January 1757, the Panis Constant, slave of the officer Paul-François Raimbault de Simblin, started pilfering at night. He climbed a picket fence around the yard of Widow Saint-Pierre; using a ladder he found leaning against the roof, he broke the window of an attic room and entered. The widow was in the attic. Terrified by the intrusion, she broke "her arm as she dropped from the attic to the lower level of the house." Constant was duly arrested. Brought before the court of Montreal, the Panis was sentenced to two hours in the public pillory, on market day, and banned for life from the jurisdiction of Montreal.

This amounted to a slap on the wrist, while the crime the Panis Constant had committed – pilfering by night – normally deserved the death penalty. For example in 1758 François Rodrigue was found hiding in a private home, with mischievous intent. He was sentenced to the gallows and the Conseil supérieur upheld the sentence. Why was the Panis treated with comparative indulgence, for the same offence? This is exactly what shocked the *procureur du roi* (Crown attorney), whose appeal to the Conseil supérieur resulted in a harsher sentence on March 26. The culprit was banished from the colony in perpetuity, remaining in prison "until the first vessel leaves the port for France."[144] The Panis Constant deserved to be sent to the gallows, but was simply banished from the colony: whereas slaves in the Caribbean were punished far more harshly than people of a free condition, slaves in New France often got off lightly.

In 1796, at a time when a person stealing a sheep could be hanged, the Panis Charlotte got a relatively mild sentence for stealing the sum of seventeen shillings six pence. As punishment she was branded on the hand with a hot iron and sentenced to five and a half months in prison.[145]

Sometimes a slave caught stealing was first sentenced to death, then pardoned. The most surprising case involved a black woman, Ann Wiley, who stole six guineas with a white man, Jean Coutencineau. On March 25, 1775, Philip Dejean, Justice of the Peace in Detroit, condemned them both to the gallows. But Detroit had no public executioner. So what should Dejean do? He ended up offering the black slave her life if she agreed to hang her white accomplice; she accepted with pleasure, hanged Coutencineau, then departed. This seems to be the first time in historical records that a female executioner executed a prisoner. The population of Detroit was very indignant that a Canadian should be hanged by a Negro. Justice Dejean was threatened with prosecution, and beat a hasty retreat to Illinois.

The black Alexander Webb did not get off so easily. He was arrested in 1785 for burglary, in the company of four other robbers, and the five men were condemned to the gallows. On the evening of June 15, the five were led to the gallows on the Plains of Abraham in Quebec. But at the last minute, just as the rope was slipped around their necks, the slave and two of the others were pardoned.[146] The same thing happened to the mulatto Thomas, known as Tom. In the spring of 1795, he was sentenced to hang for burgling the sum of forty shillings, but Governor Dorchester granted him a pardon.[147]

This is not to say that all slaves found guilty of robbery were spared death by hanging. In 1735, the black Jean-Baptiste-Thomas, a slave belonging to Louise Lecompte-Dupré (widow of merchant Jean-Antoine Magnan-Lespérance) was arrested for burgling along with François Darles, who was found guilty of receiving stolen goods. On July 22, both were sentenced to hang. But the sentence handed down in Montreal called for the gallows to be set up in front of the widow's house – the same Madame Magnan-Lespérance who owned the black slave. She was not too thrilled with the idea of a public execution on her doorstep, and appealed to the Conseil supérieur, which led to a new trial. Jean-Baptiste-Thomas and his accomplice Darles were then interrogated under torture, and the

Conseil upheld the sentence handed down in Montreal, except that the gallows would be erected in the Market Square, which came as a relief to Madame Magnan-Lespérance.[148]

The Montagnais woman Marianne was also hanged for theft. She was caught at night pilfering the home of her master, the officer Alexandre Dagneau-Douville. On September 20, 1756 the court condemned her to be hanged in front of her master's home. Dagneau-Douville likely did not relish the prospect of a hanging so close to his residence any more than Madame Magnan-Lespérance had. But this time Marianne appealed to the Conseil supérieur on the grounds that she was pregnant. The Montagnais woman was duly taken to Quebec City, where the Conseil reviewed the case and ultimately upheld the sentence, requesting that the chief surgeon at the Hôtel-Dieu, accompanied by a midwife, ascertain whether Marianne was in fact pregnant: they concluded she had made up the whole story. On November 20, 1756, at three o'clock in the afternoon, the Montagnais slave died on the gallows in Quebec.[149]

On the night of October 28, 1791, the black slave Josiah Cutan, co-owned by the merchant John Askin and the fur trader Arthur McCormick, was caught breaking and entering the Detroit house of Joseph Campeau, where he stole various items. He was arrested on the spot and taken to jail to await trial. In May 1792, John Askin bought McCormick's share and became the sole owner of the slave, who was still behind bars. On September 6, 1792, Josiah entered a plea of not guilty. The following day, witnesses were heard, the prosecutor delivered his indictment and the jury found the slave guilty as charged. On September 10, the judge sentenced him to the gallows for burglary at night, reprimanding him sharply for his actions: "This Crime is so much more atrocious and alarming to society, as it is committed by night, when the world is at repose, and that it cannot be guarded against without the same precautions which are used against the wild beasts of the forest, who like you, go prowling about by night for their prey. A member so hurtful to the peace of society, no good Laws will permit to continue in it."[150] So the black man was hanged: indeed this was the first legal execution in Upper Canada, where the history of the gallows begins with the hanging of a black slave.

We should add to this gruesome catalogue a hanging in 1827. The execution was a pittoresque affair, involving once again a black man, who was possibly still in bondage. A black Protestant, Robert Ellis, broke into the presbytery of Pointe-Lévy, along with two Monarque brothers, William Ross and Benjamin Johnson (just eighteen years old)—they were all sentenced to the gallows, but the Monarque brothers managed to escape. And so it was that on Saturday, April 21, 1827, gallows were set up in front of the Quebec prison, and Ellis was led out with his two accomplices Ross and Johnson. It was customary to allow the condemned prisoner his last words. Ross addressed the crowd for ten to fifteen minutes, after which Ellis and young Johnson spoke. Unfortunately, the press did not record the black man's spiritual testament: we only know that he maintained his innocence to the end, accepting his fate with indifference.[151]

Slaves caught stealing had a better time of it when their masters took charge of punishment. This was the case for example of the black Joe, whose master William Brown caught him stealing, clapped him in prison for theft, and paid to have him whipped. Had Joe been brought to justice, he would likely have been hanged. Evidently, thieves were happier still when they managed to flee. Such was the case of the black man Bruce, slave of Lieutenant Colonel Gabriel Christie, a seigneur. Aged 35 years or so, Bruce was "tall and well built," and suspected of having stolen liquor, soap, sugar and other things in the basement of John Jones of Montreal, on the night of September 4-5, 1777. He vanished without trace and does not seem to have been recaptured. Night burglars were generally led to the gallows. In 1794, Isaac, a black slave belonging to Azariah Pretchard of Richmond, in the Gaspé region, also fled after several burglaries; a reward of twenty piastres was offered for bringing in this six-foot-tall slave fluent in English, French and Mi'kmaq.[152] This hefty reward suggests that once Isaac was captured, he would be heading to the gallows.

SENT TO THE GALLEYS FOR RAPING A GIRL

In 1734, the Panis Jacques, aged about 40 years, was implicated in a criminal case. This Panis had belonged to several successive masters since childhood. He fled from his master Lapérade apparently after repeated beatings, then wandered through the *pays d'en haut*, reaching Michilimackinac, Illinois and later Acadia, where he married a Mi'kmaq. After she died, he married another Amerindian woman from Acadia and had five children with her: his family scattered, with two children settling at Lac des Deux-Montagnes, upstream from Montreal, while the three others remained in Acadia.

At the end of June 1734, this same Panis turned up in Champlain, just downstream from Trois-Rivières. On Midsummer Day (the feast day of St. John the Baptist), with everyone off at high mass, René Durand's daughter Marie-Joseph was staying at home to take care of the children. During the morning she went up to the woods, looking for a cow; the girl was heard screaming and then she vanished. On returning from Mass her family thought at first that Marie-Joseph Durand had been devoured by a bear, so they organized a beat, fanning out over the country. Her uncle Jean ran to the place where Marie-Joseph had been heard screaming, followed fresh tracks for one league, and finally found the Panis Jacques "adjusting his belt, with Marie-Joseph nearby wearing nothing but a blouse and her coat wide open"; she had scratches on her throat and stomach: clearly, this was a case of abduction and at least of attempted rape. The Panis was captured, and in his defence claimed to be part of a Mi'kmaq group sent by the English to take prisoners. He was willing to show where the Amerindians accompanying him were holding out. Nobody believed him, and he was taken to Trois-Rivières where the trial began on July 7, 1735.

Under questioning, the Panis denied having raped the girl; he claimed he had actually wanted to bring her back to Acadia as his wife, but he had had to grab her by the throat to prevent her from screaming. The judge noted the Panis already had a wife in Acadia, so how could he have two wives at the same time? The Panis apologized, saying the devil had made him do it.

The Panis Jacques must have been regularly tormented by the devil, because he was suspected of having attempted to kidnap another girl upstream, in the village of Berthier-en-Haut. The Panis was asked about this other case, and admitted that in Berthier-en-Haut he had met the daughter of a man named Pichion [?]. The girl's mother sent her to fetch corn on an island in the river; "as I was fishing there," the Panis continued, "the girl asked me to paddle her to the island and to wait for her there. That's what I did, but when I asked her to get out of the canoe and head home, she refused; seeing that I was getting ready to leave for Acadia, she decided to follow me; we went to Batiscan where she had relatives, but she refused to get out of the canoe; once we got to Île-aux-Oies (below Quebec), I sent her to fetch bread from Monsieur de Fonville, but he kept her and wrote her father to come and get her." "Did you have sexual relations with this girl?" asked the judge, to which the Panis replied: "Yes, but she was the one taking the initiative."

We do not know if the judge believed this story of a girl deciding on the spur of the moment to wander off to Acadia with a Panis, instead of fetching corn as her mother had requested... In any case, it was hard to believe the explanation given by the Panis, given what had actually happened to the Durand girl. On July 14, the Crown attorney argued that the Panis had been found guilty of kidnapping and deserved to be publicly hanged in Trois-Rivières. As no trace remains of the judge's sentence in Trois-Rivières, we cannot say what punishment was meted out by the trial court. However, on August 2, the Panis appealed to the Conseil supérieur de Québec; unfortunately, the sentence is not reported in the trial record. According to the anonymous author of a monograph, the Panis Jacques was deported to serve in the king's galleys, which was the usual punishment for this sort of crime.[153]

Hanged for Stabbing His Mistress
In August 1759, the Panis Marie tried to kill herself in Trois-Rivières: this suicide attempt was duly noted by judicial authorities, because under French rule a person attempting or completing suicide was

liable to be punished: the body of the "self-murdered" person was dragged face down through town, hung upside down, exposed for twenty-four hours, then thrown into the water. We know of only two suicide attempts among Canadian slaves. In November 1713, Governor Beauharnois' Fox slave Madelon was so distraught with homesickness or some other suffering that she sought to end her life. She hanged herself in the castle stables, but was "found choking, and brought [to the Hôtel-Dieu] where she was cared for"; she was admitted to the hospital on November 21, and seems to have been restored to health by December 3; but we do not know whether the governor punished her for this suicide attempt. In the other case, it was not so much the Panis Marie's attempted suicide that caught the attention of the court, as the fact that the attempt followed her armed attack against her mistresses—hitting people in authority was an extremely serious crime for a slave!

The Panis Marie, also described as a Cree woman in documents of the time, belonged to Chevalier Joseph Boucher de Niverville, the husband of Marie-Josephte Chastelain. The Nivervilles lived under the same roof as Marie-Josephte's parents, François Chastelain and Marguerite Cardin, so the Panis Marie worked for the Chastelains as well. As a result of "some mistreatment and scolding," the Panis woman conceived a hatred for her two mistresses, Madame Chastelain, aged fifty-one, and Madame de Niverville, just twenty-two. It was about half past one in the afternoon on August 20, 1759 that the incident occurred. Madame Chastelain gave an order to the Panis, who flatly refused and "angrily took a knife and struck the said woman with it, without intent to kill"; Madame Chastelain received a blow to the upper chest and another to the left shoulder. Madame de Niverville immediately intervened and the Panis woman hit her on the right shoulder and grazed her left shoulder. Blood was flowing by now, the two women screamed murder, and neighbours showed up. While the two injured women were put to bed, the Panis woman went up to the attic, shut the door, and hanged herself from a beam. The officer Nicolas-Joseph Fleurimont de Noyelle arrived on the scene with four soldiers, went up to the attic and seeing her hanging there, cut her down immediately. The surgeon Charles Alavoine turned up shortly afterwards, and laid the Panis woman on a bed: after feeling her faint pulse and noting foam at the mouth, he decided to bleed her. Half an hour later, the Panis regained consciousness, by which time Mesdames Chastelain and de Niverville had recovered from their superficial injuries. One thing at least was clear: the Panis had escaped death and could now atone for her crime.

The case was heard the same day by Jean Leproust, a practitioner filling in as judge, in the absence of the civil and criminal lieutenant general. Over several days, many witnesses were called to testify, and were confronted with the accused. Marie was subject to questioning several times, with the gunsmith Joseph Chevalier acting as interpreter. This Amerindian woman did not know her age and claimed to have been born in a Cree village. She testified that she had struck the women to scare them, but without intent to kill, so she did not deserve punishment for mistreating her mistresses. Moreover, if she had tried to kill herself, it was neither out of regret nor of fear. In any case, the crime was clearly established.

On September 11, the deputy judge convicted the Amerindian woman of "striking with a knife, as mentioned during the trial, and of subsequently hanging herself." Accordingly, "the public executioner would beat and flog her naked in the usual crossroads and places in this city"; at one of these crossroads, she would be "branded with a fleur de lys on her right shoulder," and then, after paying a fine of three livres, banned for life from the jurisdiction of Trois-Rivières.

Flogging, branding with a hot iron, banishment: given the serious crime this slave had committed, the sentence seemed disproportionately light. Perhaps people realized that under the *Code Noir* of the French West Indies and the equivalent code of Louisiana, a slave striking a master, mistress and children and drawing blood was punishable by death. Perhaps they felt that such serious rebellion could be expiated only by hanging. Whatever the case, the Crown attorney appealed Judge Proust's sentence. The Conseil supérieur showed no mercy when it convened in Montreal. On December 29, 1759, the Conseil ordered that the slave be sent to the gallows, her body to be exposed for two hours, then dumped in the public thoroughfare.[154] With the rights of authority upheld, Mesdames Chastelain and de Niverville could recover from their injuries in peace.

Two Panis Homicides

Panis committed two voluntary and intentional homicides. The first, in 1710, was pretty much a slaughter. The Panis Nicolas was mentioned for the first time in historical documents in 1709, when Quebec was engulfed in panic over a rumoured attack by the English and this Panis Nicolas took advantage of the situation to commit a few robberies. In 1710, he was suspected of stealing martens from Mr. Brousse. That same year he committed murder.

The public executioner Jacques Élie and his wife Marie-Joseph Maréchal had grown weary of hearing the public's and especially the children of Quebec's continual jeers. The executioner and his wife considered emigrating, and the Panis Nicolas offered to lead them through the woods to New England. His pay was fixed at fifty livres and a coat. He stole a canoe, which Jacques Élie boarded along with his pregnant wife, a child of five years and another of fourteen months. The Panis paddled the group as far as the Duchesne River in the Deschaillons seigneurie, and there during the night of May 22-23, 1710, the journey came to a sudden end when he killed the executioner with an axe, dumping the body into the river; he also killed the eldest child, but only succeeded in seriously wounding the pregnant woman and the fourteen-month-old infant. The woman managed to escape, dragging herself and the infant to nearby houses, as the Panis fled. The criminal was tried *in absentia*, during the woman's recovery at the Hôtel-Dieu de Québec. At the end of the trial he was condemned to be broken alive. In the convict's absence, it was decreed that the punishment "shall be carried out in effigy, using a painting attached to the pole of the public square of the Lower Town." On November 21, 1710, the executioner depicted the Panis Nicolas on a canvas, showing him being broken alive with an iron bar; this painless punishment nonetheless amounted to a public humiliation. It does not seem the Panis ever fell into the hands of justice.[155]

The other murder took place in 1762. The merchant Clapham came from Fort Pitt to Detroit to acquire a Panis man and woman. He left with them by canoe, stopping near Presqu'Isle, on the south shore of Lake Erie. He served rum to a party of visiting Amerindians. The two newly acquired slaves took advantage of the festivities, murdering their master, cutting of his head, looting his bags, burning his papers and then taking refuge in Amerindian country. The Amerindians nonetheless handed over the two Panis to Colonel Donald Campbell, commander at Detroit. The Amerindians offered to burn the criminals themselves. Campbell referred the matter to Colonel Henry Bouquet, who in turn referred it to William Johnson, Amerindian Superintendent. On October 1, 1762, Jeffery Amherst, Commander-in-Chief, finally decided the English garrison should mete out justice and not the Amerindians themselves. Major Gladwin of Detroit was ordered to bring the two accused before a court martial, but the Panis man managed to flee into the Illinois Country. The Panis woman was not so lucky: she remained under guard, was convicted and then hanged.[156]

THE BURNING OF MONTREAL

The most spectacular crime by a slave in New France was surely the one committed by the black woman Angélique (also known as Marie-Joseph-Angélique). She was the slave of a Montreal merchant, François Poulin Francheville, and had been baptized on June 28, 1730 at about twenty years of age: by then, she was pregnant by César, a black slave belonging to Ignace Gamelin. In January 1731, she gave birth to Eustache, and in May 1732, she had twins by César. Angélique then seems to have dropped this first lover for a white man, Claude Thibault.

Yet a cloud hung over this romantic relationship: in 1734 she figured that her mistress, Thérèse Decouagne (Widow Francheville), was getting ready to sell her. Angélique therefore decided to flee to New England with her lover. On the evening of April 10 or 12, 1734, she set fire to the house of her mistress in rue Saint-Paul, before fleeing, either to divert attention from her flight, or in a spirit of revenge. The house soon became a raging inferno. The neighbours realized their own homes were threatened by the advancing flames, so they rushed to move their furniture and effects to the nuns' residence at the Hôtel-Dieu. But the flames leapt from one house to the next, finally reaching the Hôtel-Dieu, and burning both church and convent. The nuns were unable to save much – this was the third fire to strike the Hôtel-Dieu. The fire continued to spread through the city and by the time it stopped, forty-six houses had been destroyed. During the conflagration, Angélique had ample opportunity to flee with her beloved.

But the long arm of the law caught up with her. Angélique was apprehended by officers of the constabulary, although her lover escaped. She was jailed and tried by the court in the still-smouldering city of Montreal. Her sentence came down on June 4:

> She shall make amends naked in her shirt, with a rope about her neck, holding in her hands a burning torch weighing two pounds in front of the main door and entrance to the parish church of the city of Montreal, where she shall be led and conducted by the hangman of the high court in a cart used to carry off refuse, bearing a sign both in front and behind marked with the word arsonist, and there, bareheaded and kneeling, shall declare that she maliciously set and caused the said fire for which she grievously repents and begs forgiveness from God, the king and justice, after which she shall have her hand cut off and raised on a post planted in front of said church, and then be conducted by said hangman in the refuse cart to the public square, there to be attached to the post with an iron chain and burned alive, her body reduced to ashes and scattered to the winds.

In the minds of the victims, this sentence was in proportion to the magnitude of the crime: the black woman would first be subjected to the most exacting and detailed interrogation under torture, then paraded in a refuse cart, compelled to make amends before the parish church, have her hand cut off, then be burned alive.

Angélique appealed to the Conseil supérieur, which meant she had to be conveyed to Quebec City. On June 12, the Conseil upheld the death sentence, although it changed important aspects of her punishment: the black woman would still be conducted in a refuse cart to the door of the parish church, there to make amends, but her hand would not be cut off; in addition, on reaching the public square, she would be hanged before burning. The Conseil took account of the black woman's partial responsibility for the disaster in Montreal. And she was led back to Montreal for the execution of her sentence, at the scene of the crime and in full view of the indignant population.

On June 21, Angélique was tortured in prison in Montreal. She confessed her crime, but only after four bouts of torture, courageously refusing to denounce any accomplice. At three o'clock in the afternoon, the clerk reached the prison and read out her sentence; the Sulpician priest Navetier heard her confession, after which Angélique was handed over to the executioner, likely the black man Mathieu Léveillé. She was conveyed on the refuse cart to the parish church, where she made amends; after this ritual ceremony, the refuse cart continued on to the public square, making a long detour past the burned houses in order to confront her with the magnitude of her crime. Once this funeral procession was over, the slave Angélique was hanged, her corpse burned, and the ashes thrown to the wind.[157]

Meanwhile, the search continued for her lover, Claude Thibault. On April 19, 1734, nine days after the conflagration, Intendant Hocquart ordered the captains of militia to arrest Thibault who was suspected of having set the fire in Montreal along with Angélique. But Thibault had a nine-day advance on the militia captains and could not be found. Two years later, in April 1736, the king authorized the intendant to stop looking for the alleged accomplice to avoid "incurring further costs related to the affair"; it should be considered "that the Negress who set the fire of Montreal avowed her guilt without identifying any accomplices. That there were only suspicions against the man named Thibault because he has fled and had some debauched relationship with this Negress, all investigation undertaken since then having turned up nothing against him."[158]

Slave Crimes Were Isolated Acts

This fire in Montreal, set by a black slave, was in no way a general revolt against society: it was an individual crime committed against a single person, Widow Francheville, in the interests of diverting attention so two lovers could escape. No massive slave revolt took place in Canada the way it had in other colonies, for example, in New Orleans in 1731, where a plot was hatched to organize an uprising. Blacks in New Orleans planned to break out in revolt during High Mass, burn houses and then flee, but the plot was revealed by a black woman. Among those found guilty, a woman was hanged and four men were broken alive.[159] It is true that a petition presented to the House of Assembly in 1799 by Joseph Papineau, to ensure owners' rights over their slaves, mentioned that the previous year, after a black woman was freed, "Negroes in the city and district of Montreal threatened a general revolt."[160] In fact, they did not threaten to revolt so much as to run away. The black woman mentioned was being sued by her master for running away. But as the presiding judge was firmly opposed to slavery, he refused to convict a person for just being a runaway slave. It seems that the other slaves were so impressed with the judge's ruling that they planned to run away themselves. At no time in our history, is there any mention of an armed insurrection led by the slave population, or even plans for one. Crimes were isolated acts directed against individuals.

Of the 4185 slaves in New France and Canada over a 200-year period, only eighteen were convicted of crimes. Yet these were slaves torn away from their native place, reduced to slavery in a foreign society, and given only the rudiments of a Christian education. One would normally expect them to have offered fiery resistance to the ordinary laws of a society in which they had unwillingly been transplanted. Yet less than twenty of these close to 4200 slaves proved to be criminals.

We should also note that corporal punishments in New France were usually less severe than in the French West Indies and that slaves were punished less severely than people of a free condition. Slaves were deported whereas Canadians were hanged – for the very same offences. And when the law was rigorously applied, the slave received the same treatment as the free person: the slave appeared before the same judge, and could appeal to the Conseil supérieur; punishment was meted out under the same conditions as for any other criminal. Surely, this can partly be explained by the fact slaves were not a particular threat to society. In any case, given the equality of slave and freeman before the law, as well as criminal convictions among slaves, it would appear that slaves were well integrated in our society.

CHAPTER NINE

Did Slaves Have the Same Rights as Freemen?

The slaves of French Canada were held in bondage, yet they were subject to many of the same conditions as their masters, taking part for example in the sacraments of the Church. Slaves appear to have had a privileged status in French Canada. But did that mean they enjoyed the same prerogatives as freeborn persons? Could slaves in fact be freed?

SLAVES COULD SERVE AS WITNESSES
According to the *Code Noir* of 1685 (and also the code of 1724), slaves had no legal capacity: they were charges under the law, they entered as such into community property, and they could only act through their masters. These provisions of the *Code Noir* were not strictly applied in New France, however. Slaves often acted as witnesses here, on the same footing as freeborn persons. They could serve as godparents at baptisms: we have already mentioned forty-six baptisms at which blacks or Amerindians served as sponsors, and the number would have been higher still if Canadians had not made a point of honour of serving as godparents to their own slaves. In any event, the number of slaves serving as sponsors is high enough for us to conclude there was little distinction between slaves and freeborn persons in this regard.

Slaves also served as witnesses at the weddings of fellow slaves: in 1750, two blacks stood in as witnesses at the wedding of Leber de Senneville's black slave Joseph-Hippolyte *dit* l'Espiègle; under the French regime this was exceptional, however, since slave owners normally served as witnesses at slave weddings, baptisms and burials, whereas under the British regime, slaves generally filled this role.

179

The role of witness on such occasions was a modest one, however. Acting as a witness at a wedding or burial was by no means as important as testifying in civil or criminal proceedings. Nonetheless, slaves witnessing a religious ceremony had their names entered in the civil registry, and in so doing they helped confer a legal character on baptisms, weddings and burials.

A SLAVE CLAIMING TO BE FREE

Slaves were sometimes involved in lawsuits, which provide an indication they enjoyed some of the same prerogatives as freeborn persons. The first lawsuit went back to the fall of 1740: Lieutenant Marc-Antoine Huart, Chevalier Dormicourt, contracted with Aubry that the latter would take the Panis Marie-Marguerite by sea to the French West Indies and sell her there.

A slave since childhood, the Panis Marie-Marguerite had belonged to a succession of masters. She was first given in 1726 to René, a voyageur from Laprairie and the partner of François-Antoine Duplessis-Fabert at Baie des Puants (now Green Bay) on Lake Michigan; he sent her as a gift to Duplessis-Fabert's wife, who lived in Montreal with the merchant Étienne Volant de Radisson; Marie-Marguerite was baptized July 8, 1730 at the age of about 12 years, and the baptismal registry indicated she belonged to Duplessis-Fabert; the following year, under the name of Marguerite Duplessis, she received the sacrament of Confirmation. Her owner died in 1733, but she continued living with Volant de Radisson, who in turn died in 1735. She now had to leave the home where she had been living for ten years, and the late Duplessis-Fabert's brother sold her to the trader Jean-Louis Fornel. In September 1740, she seems to have sought to become the property of one Bailly de Messein, and on Bailly's behalf she offered Fornel the same price as he had paid for her; Fornel turned the offer down and the Panis woman ended up belonging not to the master she hoped for, but to Chevalier Dormicourt instead.

But Dormicourt quickly regretted acquiring her. The Panis Marie-Marguerite was physically unappealing (she had only one eye), and with Volant de Radisson now dead she was no longer part of a stable household. According to Dormicourt's testimony, she had since turned to vice, debauchery and theft. As a result, Dormicourt contracted to have Aubry sell the Panis woman in the French West Indies, clapping her in jail until the ship was ready to set sail.

While in jail Marie-Marguerite managed to interest a few people in her fate. According to Dormicourt, they were "priests and monks." A legal practitioner by the name of Jacques Nouette offered to defend the slave: under the French regime, practitioners with more of less improvised legal skills could stand in when lawyers were unavailable. We do not know whether he was hired by the ecclesiastics or had simply turned up on his own initiative.

In any event, Nouette does not seem to have had much of a reputation in legal circles: nothing is known about him except that he defended the Panis woman, although Chevalier Dormicourt claimed during the trial that Nouette had no fixed address, which meant he was in a state of ignominy. This was the practitioner taking up Marie-Marguerite's defence, and deploying every possible argument to prevent her being sent into exile.

On October 1, 1740 (or perhaps a few days earlier), the Panis tightly held "under lock and key" petitioned Intendant Hocquart directly. She claimed to be a natural daughter of the late François-Antoine Duplessis-Fabert, pointing out moreover that Dormicourt "imagined her to be his slave, and held her for no reason in chains. Although the supplicant did not have the advantage of issuing from a lawful marriage, she was not born a slave, and had therefore been born free." So went the first argument.

Now came the second argument. Her liberty was being denied "even though, residing in lands under obedience to His Majesty, which are lands of liberty for all those who, like the supplicant, profess the Roman, Catholic and Apostolic faith, her condition of slavery ought to be nullified since [her residency and faith] have made her the King's subject." Nouette may have lacked a fixed address, yet he was not without ingenuity: "Even if I was a slave," he had the Panis woman say, "then my slavery would be nullified because of my being a baptized Catholic living on French soil." However, the practitioner was overstepping the mark: true, the lands of the King of France were a refuge against slavery, but an edict of 1716 had drawn a neat distinction between continental France and her colonies, this same edict stating further that any slave arriving in France did not necessarily gain his liberty; on the one hand, Amerindians who were baptized according to the Catholic rite from 1627 onwards acquired the status of "French naturals," but on the other hand, Raudot's ordinance of 1709 had legalized slavery. The practitioner was thus raising two serious issues: the Panis woman claimed to be the illegitimate daughter of an officer, adding that even if she had been born a slave, the facts of her baptism and residency on French soil had freed her from bondage.

Intendant Hocquart studied the petition, and referred the case to the trial court, the provost of Quebec. The civil and criminal lieutenant general slapped Dormicourt with a summons to appear on October 4. How did he respond to the Panis woman's claims?

[He said he was] astonished to see priests and monks secretly arming against him without prior warning, in order to snatch away his slave, and to see clergymen groundlessly attacking the reputation of an honest man [the late Duplessis-Fabert], while treating a rascally wench and a libertine gently and with all consideration, whereas she ought to be shamefully pitched out of the colony, to put a stop to her perverted debauchery and prevent further scandal [which she was causing]: she ought moreover to be sold off in the islands rather than brought to justice for household burglary.

After this indictment of the ecclesiastics and his Panis woman, Dormicourt addressed the matter of her supposed natural descent: "They simply made up the claim she was the daughter of the late Monsieur Duplessis. This is a calumny, and I demand a retraction.

They have slandered an honest man without evidence: there is simply no way to establish any relationship of the sort." Dormicourt then told the court how this Panis woman had arrived in Montreal as a slave, belonging as a slave first to Fornel and then to himself.

But what about her family name? Dormicourt objected that "said slave had always borne the name Marguerite Radisson, because Monsieur Radisson had had her baptized. And even if she bore the name of Duplessis, that proved nothing. It is customary in this country for slaves to bear the name of their master, even in the absence of any relationship of paternity or filiation." Dormicourt concluded that a family name proved nothing. The only way to prove descent, he said, was if the father acknowledged it, or the baptismal certificate specified it, whereas this slave had been baptized in Montreal "as originating from the Panis nation, without mention either of father or mother"; the Panis were recognized as slaves in our society, and several gentlemen had sent Panis to the French West Indies, there to serve as slaves. Moreover, Dormicourt continued, even if a French father acknowledged a female slave as his daughter, that would not change her condition of servitude: "A child born to a slave mother and a French father shall be a slave: such is the law in America. And this same law must be applied to 'savage' slaves in this country: the King alone is empowered to rule on this issue or to change the law."

Dormicourt concluded with an *ad hominen* argument: the Panis Marguerite had always acknowledged she was a slave, and the previous month she had tried to get Monsieur Bailly of Montreal to buy her, offering on his behalf the same sum as Fornel had paid for her: "Without the misplaced charity of some ecclesiastics, she would never have considered becoming free." And who was this woman protected by the clergy? "She is a disreputable subject whose debauchery can cause a good deal of disorder and scandal: he preferred selling her off than charging her with household burglary; she is a rascally wench and a libertine, a thief, a drunkard with many other faults besides – this is the subject who has roused the charity of the clergymen." In short, Dormicourt requested permission to transport his Panis immediately to the French West Indies.

The court felt it important to know in what capacity she had been baptized, and therefore ordered Nouette to produce her baptismal certificate within a fortnight. This fifteen-day delay was a disadvantage for Dormicourt, since it was late in the navigation season, and her departure for the Caribbean was now compromised. Accordingly, Dormicourt enjoined Nouette on October 6 to "provide security [...] for damages, costs [legal fees], procedural costs, plus interest given the longer detention period."

The Panis woman now had the burden of proof: she had to prove her natural descent, and the court had instructed the practitioner Nouette to provide such evidence by producing the baptismal certificate. However, on the advice of the practitioner or clergymen, the Panis woman decided not to wait for the certificate. Perhaps she knew this piece of evidence would work against her; in fact, the baptismal certificate reads as follows: "The eighth day of July, one thousand seven hundred and thirty was christened Marie-Marguerite, a Panis twelve years of age, belonging to Captain Duplessis." It would be better for her not to present this certificate in court. On October 8, she petitioned Intendant Hocquart again, requesting leave to appeal to the Conseil supérieur, "whereas the case needs to proceed swiftly," and asking that Dormicourt be slapped with a 3000-livre fine: evidently, she wasn't pulling any punches. The intendant granted the appeal.

The Conseil supérieur met in special session on October 17. Until then, the Panis had borne the burden of proof, but now Nouette claimed Dormicourt was the one bearing the burden of proof: "Here is a girl who claims to be free, while another claims her as his slave, without any written proof thereof, without that possession which would prove her servitude: is she required to prove the very state of slavery she is contesting? It is this ridiculous affirmation that we are appealing." In other words, Nouette argued, it was up to Dormicourt to prove she was his slave.

Dormicourt retorted that Nouette could not serve as counsel to a slave, since a slave had no civil rights, and could neither go to court nor validly contract an agreement without the consent of her master: she could only be defended by a Crown attorney. And as for the practitioner, he had no fixed address and could not serve as guarantor for any damages. After these new *ad hominem* arguments, Dormicourt argued against the idea of relying on the baptismal certificate, for two reasons: first, a baptismal certificate could not be a sufficient basis, since it did not indicate the fathers and mothers of Amerindians, the baptized person only being described "as a savage, Panis or whatever, belonging to so-and-so" – in other words, the baptismal certificate was only proof of baptism; and second, it would take far too long to get the evidence, "because I am about to transport this Panis woman to the Caribbean, and if she missed the sailing, I would find it too burdensome to provide her with food and lodging until next autumn. I would prefer to consent to her discharge," Dormicourt added, "provided I am reimbursed the full purchase price, as well as the cost of maintaining her in jail, and court costs." He added, somewhat mischievously: "Since so many charitable persons are interested in the welfare of a disreputable subject given to debauchery, drunkenness and household burglary, this proposal may well rouse their indiscriminate zeal and supposed sense of charity."

The Conseil supérieur decided that same day to refer the parties to the intendant, who called on his sub-delegate, Estèbe, to hear Dormicourt and Nouette one last time. Dormicourt called two witnesses, René Bourassa and Nicolas Sarrazin: both testified they had been at Baie des Puants in 1726, had received a one-eyed Panis woman from a "savage," and had sent this Panis woman as a present to Madame Duplessis-Fabert; they also testified they had regularly seen this Panis woman living in the Radisson household where Madame Duplessis lived, and the woman's name was Marguerite. This compelling evidence weakened the Panis woman's case.

But the Panis applied to the intendant for a new delay (perhaps to be sure she would miss the sailing); she argued that her witnesses were unwilling to appear unless forced to do so, and they had vital evidence to present. What was this evidence? She claimed it showed she was the daughter of the late Duplessis and a freeborn woman;

the Jesuit Father Saint-Pé knew that Duplessis had had a child born free, raised in Radisson's household: she was none other than this child herself; she had lived in a free condition in Radisson's house, but on Duplessis-Fabert's death, the latter's brother had sold her as a slave to Fornel. She therefore requested that the court summon Duplessis-Fabert's brother, who was commander of Fort Saint-Frédéric. In the meantime, Nouette agreed to pay seven livres ten sols per month for her food and maintenance in jail. The intendant granted this new delay, and the following day, October 18, at the Panis woman's request, the bailiff summoned three people to testify: Joseph Denys de Laronde, the Jesuit Father Saint-Pé and Louise de Ramezay, a Montreal woman then visiting Quebec City.

The inquiry risked stretching out indefinitely just as the navigation season was coming to a close. Weeks would go by if the court were really to bring Duplessis-Fabert from Fort Saint-Frederic on Lake Champlain to hear his testimony in Quebec City. Dormicourt petitioned the intendant again: the inquiry sought by the Panis had not actually taken place because the witnesses called by Nouette had not turned up; moreover, Dormicourt claimed the scheme of bringing Duplessis-Fabert from Lake Champlain was a "frivolous red herring because Monsieur was not about to testify against himself"; all this scheme did was drag out the case, preventing "said slave from departing for [the islands of French] America once the ships are ready to set sail." Dormicourt therefore requested leave to put his slave on board a ship immediately.

Nouette tried to counter this new threat by calling for a further twenty-four-hour delay. Intendant Hocquart decided there had been enough delays already. On October 20, he signed an ordinance declaring that Marguerite Duplessis *dite* Radisson was indeed the slave of Chevalier Dormicourt; the intendant dismissed the Panis woman's appeal, upheld her status as a slave and ordered her to pay costs, based on Bourassa and Sarrazin's testimony as well as the fact that none of her witnesses had appeared despite her petition of October 17.[161]

In this slave's case, justice followed its normal course. She was the only slave under the French regime to set the workings of the justice system in motion, all the way from the trial court to the Conseil supérieur and ultimately the intendant himself.

A BLACK WOMAN CLAIMED THE CONQUEST HAD MADE HER FREE

We know of only one slave who demanded her freedom under the military regime: the black Étiennette, slave of Geneviève Gamelin of Montreal. She claimed that she had become free through the conquest of Canada.

The story went back to the taking of Sarasto (Saratoga) in 1745. She had been an infant only a year or so, when Canadians and Amerindians took the town by storm, capturing a portion of the population. Among the prisoners were a black man and woman, the father and mother of the little black infant Étiennette (also called Eskenne): the prisoners were forced to walk north to Canada, the father carrying his daughter on his back. In Montreal, the prisoners were parcelled out: the father and mother became the property of Luc Lacorne Saint-Luc; the girl meanwhile belonged to the Abenaki Pierre-Nicolas, who immediately sold her for 500 livres to the merchant-bourgeois Joseph-Jacques Gamelin; on March 7, 1746, the black infant girl was baptized and continued living in the Gamelin household.

Montreal capitulated to the British in September 1760. Nine months later, in June 1761, the black woman demanded to be released so she could return to the English colonies which she had left as an infant. How can this sudden nostalgia be explained, since Montreal had in fact become her home, and she had never known any other family than the Gamelins? Did Étiennette want to break free from authority which she found unbearable? Given that she was now about seventeen years old, perhaps she had fallen in love with a black or English soldier from New York during the occupation of Montreal. In any event, her mistress Geneviève Gamelin did not want her to leave.

On June 6, 1761, the black Étiennette appeared before the Militia Court in Montreal and asked leave to return to New England: she said she was a native of that country, and by virtue of the Capitulation of 1760 she must be regarded as a free British subject.

The black woman was citing the Articles of Capitulation, although only Article 47 referred to slavery: Vaudreuil had requested that "The Negroes and panis of both sexes shall remain, in their quality of slaves, in the possession of the French and Canadians to whom they belong; they shall be at liberty to keep them in their service in the colony or to sell them; and they may also continue to bring them up in the Roman religion." To which Amherst replied: "Granted, except those who shall have been made prisoners."[162] This reply was ambiguous: either the people of Canada could not claim back their slaves who had been captured by the English, or slaves previously captured from the English would no longer be held in bondage by Canadians. Perhaps the black Étiennette sought to use this second interpretation, as if to say: "I was once captured from the English, so I am no longer a slave of Canadians."

In our view, Étiennette was likely citing ordinances recently issued by military governors. Indeed, the authorities had begun an investigation to release captives from the Thirteen Colonies who had been taken or adopted by Canadians. On May 13, 1761, Governor Gage published the following ordinance in Montreal: "As several English children and others taken during the war are at this moment among the inhabitants, in the town as well as in the country, notwithstanding the orders long since repeated on the subject; all persons of whatever rank are hereby ordered to bring all the English children, women, or men, whether prisoners or deserters;" Canadians not complying with this ordinance could face a fine of 100 écus (more than 600 French livres) and six months' imprisonment.[163] In Trois-Rivières, Governor Burton learned that English children and servants in captivity had still not been reported to the authorities: on May 31, 1761, he summoned all persons to report within a fortnight "the name, age and sex of English children and domestics who reside with them, whether they have received them as a gift, or have purchased them from Indians."[164] The following June 6, Étiennette appeared before the military court, in her bid to return to New England.

Her mistress, Geneviève Gamelin, appeared in the Militia Court to assert her ownership rights over the slave: she told the officers under what circumstances the Gamelin family had come into ownership of the black in December 1745, at a cost of 500 livres, and she said the slave had been raised and maintained continuously in the Gamelin household ever since, without ever being claimed by anyone. Lacorne Saint-Luc, who had bought the black woman's parents in 1745, backed up Geneviève Gamelin's testimony. After hearing the parties, the Militia Court produced a verbatim of the case, transmitting it to the governor of Montreal.[165] Unfortunately, Governor Gage's ruling in this case has not survived the ravages of time, and we have to let the matter drop just when the story begins to get interesting.

THE SAME JUSTICE FOR SLAVES

If slaves in New France and colonial Canada had been subject to the *Code Noir*, they would have lost significant legal advantages. According to Article 31 of the *Code* of the Islands of French America, and also of Louisiana: "Slaves shall not be a party, either in court or in a civil matter, either as a litigant or as a defendant, or as a civil party in a criminal matter. And compensation shall be pursued in criminal matters for insults and excesses that have been committed against slaves"; naturally, the *Code* of 1685 granted the same criminal sanctions on slaves as on free people, but the 1724 version issued for Louisiana removed the requirement that the Conseil supérieur uphold punishment by whipping, branding the fleur de lys or cutting the slave's ears off, when the sentence was being imposed by a trial court.[166] In other words, the last edition of the *Code Noir* left a slave sentenced to corporal punishment at the mercy of a lower court; the slave had no legal right to be a party either as litigant or defendant.

Slaves were better treated by the courts in Quebec, where the *Code Noir* was not in full force. A slave could be a plaintiff in a civil case. In December 1727, the Panis Catherine belonging to the wife of Louis Maray de Lachauvignerie filed a lawsuit against the surgeon

Benoist, in whose household she worked as a domestic servant. The surgeon wrongfully seized the Panis woman's clothes because of a debt Madame de Lachauvignerie owed him. The Panis first had the bailiff serve a summons on Benoist, then she appeared in the court of Montreal, which found in the slave's favour. In November 1761, the black Louise appeared before the Militia Court in Montreal with a view to getting Widow Loranger to pay her 396 livres worth of tobacco, but the widow claimed to be owed sixty livres by Louise's husband for having "laundered and mended his clothes" while he was a slave of one Monsieur Martel. The Militia Court dismissed the two parties without pronouncing in favour of either. Undeterred, the black woman appealed this decision and won, the appellate court taking the view that maintenance of a slave was the master's responsibility, not the slave's.

The most interesting civil suit was the one we referred to above, brought in 1740 by the Panis Marie-Marguerite against her master. We saw how complicated this suit turned out to be: the Panis woman petitioned the court, the owner filed his own counter-petitions, after which the Panis woman requested and obtained additional delays. It seemed like an ordinary lawsuit involving two persons of a free condition, whereas if the slave had been subject to the *Code Noir*, she would have been stopped in her tracks from the outset.

There was no distinction between slaves and persons of a free condition in criminal court either: it was the same justice for all, because slaves in Quebec were not subject to the restrictions imposed in other French colonies by the *Code Noir*. In Detroit in 1762, a Panis man and woman murdered the man who had come to buy them. Amerindians asked the governor to let them punish the couple according to their own justice, but since the guilty parties were part of society, the authorities preferred to give them a proper trial. We should also note that the slave could get a writ of *Habeas Corpus* and appear before a judge just like a free person. According to a long-established custom, masters who wanted to punish their slaves locked them up in prison and left them languishing there to think things over, for as long as the masters deemed necessary, but from the 1790s, slaves were brought before the judge. This judge was William Osgoode, an outspoken opponent of slavery, who released any black who was sued in court as a slave.

Slaves could thus invoke *Habeas Corpus*, but they also had the right to a trial by jury, as in a Detroit case in 1792, involving the black Cutan, who faced a jury. Slaves also had the right of appeal to a higher court: in 1734, the Panis Jacques was found guilty of rape, and appealed to the Conseil supérieur. That same year, the black Angélique was sentenced to burning at the stake in Montreal for setting fire to the city, and she appealed to the Conseil; she was led to Quebec, and the sentence was ultimately changed to strangling before burning. In 1756, after being sentenced to the gallows in Montreal, the Montagnais Marianne appealed to the Conseil supérieur in Quebec City on the grounds she was pregnant. The Conseil suspended execution of the sentence long enough to have a surgeon ascertain whether she was in fact pregnant. Finally, some slaves sentenced to death were granted a pardon at the foot of the scaffold, but in cases where the slave was not pardoned, the punishment meted out was no different than it would have been for a free person convicted of the same crime. In other words, when a slave appeared before a judge, he was a man like any other.

Slaves with Québécois Surnames

It was only normal that slaves should have Christian first names, but the fact slaves bore family names (usually the names of their masters) strikes us as a social promotion of sorts, outwardly putting slaves on the same footing as free people. During the 1740 trial of the Panis Marie-Marguerite, Chevalier Dormicourt said: "It is customary in this country for slaves to bear the name of their master, even in the absence of any relationship of paternity or filiation." This custom was practiced by slaves in general, although less often by Amerindians than by blacks.

The following is a list of family names which Amerindian slaves borrowed from Québécois families (although we have left out names drawn or apparently drawn from Amerindian languages).

Alavoine	Desautels	Hamelin	Longueuil
Auger	Desforges	Hay	Magnan
Belhumeur	Doyon	Hervieux	Maillot
Blondeau	Duchesne	Lafleur	Marin
Boileau	Dufresne	Laframboise	Monplaisir
Bourdeau	Dufy	Laprise	Porlier
Bourdon	Dulude	Laronde	Radisson
Campeau	Dumay	Larose	Raimbault
Cardinal	Duplessis	Laviolette	Rapin
Chauvin	Fily	Leduc	Riberville
Christie	Foster ·	Lefrançois	Saint Luc
Content dit Bourdon	Francheville	Legardeur	Saint-Sauveur
Courchaîne	Gagné	Lépine	Sanssouci
De Berey	Gamelin	Lespérance	Viger
Decouagne	Giasson	Lestage	Youville
Defond	Guillory	Léveillé	

Of these sixty-three surnames, at least thirty were borrowed by Amerindian slaves from their masters: we are sure about this fact because the slaves used the surname of their masters as long as they resided with the latter; as for other surnames, they may reflect a former master-to-slave relationship which it has been impossible for us to establish.

It is surprising how few Amerindian slaves bore the name of a Canadian family. Apart from children, we counted only 158 Amerindians with such names, or a tiny 5.9% of the total of 2683 Amerindians. It seems that Amerindians were integrated into Canadian society and did not care about surnames.

The situation was different for blacks. Of a total of 1443 blacks, 469 or 32.5% took a family name – almost one third. Whether they were slaves or freedmen, blacks seemed to have been more aware than Amerindians of the importance of a surname. Only fourteen of the family names adopted by blacks were French: Beauménil, Céré, Couture, Hubert, Lamour, LeJeune, Lenègre, Lepage, Léveillé, Marié, Paul, Saint-François, Saint-Julien, Rosier (for Desrosiers); the black Hubert took the name of his godfather, Father Hubert, and the black Lejeune the name of the Jesuit who had taught him; the blacks Lepage and Rose definitely took their masters' surnames. The reason so many blacks had English names is that they mostly came from English colonies and overwhelmingly belonged to English masters.

THE CONDITIONS OF FREEDOM

In any case, slaves naturally dreamed of gaining their freedom; they wanted to be free to marry the person they loved, like the black Jacques-César, or they wanted to be free because liberty is one of the deepest human needs. The black Joseph Beauménil longed to be free and therefore did research into his own condition. In 1768, at the age of twenty-one, he was sold by Joseph Cureux *dit* Saint-Germain to Michel Fortier, in 1785, nine years after the death of the latter purchaser, the black Beauménil petitioned Justice Pierre Panet "with good cause, given that he was aware of the agreements concerning him entered into by Messrs. Saint-Germain and Fortier"; he requested a copy of the deed of sale, "as he is a part thereof, and keenly interested in its contents". Justice Pierre Panet considered this curiosity legitimate, and authorized the notary Antoine Panet to issue a copy of the deed, "for a reasonable fee"; the notary produced the copy, providing it free of charge, doubtless because the black man was so poor. Fortunately it did not cost anything, because the black only discovered one important fact in the document: he had been sold in the company of another black for a total sum of 200 pounds, Quebec currency; the deed of sale established no time limit on his servitude.[167]

Normally this limit on servitude could only be established by legal emancipation. Under the French regime, a slave could only be emancipated in a formal notarized document – a mere verbal declaration was not enough. In 1736, Intendant Hocquart issued an ordinance with royal authorization on the procedure for emancipating slaves: given that "many individuals of this colony had freed their slaves, without any other formality than granting them their freedom verbally," and considering it was necessary "to find an invariable manner for establishing the status of slaves who could be emancipated at a later date," he advised "that in future all individuals in this country, of whatever quality and condition, who want to emancipate their slaves, will be required to do so by a notarized document, of which a copy shall be kept and minuted, and shall also be registered at the nearest royal court"; any other emancipation not following this procedure would be null and void.[168] The law was clear: only a notarized act of emancipation could release a slave from bondage.

Emancipation was a rare event under French rule, judging from the registries of notaries. Yet here and there, historical records mention freedmen or free Panis. Some of them may have been verbally freed from bondage before 1763, while others may have been formally emancipated in their masters' will and testament, since this latter means of emancipation satisfied the ordinance of 1736. Under the British regime, emancipation was common and it became more and more frequent during the late eighteenth century: emancipation could be established by notarized act, as under French rule, or where the master provided written permission for his slave to marry; or the master could specify in his will that at his death his slaves would regain their freedom. For example, when the black Louis-Antoine willingly returned to bondage in 1761 to marry the black Dominique Gaudet, it was understood they would remain slaves until their master's death, which took place in 1789. In 1774, the Sioux Jacques, slave of the surveyor Claude Gouin of Detroit, married the Chickasaw Marie-Louise, slave of the bourgeois Antoine Cuillerier: the two would remain slaves until Claude Gouin and his wife had died. In 1797, the widow of the voyageur Antoine Janis made her will, and specified that on her death her Amerindian slave Marie-Antoine-de-Pade would be emancipated.

Emancipation sometimes depended on other conditions. On September 3, 1796, the merchant John Shuter bought the black Jack on credit, and that very same day Shuter committed in a notarized agreement to emancipate Jack six and a half years later, on condition that he conduct himself well. Jack satisfied this condition and obtained his freedom on November 2, 1803.[169] On August 25, 1797, the innkeeper Thomas John Sullivan of Montreal also bought the black Manuel on credit, immediately committing to free him in five years, if he conducted himself well; the black agreed to this condition, but lacked Jack's loyalty and patience, and ran away on March 1.[170] Purchased in 1797, the black Rubin received the assurance of his master, the merchant John Young, that he would be released from bondage after seven years if he conducted himself well.[171] We should add that these three cases came at the end of the slave-owning era in Canada: by now, the legality of slavery was in doubt, and owners sought to ensure the continuing services of their slave by promising emancipation at a future date.

In at least one case emancipation was granted provided the slave disappeared forever. On May 12, 1794, Seigneur François Boucher de Laperrière and his wife Marie-Charles Pécaudy de Contrecoeur agreed before the notary Racicot to emancipate their black Jacques, aged about twenty-one years, on condition that "he go up to the *pays d'en haut* and remain in the farthest trading posts there"; coming back to the St. Lawrence Valley would mean returning to bondage, in which case they could dispose of or sell him as they saw fit.[172] Clearly, the Laperrières were afraid that the black knew their house-hold all too well: they felt the need to send him to the most remote trading posts in the Great Lakes region, never to return. Slave owners under the French regime had been consumed by this same fear of the all-knowing slave, and for this reason some proposed deporting Panis to the French West Indies once they reached adulthood.

Finally, in granting emancipation, some masters added a few gifts as a sign of their satisfaction. In 1750, Josué Boisberthelot de Beaucour's widow made her will and promised to free her Panis slave Gabrielle *dite* Arthémise; she promised at the same time to leave "my stockings, shoes, my two little mantles"; this small gift hardly amounted to much, but the Boisberthelot de Beaucour family had fallen into poverty, and in any case, the widow's death in 1759 meant that the Panis woman would have to wait nine years to inherit the stockings, shoes and two mantles bequeathed by her mistress! In 1796, in undertaking to free the black Jack, the merchant John Shuter promised him a new set of clothes: a coat, jacket, breeches, a hat, shoes and stockings – the black man would at least cut a fine figure among free people. In 1797, the widow of Antoine Janis specified in her will that she would leave her bed and cover to the Amerindian Marie-Antoine-de-Pade, as well as "six pairs of the best bed linen to be found on her death, and all the testator's used clothing," including "towels and napkins, a copper crucifix, a mirror, an empty chest and a cupboard as is" – a complete trousseau plus furniture!

EMANCIPATED SLAVES

In his will of 1802, Seigneur Antoine Juchereau-Duchesnay preferred not to free his slaves: "I specify that my Negro François Williams not be sold, but since complete liberty would be more disadvantageous than advantageous given his age, I specify that he choose a master among my five children, legatees under this will, and that the master he chooses shall be bound to care for him in sickness and in health. I also grant the same liberty to his wife Mondina *dite* Olivier of Saint-Thomas-de-Montmagny and to her two daughters for the time they are required to serve me or to remain in my possession."[173] The slave thus enjoyed security as long as he remained with his master but lost this security as soon as he was freed. Seigneur Juchereau-Duchesnay therefore concluded his black should remain in bondage. It was a wonderful idea to free slaves, but in gaining that liberty which humans everywhere naturally desire, these slaves should not become a burden for society.

The freedman could make a go of his new life if he learned a trade. But in inquiring whether Amerindian and black slaves practised specific trades during their years of bondage, we found that blacks practised the most diverse trades, whereas Amerindians worked only as servants or boatmen. And emancipated blacks also had this greater range of skills than Amerindian freedmen.

It was understandable that Amerindians should work as boatmen, since that was a trade they had grown up with: Amerindian freedmen therefore signed up for work especially in the *pays d'en haut*. This is illustrated by the following examples drawn from the historical record:

BOURDON, Joseph, Panis
April 2, 1719, signed up to go to the pays d'en haut at a salary of 120 livres of beaver; April 29, 1726, signed up for work in the pays d'en haut at a salary of 160 livres (currency of France); June 11, 1728, signed up for the journey to Michilimackinac at a salary of 171 livres, payable in beaver and deer skins; April 20, signed up for work in the pays d'en haut at a salary of 160 livres, payable in furs; July 2, 1732, signed up for the round trip to Illinois Country at a salary of 200 livres, payable in furs, plus the skins of any animals he hunts, which he can bring back in the canoes, at no additional cost; May 18, 1735, signed up for the trip to Michilimackinac at a salary of 150 livres in furs.

JEAN, Panis
May 13, 1718, signed up for the journey to Michilimackinac (this commitment was later cancelled); August 16, 1718, signed up to go to Detroit at a salary of 75 livres of beaver skins (the return journey was unpaid).

JEAN-BAPTISTE, Panis
September 25, 1710, signed up to work for the commander of Fort Detroit for 150 livres; August 21, 1712, signed up to go to Detroit at a salary of 200 livres; May 24, 1726, signed up for work in the pays d'en haut and the Illinois Country, at a salary of 210 livres, payable in furs; August 21, 1727, signed

up for work in the pays d'en haut at a salary of 250 livres; May 25, 1732, signed up for the trip to Michilimackinac at a salary of 120 livres in furs, in addition to a deer skin (this commitment was later cancelled); July 12, 1732, signed up to go to Detroit at a salary of 60 livres (the return journey was unpaid).

We found eighteen Amerindian freedmen working as voyageurs, paddling canoes laden with trade goods to the pays d'en haut, and bringing them back laden with furs. We consider these eighteen Amerindians as freedmen because their employment contract specified they were free, or they kept their earnings to themselves. We know of two other Amerindian freedmen who accepted employment in the St. Lawrence Valley itself: when the Panis Pierre died in 1703, he was described as an "employee" of the Saint-Joseph farm which belonged to the Hôtel-Dieu de Montréal; from 1708 until his death in 1720, the Panis Joseph Riberville was employed by Guillaume de Lorimier, of Lachine. The Chickasaw Marie-Louise was a servant in Quebec City, employed in the Porlier-Benac household, before getting married in Detroit in 1774, and when she was buried in Quebec City in 1810 at the age of 70 years, she was still described as a servant. We identified only two Panis who became soldiers: the Panis Jacques staying at the Hôtel-Dieu de Québec in April 1712, and the Panis Charles who fomented a mutiny at Fort Niagara in 1730. We should also mention a Panis woman, Marguerite, who seems to have operated a business since she provided effects and lent money to a man named Jolibois; she sued him in court for the sum of fifty-three livres and in 1761 the Militia Court in Montreal ordered Jolibois to repay his debt in instalments of twelve livres per month.

Far fewer blacks were emancipated than Amerindians, yet the occupations of freed blacks were more varied. Some were soldiers: Benjamin Butcher served in the American army of occupation in 1775, Joseph Hunter in the French army in 1756, Jacques Paul in Brigadier Janson's regiment in 1783, and John Williams in the Canadian Volti-geurs before 1816. Others worked on board ships:

Caesar Brown, Peter Carter, John Dickson, John Griffiths, Nicholas Jones, Joseph the mulatto, John Linds, Joseph McIntyre, Edward Parkinson and Richard Thompson. John Ross worked as a hand on a brig, then at Quebec; Margaret Sinclair was cook on board the *Quebec* in 1803. Robert Boston, Cato Giles, Jacques Robertson and Henry Thompson were farmers. In 1816, William Lee was a dressmaker: James Black went from raftsman to upholsterer in 1787, but in 1817 he was described as a cabinetmaker. James Payne was a carpenter in 1802, George Crane a saddler in 1810, the mulatto Eber Welden an apprentice shoemaker in 1792, while John Curtain was a painter in 1818 and a longshoreman in 1825. Nicolas Jackson was a hairdresser in 1820. Nafrechoux's former slave François-Dominique *dit* Mentor was described as a goldsmith in 1773. Jean-Barthélémy built barrels in 1795. The black Jacques-César served as beadle in Saint-Philippe-de-Laprairie around 1784. James Richard was a music-lover, playing in the Royal Newfoundland Fencible of Infantry band in 1809. One black man had a profession nobody admired – George was public executioner in Quebec in 1805, and was likely the poor man roughly handled by a crowd on a market day in 1806.

Freed blacks signed up for work on a long-term or short-term basis. Louis Marié, who lived in the household of the merchant Louis Lecompte-Dupré in 1692, voluntarily let himself out in 1696, before a notary, to Jean Cailhaut *dit* Baron of Laprairie, to cultivate the land. This three-year contract specified that the black man would receive annual wages of 360 livres. The black woman Charety signed up for ten years as a servant to John McIntyre, innkeeper in Soulanges. The contract specified she would receive food and lodging, plus five shillings a year, and although her salary was not high, she was guaranteed a roof over her head for a ten-year period. When the black Charles died in 1807, Joseph Lafricain signed up for two years as a carpenter at a salary of 1200 livres (old currency). To get up to Michilimackinac where he was to work, he would be middle paddler, which meant the journey would not be much of a strain.

We identified forty-one other black freedmen who were simply described as day labourers, although their occupation was not recorded: they worked from day to day, depending on whatever needed to be done.

To make a meaningful comparison of the ways Amerindian and black freedmen ensured their livelihood, we would need a much longer list of freed slaves, but historical records surviving to our day are incomplete.

Still, of one hundred two freedmen whose occupations we know, seventy-eight were blacks and only twenty-four were Amerindians. There were twice as many Amerindian slaves as black ones, however. Perhaps fewer Amerindians were emancipated than blacks. Perhaps Amerindians deserted in greater numbers than blacks. Perhaps the difference stemmed from the fact more blacks reached adulthood. Another possible explanation is that blacks aspired to live the way whites did, whereas Amerindians did not seem to care as much.

The fact is that some freedmen posed a challenge to society, although fragmentary historical records make it impossible to assess the challenge. We can only gather shreds of evidence here and there. The Panis Marie, buried at age twenty-two in 1732, had no fixed address; the Panis Jacques travelled the colony from one end to the other, before finally being arrested in 1734 on a charge of rape; in 1710, the Panis Nicolas stole an axe, a canoe and then murdered the people he was hired to lead to New England; in 1800, an elderly black was described as a beggar—we do not know whether to say he was "poor, but free" or "free, but poor"...

As long as slaves were held in bondage, society was hardly interested in their fate; but once slaves were freed, society was extremely concerned about its own security. In petitioning the House of Assembly in 1800 to regulate the status of slaves, Montreal slave owners declared they were "deeply sensible that this class of men who are now let loose on society, and live an idle and profligate life, may be tempted to commit crimes, which it is the duty of every citizen to endeavour to prevent."[174] Society had profited handsomely from slavery, but slavery in turn could come back to haunt society.

CHAPTER TEN

Debauchery and Marriage

A merindian and black slaves lived in a society whose mores were not their own. As we have already seen, slaves adapted quite well to those mores, since only a small number were ever convicted of crimes. Whether it was hard or easy for them to abide by the law ultimately depended on how severely justice was meted out. But morality is not the same as justice, and individual slave behaviour was not conditioned by the criminal justice system. In this chapter, we will assess individual slave behaviour.

"Debaucherous Unions"
The arrival of native Amerindian women in Quebec society continually raised the delicate question of relations with their masters and compatriots. Throughout our colonial history, Canadian men were powerfully attracted to "savage" women, while Amerindian men do not seem to have had any particular interest in Canadian women. The Jesuit Charlevoix praised Amerindian men in this respect: "None of them ever took any liberties with French women, even when they had taken the latter prisoner. They were not tempted to do so, and it is to be hoped that French men develop a similar distaste for Amerindian women."[175] Canadian men sought the maximum advantage in buying Amerindian women slaves. Their natural attraction for these slave women was greatly stimulated by living with them on a day-to-day basis.

Some people completely lost their heads. In 1726 Pierre Chauvet *dit* Lagerne, the forty-year-old widower of Marie-Madeleine Gaudin, kidnapped an Amerindian woman he was in love with in Sainte-Anne-de-la-Pérade. One night, he stole into Seigneur Tarieu de

Lanaudière de Lapérade's residence and left with the Fox or Panis Marie-Madeleine, aged about twenty-nine. On July 17, Intendant Dupuy published an order directing officers of the militia to take this slave "back from the hands of said Lagerne" but in the end, things worked out well for the lovers – they were dispensed from publishing three wedding banns, and married on November 7 at Beauport. The Sioux Marie-Marguerite-Caroline was the slave of Claude Landry *dit* Saint-André. After having a child out of wedlock with the voyageur Champagne in 1753, she became the mistress of Firmin Landry *dit* Charlot, giving him five children out of wedlock. She was pregnant again in the summer of 1771; to stop the scandal, her owner agreed to sell her to Landry *dit* Charlot on the express condition that he marry her, which he did on July 17, 1771.

Canadian men were also attracted to black women. Claude Thibault may have hoped for the perfect love tryst in 1734, on fleeing Montreal with the black Angélique. But she created a diversion by setting fire to the house of her mistress, Widow Francheville, and when the fire spread to other houses in the city, Thibault was suddenly implicated in a spectacular crime. Charges were later dropped against him, on the grounds that he was suspected "only of fleeing and having a debaucherous union with this Negress."

A rather mischievous article by a Montrealer in the *Quebec Gazette* described biracial relationships in Montreal society: "The greatest harmony and understanding exist between the two sexes. Black women and white men mingle by night, forming a general company, where our young people throw off the annoying constraints of convention, and unwind from workaday tasks by indulging in innocent pleasures. The other day, following the rules of politeness, a young lieutenant saluted the black woman with whom he had been dancing: 'How did you get over your fatigue this morning, E., after being out last night?'"[176] People could also "unwind from workaday tasks" in Quebec City, by indulging in the same sort of dubious pleasures. In 1798, in the account of his parish rounds, the parish priest of Quebec put an asterisk beside the infamous home of the black Joseph Beauménil in Anse-des-Mères, which was a lodging-house for "*meretrices*" [Latin for prostitutes].[177]

Our goal is not to entertain the reader by digging into the more salacious aspects of slavery, but rather to examine the problem of master-slave and slave-slave relations. There would be no point trying to develop a sort of Kinsey Report since the archival material is fragmentary and the only significant clue we have is the birth of illegitimate children.

A Majority of Illegitimate Children

Of 1205 slave women aged 14 and over, we identified 213 or 17.7% who gave birth to one or more illegitimate children: 158 or 17.2% of 921 Amerindian mothers bore children out of wedlock, while a slightly higher proportion of black mothers – fifty-five or 19.4% of 284 – gave birth to illegitimate children.

Some slave women were several months pregnant once they reached the colony. Slave women being brought from the *pays d'en haut* and the Mississippi basin had ample opportunity for sexual relations with French paddlers during the long canoe journey. For example, in 1717 Michel Bisaillon brought a Panis woman from the Missouri tribe. On September 19 she gave birth in Laprairie to a daughter, the priest noting that the father was unknown and she had recently been brought out of her country. On October 22, 1741, the officer Clément Laplante-Lérigé's Amerindian woman gave birth to a son in Laprairie, father unknown. The civil registry mentions she had come down from the *pays d'en haut* earlier that year. The place where a slave woman lived was no guarantee against illicit relations. In June 1764, a Panis slave at the Jesuit mission across the water from Detroit gave birth to a daughter, although she was unmarried. Moreover, when a slave mistress set a bad example, the slave not surprisingly followed suit. On April 9, 1752, at Fort Saint-Joseph (on the south-eastern shores of Lake Michigan), Marie Réaume, widow of Augustin Larchevêque, presented the illegitimate son she had had with Louis Chevalier for baptism. The following day, her Panis slave Marie-Jeanne baptized her own illegitimate child. The mistress and her slave both had illegitimate sons, so everyone was happy.

Some slave women went beyond just one illegitimate child, to have two, three, four or more. We identified nine slaves who had four illegitimate children. Some slave women had five: between 1752 and 1759, Lamothe's Panis slave Barbe, in Detroit; between 1761 and 1773, Courtois's Panis Marguerite, in Detroit; and between 1788 and 1794, Pelletier's Panis Marie, also in Detroit. Two slave women had six children out of wedlock: between 1754 and 1769, Labutte's Panis Charlotte, in Detroit; and between 1753 and 1769, Landry *dit* Saint-André's Sioux slave Marie-Marguerite-Caroline.

We found several cases of unwed mothers bringing twins into the world. For example, in May 1732 Poulin de Francheville's black slave Angélique had twins out of wedlock with Ignace Gamelin's slave Jacques-César, but the twins died that same year. On January 2, 1790, George Maldrum's unmarried Panis slave Dorothée had twin girls, Suzanne and Dorothée. On March 30, 1795, Jean-Baptiste Meloche's Panis slave Madeleine gave birth to twins, Charles and Charlotte. Of 341 illegitimate slave births, six were twins.

We might expect that the places with the greatest concentration of slaves also had the greatest numbers of illegitimate slave children, but this was not the case. In Montreal a total of 1525 slaves had only thirty-three illegitimate children, whereas in Quebec, a total of 970 slaves had only eighteen illegitimate children. Children born out of wedlock were actually more common in the *pays d'en haut* than in the centres of New France. In the little city of Detroit, a total of 650 slaves had 177 illegitimate children, whereas in Michilimackinac, a total of 160 slaves had 35 such children. But Detroit and Michilimackinac also saw many illegitimate births among free persons, since these wilderness settlements were far removed from the conservative and more tightly-controlled centres of the St. Lawrence Valley.

Of 573 children born to slaves, 341 or a very high proportion of 59.5% were born out of wedlock. Amerindian slaves had more illegitimate children than black slaves. Two hundred fifty-five or 75.9% of 336 children born to Amerindian slaves were illegitimate, while eight-six or 32.1% of 237 children born to black slaves were illegitimate. The difference between the two groups is extremely significant: one third of black slave children and three-quarters of Amerindian slave children were illegitimate. Was this due to chance, or did it reflect the strong attraction Canadian men felt for "savage" women?

DID QUEBEC MEN FATHER THESE CHILDREN?
When a slave gave birth to an illegitimate child, who was the father? It is hard to say, because the civil registries usually maintain strict silence about the matter. The records of 314 of 341 illegitimate children mention the father was unknown or uncertain (which amounts to the same). But was this unknown father a Canadian, an Amerindian or a black? The priest did not describe the child at any length in the baptismal registry: he wrote "unknown father" and left it at that. The slave population made up a tiny minority within society, so these unknown fathers were most likely Canadians. Neighbours or masters could enjoy sexual relations with Amerindian or black slave women living under the same roof, thereby increasing the overall number of slaves at no additional cost… Having said that, the "unknown father" indicated in the registries remains an unknown father.

Civil registries duly identify twenty-seven slave children. We identified four slave owners who yielded to the charms of their slaves:

Mouet de Langlade, Charles. Before 1754, he had a son named Charles with his unnamed Amerindian slave (Michilimackinac).

Villeneuve, Constant. On April 30, 1759 at Michilimackinac, his Panis slave Charlotte gave birth to a Panis named Charlotte: the slave designated her master as the father.

Sanscrainte, Jean-Baptiste. On 7 October 1760, at Michilimackinac, his unnamed Amerindian slave gave birth to a son named Jacques.

Bourassa, Daniel. On 7 April 1794, at Michilimackinac, the Panis Régis, son of Daniel Bourassa and his Panis slave, was baptized; this Panis had a daughter with an unknown father in 1792, and she had another daughter in 1797.

The sixteen other white fathers of illegitimate children we identified were not the masters of the slave mother.

The following is a list in alphabetical order of the natural fathers we identified:

Bourassa, Daniel	Michilimackinac
Champagne, voyageur	Detroit
Chevalier-Lullier, Charles	Michilimackinac
Dion, voyageur	Michilimackinac
Duschesne	Quebec
Fleur d'Épée, Louis	Michilimackinac
Jasmin, voyageur	Michilimackinac
Lamothe, voyageur	Michilimackinac
Landry *dit* Charlot	Detroit
Larche, François	Montreal
Lespérance, Jean-Marie	Michilimackinac
LeVerrier, fils	Quebec
Lorrain, Joseph	Montreal
Magnan, Jean	Montreal
Mouet de Langlade, Charles	Michilimackinac
Sanscrainte, Jean-Baptiste	Michilimackinac
Villeneuve, Constant	Michilimackinac
Villeneuve, Daniel	Michilimackinac
"Yonce," English officer	Boucherville

In all of these cases, the mothers were Amerindian slaves, which provides once again an indication of the attraction Canadian men felt for "savage" rather than black women... Among blacks, the reverse occurred. Black men were attracted to Canadian women, but once the woman gave birth, the black father married her, at least if we can judge from the rare examples turning up in the archives. In November 1749, the Canadian Marie Talon married the black Pierre-Dominique Lafleur, slave of Jacquin *dit* Philibert's widow, and gave birth the following April; in September 1783, the Canadian Marie-Élisabeth Mondina gave birth to a daughter: the month before, she had married Antoine Juchereau-Duchesnay's black slave François Williams.

THE NATURAL CHILDREN OF SLAVE MOTHERS SHALL ALSO BE SLAVES

When a slave woman gave birth to a child whose father was unknown or was a free man, what was the child's status? The *Code Noir* of the Caribbean stipulated that the illegitimate child of a slave woman was a slave like its mother, whatever the condition of the father. Although the *Code Noir* was never officially adopted in Canada, this principle was invoked at the trial of the Panis Marie-Marguerite in 1740. The owner of this Panis woman testified: "According to the law in America [Louisiana and the Islands], a child born to a slave mother and a French father is deemed a slave, and this law should be applied in our own country."[178] The reasoning behind this principle was as follows: the father is always uncertain, whereas only the mother is certain, therefore, *fructus ventrem sequitur* – the child has the same status as its mother.

This principle was applied at least four times in Canada. Around 1739, Jean-Marie Lespérance had a daughter named Marie-Joseph with Claude Marin de Laperrière's Ojibwa slave Rose; but when the child was buried in Montreal in 1749, she was recorded as a slave belonging to one Lécuyer. In July 1746, Chevalier's slave gave birth to a daughter whose father was Louis Fleur d'Épée; she was entered in the baptismal registry as Chevalier's property. In 1760, an Ojibwa woman and an unnamed French father had a baby. The child was sold to Antoine Cuillerier who still owned it in 1764. In 1766, Claude Landry *dit* Saint-André's Sioux slave Marie-Marguerite-Caroline gave birth to a daughter, Suzanne, whose father was Firmin Landry *dit* Charlot. When the latter bought the Sioux woman and married her, the daughter Suzanne remained Claude Landry *dit* Saint-André's slave until the parents were able to redeem her. Even where the father was of a free condition, we see that the natural child of a slave mother was also automatically a slave.

A fortiori when the father was unknown. The mother's master saw the number of his slaves increase, and could dispose of illegitimate children as he saw fit. On August 16, 1752, in Detroit, when the illegitimate son of the Panis slave Barbe was baptized, the slave owner Guillaume Dagneau-Douville de Lamothe vowed he would only sell the child to Catholics. In April 1759, when Joseph Cabassié's Panis slave Marie-Anne gave birth to an illegitimate daughter, Françoise, Cabassié gave the child to Jean-Baptiste Petit *dit* Milhomme who kept her as his personal property. In January 1763, when a Panis slave woman in prison gave birth to a daughter, the commander of Detroit immediately gave the child as a slave to the bourgeois Pierre Barthe. In May 1772, Marguerite, a Panis slave belonging to Charles-Martin Courtois, gave birth to an illegitimate daughter, and the child was immediately given to François Lebeau; the following year, the same slave had another child out of wedlock, who was immediately handed over to Berthiaume "as a gift to serve as his slave." In November 1772, when Jean-Baptiste Chapoton's slave gave birth to a bastard girl, Chapoton immediately gave the child to one Madame Pelletier, who became the slave child's mistress as was made clear in the child's burial register a few days later. In December 1774, when a Panis slave woman belonging to Alexis Trottier-Desruisseaux gave birth to an illegitimate child, the master gave the child to Alexis Maisonville who kept it as a slave. The father's status therefore was of no consequence: the natural children of slave mothers were slaves like their mothers. And from time to time masters could make friends at low cost, simply by giving away the children their slave women had.

The fact the illegitimate child of a slave belonged to the master was so well-established that many times the child's mother was not even identified in civil registries. The Panis Bonaventure was born in 1751 to a Panis woman belonging to Charles Chauvin. When the infant boy was buried in May 1753, the registry showed he belonged to Chauvin, without any mention of the mother. In October 1757, the Panis Nicolas was buried. Born the previous month to a Panis woman belonging to Simon Gendron *dit* Potvin, he was mentioned in the burial register only as the child as Nicolas, the slave of Gendron *dit* Potvin, without identifying the mother. When Pierre Chesne-Labutte's Panis child Pierre was buried in January 1759, the registry made no mention of the mother; the same happened in May 1766 at the burial of the Panis Marie-Joseph, daughter of Gabriel-Christophe Legrand's slave, in August 1759 at the burial of the Panis François-Prisque, son of Labutte's slave, and in May 1778, at the baptism of the Panis Marie-Louise, daughter of Lagotherie's slave. And we could cite many more examples as late as 1796. It was common practice under both French and British rule, to identify an illegitimate child's master rather than its mother: possession was more important than affiliation. Slavery in French Canada was not always particularly humane...

SLAVE MARRIAGES

There were not that many marriages between slaves; we identified only seventy-three. Slaves were allowed to marry. According to the *Code Noir* of the Caribbean, slaves needed the consent of their masters, but not of their own parents, and it was strictly forbidden for priests to conduct weddings if it appeared that masters had not first given their permission. At the same time, the *Code Noir* of the French West Indies forbade masters "from using any constraints on their slaves to marry them against their will," and these provisions also featured in the *Code Noir* of Louisiana. Although Canadian slave owners had no obligations in this regard, they generally fulfilled these provisions.

When Colonel Campbell's slaves Jean-François and Jeanne married in Montreal on January 20, 1785, the minister noted the marriage was taking place at the owner's request; there was some urgency, since the bride was pregnant. Similarly, when the black slave York married the black woman Margaret McLeod in Montreal on January 22, 1786, they both had to get permission from their respective masters.

Slave owners did not always willingly or quickly grant their slave leave to marry the slave of another master, since one of the two masters would necessarily lose his property. This was the case, for example, with the black Jacques-César, belonging to the merchant Ignace Gamelin, and the black Marie-Élisabeth, belonging to the Dowager Baroness de Longueuil. Gamelin readily gave his consent. In consideration of the services that Jacques-César, aged about fifty-two years, had provided over a thirty-year period, Gamelin allowed him to marry on January 21, 1761, granting him his freedom at the same time, but not "under any other conditions or for any other marriage than this." But, unfortunately for poor Jacques-César, the Baroness de Longueuil could not make up her mind. Was the reason that Jacques-César had already had three illegitimate children with the dreaded black Angélique, who had set fire to the city of Montreal in 1734? Or that the Baroness did not want to give up her thirty-nine-year-old slave? Months went by, then a year, then another year. Finally, on January 26, 1763, the Baroness gave her consent and freed her slave, but on condition that the newly-wed couple remain in her domestic service for three more years. On this basis, the wedding finally took place in Longueuil, on February 5, 1763; in the wedding registry, the priest duly noted that Gamelin had consented in 1761 and the Baroness in 1763; he annexed their declarations of consent to the registry.

The merchant Dominique Gaudet experienced roughly the same dilemma in 1761 when his fifteen-year-old black slave Marie-Catherine Baraca fell in love with the twenty-year-old black Louis-Antoine. The latter had been free from childhood, but the merchant Gaudet had no intention of losing his slave Marie-Catherine. The person who found a way out of this situation, on March 26, 1761, was none other than Louis-Antoine himself who accepted before a notary to return to slavery, selling himself to Gaudet.

Slave owners allowed their slaves to marry, sometimes adding specific conditions. The state took the same approach to slaves it owned. For example, in the early 1740s, the hangman in Quebec City was a 25-year-old black, Matthieu Léveillé. Intendant Hocquart decided to find him a suitable wife, importing a black slave woman for this purpose, at the state's expense. Unfortunately, mail was only sent to France once a year at the time, so sending an official letter, getting the necessary permission, setting the administrative machinery in gear, placing the order in the Caribbean and finally shipping the slave to Quebec took several years, the slave woman only arriving in 1742. In the meantime, Léveillé had fallen seriously ill, was committed to the Hôtel-Dieu de Québec, and finally died on September 9, 1743, still officially employed as public executioner and still unmarried. This left the black woman Angélique-Denise high and dry. She had been brought north from the islands to marry, and had been left languishing in Quebec until the executioner was restored back to health – but now her black fiancé had died. What future lay in store for this black slave? The sacrament of marriage was now out of the question, so she was baptized instead, on December 23, 1743, while awaiting orders from the king. On March 30, 1744 the Minister wrote to the Intendant: "Once you have found a white man to replace the now deceased Negro as public executioner, it would be desirable that you resell the Negress originally obtained for this Negro, at cost price if possible."[179] And the unlucky young woman was sent off to new horizons.

Marriage Involved the Same Requirements

As a Church sacrament, marriage evidently involved the same rights and obligations for slaves as for free people. Slaves had to publish the banns of marriage, and witnesses had to participate in the wedding itself. The intention to marry was normally published by three banns from the pulpit, but the number of banns could be reduced, subject to certain fees. It was common practice in Canadian society and elsewhere to publish just one bann, although poor people were sometimes forced by a lack of funds to have their banns published on three successive Sundays. We found no slave wedding where the priest had actually been compelled to publish three banns – probably slave owners did their best to keep up appearances.

Most of the time, slave couples followed the general practice in society, and received an exemption from two callings of banns. For example, the blacks Joseph and Marie-Louise, who belonged to Lagorgendière and Contrecoeur respectively, and whose marriage took place in Montreal January 12, 1750; the blacks Jacques and Marie, slaves of Lacorne Saint-Luc, who wed in Montreal on May 24, 1757; Juchereau-Duschesnay's black slave François Williams, who married a Canadian in Quebec City on August 5, 1783. We should add here that in each of these cases, we would have expected a total exemption from callings of banns because the bride was already pregnant; the Canadian woman marrying Juchereau- Duchesnay's black slave was actually six months pregnant.

Some slaves got an exemption from callings of banns. Such was the case for Charles and Charlotte-Elisabeth, black slaves belonging to the Baron Lemoyne de Longueuil, who married in Montreal on August 29, 1719; and for Joseph *dit* Neptune, Governor General Vaudreuil's black slave, who married the black woman Marie-Françoise in Montreal on February 27, 1759. We identified another bann exemption case: Dominique Gaudet's black slaves Pierre Baraca and Marie-Anne were married in Lachine on July 11, 1746, but four months earlier, the mother had had a daughter baptized whom the parents concealed after the marriage ceremony, by which time the young bride was pregnant again. The exemption was simply to avoid publicizing this situation.

A key requirement at weddings of slave and freeborn alike was to be accompanied to the altar by witnesses. What did slaves do? We have already seen that slave owners considered it their duty to stand in as witnesses at baptisms and funerals; they sometimes acted in the same capacity at the weddings of their slaves. In February 1763, when Jacques-César married the black Marie-Élisabeth, the bridegroom's master Ignace Gamelin and Christophe Gamelin-Lajemmereais both served as witnesses, while the young Dowager Baroness de Longueuil accompanied her black slave Marie-Élisabeth to the altar. At the December 11, 1783 marriage of the black William Deane with the black Nancy Hill, at the Anglican Church of Quebec, the merchant Thomas Hackett and the clerk John Lane served as witnesses.

Sometimes, a situation occurred that may be unique to slavery in Canada – slaves served as witnesses at marriages, alongside free people. At Lachine, on July 11, 1746, at the marriage of the black slaves Pierre Baraca and Marie-Anne (who was already pregnant), Marie-Anne Cuillerier, wife of the owner of the blacks, and Chevalier de Lacorne's slave Joseph, served as witnesses. In January 1750, in Montreal, another Joseph, Fleury Deschambault deLagorgendière's black slave, married Pécaudy de Contrecoeur's black slave Marie-Louise. At their wedding, François and René Pécaudy de Contrecoeur served as witnesses, along with Gamelin's black slave César and Hervieux's black slave Joachim.

But weddings could also be family affairs for blacks, since black slaves sometimes stood in as witnesses when other blacks got married. On April 21, 1750, Hervieux's slave Jasmin and Madame Lestage's slave Valentin served as witnesses at the wedding of Leber de Senneville's black Joseph-Hippolyte *dit* l'Espiègle and Soumande-Delorme's black Marie-Madeleine. Likewise at Lachine in 1761 the blacks Joseph-Hippolyte and Charles served as witnesses at the wedding of Dominique Gaudet's black slaves Louis-Antoine and Marie-Catherine Baraca. These were exceptional cases under the French regime. Under British rule, slave owners – particularly English-speaking slave owners – generally did not bother to attend the religious ceremonies of their slaves.

Children Belonged to the Mother's Owner

As we have already seen, the illegitimate children of a slave woman automatically became the property of this slave's master, whether or not their father was known. This provision strikes us as understandable, because if the slave woman was unmarried, there was no question of a family. But what happened to children born to married slaves? According to the *Code Noir* of the French West Indies and Louisiana, female slaves marrying their masters became free and their children free and legitimate. As for children born from marriages between slaves, they "shall be slaves, and if the husband and wife have different masters, they shall belong to the masters of the female slave, not to the master of her husband." Moreover, if a male slave married a free woman, their children would be of the same condition as their mother and would be free, whereas if the father was free and the mother a slave, "the children shall also be slaves." The law remained the same, whether the child was legitimate or not – the child would be of the same condition as its mother. These provisions were fulfilled in Canada, even though the *Code Noir* was never officially adopted. We collected many examples.

The slave owner generally declared that he owned the legitimate children of his slaves, without paying any attention to the parents of those children. We will provide a few examples here, in chronological order, to show how frequent this attitude was. In 1746, a widowed black slave, whose husband had died shortly beforehand at Saratoga, and who belonged to the officer Liénard de Beaujeu, had her daughter buried in Quebec City: the act of burial noted the child belonged to Beaujeu but made no mention of the mother. In 1755, Louise, the legit-imate daughter of Fleury Deschambault de Lagorgendière's blacks, was born, then died, but the parents were mentioned neither in the baptismal registry nor in the act of burial – it was enough to say the infant girl belonged to Fleury Deschambault de Lagorgendière. When Joseph, the six-day-old legitimate son of Governor General Vaudreuil's black slaves, was buried at Pointe-aux-Trembles in 1757, the act of burial described him only as a little "Negro" belonging to the governor. In 1784, in Detroit, when the twins of Bernard's black slaves were buried, the act of burial mentioned their owner by name, but not their parents. The same thing happened in 1791, at the burial of the four-year-old legitimate daughter of two of Colonel Campbell's black slaves, and again in 1797, at the burial of the legitimate son of two other of the colonel's slaves. Evidently, legitimate children belonged to the parents' master.

This ownership of the legitimate children of slaves had another consequence: the slave owner could dispose of the children as he saw fit. In 1755, Soumande-Delorme's black female slave had a legitimate child, but by the time the child was buried at Quebec in 1758, it belonged to Captain François Mercier: the mother's owner had given or sold the infant to the captain. When the free black Louis-Antoine accepted in 1761 to return to slavery in order to marry Dominique Gaudet's black slave Marie-Catherine, the contract specified that Gaudet would own any resulting children, and sell both parents and children as he saw fit.

The most important case arose in 1729 when the two sons of the first Baron de Longueuil divided up their late father's estate, which included the black slave Charles, his wife Charlotte-Élisabeth and their five children. Chevalier Paul-Joseph Le Moyne de Longueuil inherited the slaves Charles, Charlotte-Élisabeth and three of their children: eight-year-old Charles-Claude, three-year-old Marie-Charlotte, and one-year-old Joseph. The second Baron de Longueuil inherited only two of the slave children: six-year-old François, and five-year-old Marie-Élisabeth, but he also got two Panis slaves from his brother by way of compensation. As a result, the parents and three of their children were handed over to Chevalier de Longueuil while the two other children, aged six and five years respectively, were handed over to the second baron. This division of property had not completely eradicated the family unit, since the youngest of the children would continue to live with their parents, but the fact remained that being separated from one's family at the age of five or six years was harsh. The *Code Noir* of the Caribbean and Louisiana prohibited the separate sale of parents and their young children before puberty, but as the *Code Noir* was never formally adopted in Canada, slave owners did as they pleased in this regard.

Marriages Between Slaves

We have considered at some length the conditions under which slaves could marry and the fate reserved for their legitimate children, but we have not yet presented a statistical profile of slave marriages. This profile is a real challenge, because vital records have not all survived. We are thinking, for example, of records at Lac-des-Deux-Montagnes, which disappeared in a fire; the only known copies unfortunately made no mention of Amerindians; baptismal registries identified some children as legitimate, without mentioning the marriage of their parents; and it often happened that the act of baptism or burial of a child did not specify whether the parents lived as husband and wife. Given that information about slaves in civil registries was hopelessly vague, we will only use definite references to slave marriages in our statistical portrait.

We only found eleven marriages between Amerindians.

Since slave owners sometimes had both Amerindian and black slaves, the question naturally arises whether there were any mixed-race slave marriages. To our surprise, we only identified four such marriages: in each case, the husband was black (no Amerindian married a black woman), which might lead to the conclusion that black men were not particularly attracted to Amerindian women.

The first such marriage took place on April 10, 1752 at Detroit, when two slaves belonging to Albert Parent's widow (née Marie-Suzanne Richard), married – the black slave Charles and the thirty-year-old Panis slave Marie-Marguerite who was baptized six days earlier. At the wedding, the bride was three months pregnant. On July 9, she gave birth to a daughter named Catherine, described in the records as a "Negress." We could not determine whether the couple had any other children.

Another marriage was contracted around 1756 between a black man and a Panis woman, according to an act of burial of April 12, 1767, for on that day Marie-Madeleine, the eleven-year-old legitimate daughter of the black Charlot and the Panis Marie was buried at Lachine; the following May 15, the father was buried at the age of fifty years and was identified as the husband of the Panis Marie. This leads us to conclude that the marriage took place around 1756, but it is also possible this was the couple that got married in Detroit in 1752.

The third mixed-race slave wedding took place in 1780, when the black Jacques-Caton and the Métis Marie, two slaves belonging to the bourgeois Jacques Duperron-Bâby, got married. The wedding was held at the owner's request in order to legitimize the couple's child. Actually, the Métis Marie had a son baptized somewhere between January 10 and 19, 1780, although the vagueness of records makes it impossible to say whether the wedding took place during the fortnight preceding the infant's birth, or sometime afterwards.

Finally, around 1798, the black slave Jollock Kellings belonging to the merchant George Gregory, took an Amerindian wife, Josette Christie, who had come to Quebec at a young age from the *pays d'en haut*. The following year, when their one-year-old son was buried at Sainte-Anne-du-Bout-de-l'Île, the priest described the infant as a "Negro" but did not know whether the parents were married or not; from 1803 on, they were described as husband and wife.

This brings the total of slave marriages we identified to seventy-three, which can be broken down as follows:

Marriages between Amerindians	11
Marriages between Amerindians and blacks	4
Marriages between blacks	38

We should note that very few of these slave marriages involved lawful unions between Amerindians and blacks. And if we recall that the Amerindian slave population was twice the size of the black slave population, it seems surprising to find just eleven marriages between Amerindians, and fifty-eight between blacks. This does not mean that Amerindians avoided getting married, since thirty-four Amerindian slaves married whites: a more plausible conclusion might be that Amerindians married whites more readily than other Amerindians...

We would be able to determine with reasonable accuracy the average age at which slaves married, but only if we established the age of husband and wife at each wedding, and could rely on a sufficiently large sampling of such marriages. The records only indicate the age of six Amerindian husbands, and even then the age given was a guesstimate. Of these six husbands, five were twenty-three years old or less, the youngest couple being René Bourassa's twenty-two-year-old slave Charles, who married seventeen-year-old Marie.

More complete information about the age of black slaves appears in the records. The registries provide the age of thirty spouses, but not always the age of husband and wife together. The records such as they are indicate that the average age of husbands on marrying was 32.3 years, while that of wives was 24.9 years. This average was only obtained from a relatively small sample of thirty individuals. The youngest couples were twenty-year-old blacks, while the oldest was Gamelin's fifty-two-year-old slave Jacques-César, who married the Baroness de Longueuil's black slave after waiting two years. Six wives were twenty years old or less and one was just fifteen – Dominique Gaudet's slave Marie-Catherine, for whom the free black Louis-Antoine consented to return to slavery.

Cases of large age differences were rare, the most striking being the marriage in 1719 of slaves belonging to the Baron de Longueuil, when the thirty-five-year old black Charles married the twenty-year-old black Charlotte.

At least six of these seventy-three unions were so-called "obligatory marriages" given that the bride was already pregnant. For example, in 1797, the black Paul Cramer Polydore walked down the aisle with the forty-year-old black slave Margaret Wimble. She had already given him four illegitimate children, and was pregnant again – neither of them should have found this surprising.

6 children	Jean-François and Jeanne, black slaves belonging to John Campbell, married in the Anglican Church of Montreal in 1785.
7 children	Charles and Charlotte-Élisabeth, black slaves belonging to the Baron de Longueuil, married in Montreal in 1719
	Francis Smith and Dorothy Hutchins, black slaves, married at the Presbyterian church of Quebec in 1788
8 children	Robert Jackson and Catherine Stephens, black slaves, married at the Anglican Church of Quebec in 1795

We would have liked to calculate the average size of slave families, but how could we have done this? Many slave children were baptized without being identified, and in an age of high infant mortality (and it was even higher among blacks) it often happened that newborns were not even baptized, which meant they never appear in official records. With such fragmentary documentation, we were only able to identify four families with six or more children as the preceding table indicates.

These four examples only concerned black married slave households; we never identified more than three children per Amerindian slave household. The statistical profile of slave households might change if we could access more information, but this is impossible at the present time.

CHAPTER ELEVEN

Do Canadians Have Slave Blood?

There were many marriages between black slaves, but few between Amerindian slaves. This does not mean that Amerindian slaves remained single, however. Charlevoix noted that
many white Canadian men had a pronounced liking for "savage
women" and while many such men were quite content to have
sexual relations with "savage women," some nonetheless felt the
need to marry such women before God; some Amerindian men
also formed permanent unions with white Canadian women.

"French and Amerindians should form only one people and one blood"

As Canadians returned from the *pays d'en haut*, they brought back
mainly Panis, which raised the inevitable problem of illegitimate
children and of marriage between Canadians and Amerindians.
This problem went back a long way. Around 1648, the Jesuit Pierre
de Sesmaisons recommended to the Pope that the French of New
France be allowed to marry "savage women," even those who had
not been baptized. He claimed this would produce numerous
benefits, such as the strengthening of alliances with native tribes:

> This will diminish the number of savages while increasing
> the number of Christians [...]. These marriages will greatly
> promote the peopling of this great country where God is not
> [currently] well served, since French men will marry here,
> and will no longer return to France in order to take wives,
> which in turn hinders them shortly afterwards from coming
> back to the colony [...]. These reasons seem pressing enough

to incite His Holiness to allow the French who live in New France to marry savage girls, even when the latter have not been baptized and are not even very well educated.[180]

The Jesuit's memo is interesting, but more important still was the policy advocated by the minister Colbert, which favoured the complete integration of the native Amerindian and French populations in New France. In writing to Intendant Talon in 1667, Colbert regretted that the Algonquins and Hurons had not yet been integrated into French society: "You have started to address this long-standing neglect, and you must try to attract these [Amerindian] people to those who have embraced Christianity in the vicinity of our homes, and if possible to mix them together so that over time, living under only one master and one system of law, they will form only one people and one blood." The following year, Colbert accused the Jesuits and the authorities of not working hard enough to civilize converted "savages, whether by uniting them in marriage to the French or in getting their whole families to live among our own."[181] Colbert's policy on the settlement of New France clearly called for bringing French and "savages" together in marriage, so that they formed only one people and one blood.

During the seventeenth century many attempts were made to bring this about. Champlain adopted three young Amerindian girls, Foi, Espérance and Charité, intending to raise them in the French manner, but ultimately the girls headed back to the forest. The Ursulines of Quebec founded a "convent for Indian women"; the Sisters of the Congregation in Montreal raised among others two Potawatomi girls, who had been presented as slaves by the Iroquois to Governor Courcelle: "they learned the French language and were raised in the European manner, so that the elder of the two girls is fit to marry a French man, but it is to be hoped that she will receive a dowry, to serve as an example to others, and to fill them with the desire to be raised in the French manner."[182]

The eighteenth century saw more of these marriages between French men and "savage" women of a free condition. On August 15,

1718 in Montreal, Marianne You, a twenty-four-year-old Miami Amerindian and daughter of Pierre You d'Youville Ladécouverte and of the Miami woman Élisabeth, married a Canadian named Jean Richard, son of Guillaume Richard and Agnès Tessier. A more interesting case occurred in the Hamelin family, where on November 27, 1738, in Michilimackinac, the merchant Charles Hamelin, son of Jacques Hamelin, seigneur of Grondines, married the Sauteux or Plains Ojibwa woman Marie-Athanase who had already given him four illegitimate children. He legitimized them the day of his wedding. Marie-Athanase died in 1745, but the merchant continued to enjoy the company of Amerindian women. Another Plains Ojibwa woman named Marie-Anastasie, gave him an illegitimate son in 1746, and they finally married on February 4, 1748 – his second marriage to an Ojibwa woman. Charles Hamelin's son, Louis Hamelin, faithfully maintained his father's tradition. Between 1769 and 1779, he had five illegitimate children with the Plains Ojibwa Marie-Joseph Lesable, and on August 19, 1787 in Michilimackinac he finally married the mother of his children. No matter what various people may have claimed about the matter, we could easily provide a long list of such marriages between white Canadians and "savage women" of a free condition.

Allowing Canadians to marry "savage" women could at best have been a means of ensuring that the wife received a Christian education; it was at least a way of providing settlers with wives. But these marriages were not without serious drawbacks, as Marie de l'Incarnation had already noticed: French men were likelier to become "savage" than "savage" women to become French. Husbands had to be prevented from giving themselves up to the savage lifestyle: in 1673, for example, when Nicolas Pelletier was allowed to marry a Montagnais woman, it was only on condition that he live with his wife in his home among the French and not in the forest among the "savages," and that the children be raised in the French language and manner.[183]

In the eighteenth century authorities in New France enforced a kind of prohibition. In 1706, Governor Vaudreuil ordered Lamothe from Detroit, to prevent French men from marrying Amerindian women, and as Governor Vaudreuil wrote to Intendant Raudot in 1709, Lamothe complied with this order, "as he is convinced that bad blood should never be mixed with good, given the experience we have in this country, where all French men who married savage women have become lazy libertines, and unbearably independent, and the resulting children have proved just as lazy as the Amerindians themselves, and we must not allow these kinds of marriages to take place."[184] This was a far cry from Colbert's project of marrying French men to Amerindian women so that they should form "only one people and one blood."

The problem was different for Amerindians living in bondage, however: they came from deep in the interior of the continent (mostly the Upper Missouri), had often been removed from their families at a very young age, were accustomed to Canadian family life, and as Amerindian slaves thus stood better chances of being integrated into French society. In 1726, Mgr. Saint-Vallier willingly blessed the marriage of the Panis, Marie-Catherine Desbois, and a French Montrealer, François Sainton *dit* Carterel. Amerindian slaves were intimately involved with the French population, so it was

GRAPH V
SLAVE MARRIAGES
(FOR 4,165 SLAVES)

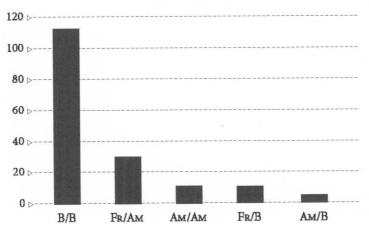

natural that such unions should be solemnized in marriage. In fact, the Panis were repeatedly described as "sauvages francisés" or "savages integrated into French society."

By the time Mgr. Saint-Vallier blessed this Panis-French marriage, slaves and Canadians had already been getting married for twenty years. The first case seems to have been in 1705: the Panis Laurent Léveillé got the nineteen-year-old Canadian minor Marie Demers pregnant; the Panis probably belonged to the Boucher de Boucherville family, because on November 22, 1705, when he ended up marrying the young Canadian woman, the seigneur of Boucherville stood in as witness at the wedding, which took place without the publication of banns. More than thirty of these marriages between Canadians and Amerindian slaves would follow in due course.

In addition, in historical records between 1713 and 1812 we turned up a small number of marriages between Canadians and black slaves. The last of these marriages was contracted by a black man born in the slave era.

MARRIAGES BETWEEN CANADIANS AND BLACKS OR AMERINDIANS

All in all, we identified eleven marriages between Canadians and blacks and thirty-four more marriages between Canadians and Amerindians. A total of forty-five white people (who were either French or had been integrated into French society) joined blacks or Amerindians in wedlock. Among mixed-race weddings, we found only one case where a Canadian man married a black woman – and there is no way to make sure this man, Joseph Provençal, was actually white: in all other such cases, black men married Canadian women.

Things were more balanced in the case of marriages between Amerindians and Canadians: of these thirty-four marriages, four Amerindian men married Canadian women, whereas twenty Canadian men married Amerindian women.

At the time of marrying, three black and five Amerindian spouses were still slaves. The black François Williams married the Canadian Marie-Élisabeth Mondina, yet continued to live in bondage; the

Panis slave Louise and the Sioux slave Marie-Marguerite-Caroline were only freed when they married Canadians. The others were former slaves, emancipated at an unknown date.

Some slaves were entered in the marriage register without any surname: the Fox Joseph Le Renard married under the name Joseph alone and it was only at a later date that he adopted the surname Le Renard; the Panis François, husband of Madeleine Lamontagne, never seems to have cared much about surnames. Other slaves known only by their first names at the time of marriage made sure their children acquired surnames. The Panis Jean-Baptiste married Marie-Geneviève Desforges *dite* Saint-Maurice and simply adopted his wife's last name; his son was known as a Desforges *dit* Saint-Maurice. The Panis Joseph married an English servant named Mary Anne "Ouidech," and assumed the surname Riberville, by which name his children were later known. Doyon's Panis Nicolas came to be known by the surname of Doyon *dit* Laframboise, which is confusing for genealogists if they do not realize Nicolas Doyon was actually a Panis.

As mentioned earlier, registers do not always record the ages of each spouse: sometimes the husband's age is indicated, sometimes the wife's, and sometimes nothing at all is given. The historian can only rely on the specific facts provided. Of the twenty spouses whose age is known, none were extremely young: only three were under twenty-one years of age. The oldest to marry was the sixty-three-year-old Panis André Rapin *dit* Scayanis who tied the knot with a fifty-eight-year-old Canadian.

These marriages between Canadians and Amerindians or blacks followed customary practice. Where a man or woman planning to get married was a slave, then the prospective spouse had to obtain consent from the slave's master. This was the case for the black Pierre-Dominique Lafleur who wanted to marry the Canadian Marie Talon; he got permission in writing on November 27, 1749 and married two days later. Slaves could also be granted their freedom, which was the case for the Panis Louise in 1776 who wanted to marry Louis Brunet, and for the Sioux Marie-Marguerite-Caroline in 1771, who had first to be purchased by her fiancé. This was because according to the *Code Noir* the marriage of a slave with a free person did not change the condition of the slave, unless the master freed the slave by a formal act. After marrying the Canadian Marie-Élisabeth Mondina in 1783, the black François Williams remained in slavery.

Banns were published in church. Dispensing with the three banns was considered a sign of great poverty. People who were comfortably off managed to publish at least one wedding bann. Sometimes the publication of three banns was dispensed with: it was considered better not to publicize the marriage when for example a widower remarried soon after his previous wife had died, or there seemed to be an excessive age difference between spouses, or the bride was noticeably pregnant. Banns were dispensed with in the cases of the Panis Laurent Léveillé in 1705, when he married a pregnant minor, and of Firmin Landry *dit* Charlot, when he married the Sioux slave who had given him five illegitimate children and who was pregnant again. In other cases of dispensation of the three banns, no explanation was given; was the bride pregnant, or did a Canadian prefer to keep quiet about his marriage to an Amerindian woman?

Witnesses are needed at weddings, and these weddings between slaves and free persons were no exception. At the 1705 wedding of the Panis Laurent Léveillé, Seigneur Pierre Boucher de Boucherville, likely the Panis's master, served as witness; Captain Jacques-Pierre Daneau Demuy filled the same role at the 1752 wedding of the Panis Geneviève Caris; so did François-Augustin Bailly de Messein, at the 1770 wedding of his former Panis, Marie-Anne, when she married the widower Montpetit.

Of the marriages we studied, three cases of second marriages show that once their Canadian husbands had died, some Canadian women were willing to share their lives with Amerindian men, whereas once Canadians survived a first marriage with an Amerindian, they were more likely to marry a white person the second time around. And if children from the first marriage survived, intriguing blended families resulted. For example, Marie Gareau had eight children with the Panis Nicolas Doyon; she then married Charles Langevin, with whom she had more offspring: subsequent unions between some of the step-brothers and step-sisters resulted in at least two illegitimate births.

MÉTIS AND MULATTOS

In our inventory we included all Canadians who married slaves, whether Amerindian or black, and also all those who had illegitimate children born of slaves. To these Canadians can be added a German who became fully integrated into French society (De Raby), the English servant "Ouidech" who was also fully integrated, and an Englishman (the officer "Yonce" – his name may have actually been Hughes), for a total of sixty-two mixed-race couples in French Canada made up of free persons and slaves.

Apart from the Englishwoman "Ouidech" and the English officer "Yonce," we found sixty cases of French Canadian families intermarrying or otherwise forming unions with Amerindians and blacks. Not all of these marriages resulted in children however: among French Canadians, forty-eight people had a total of 103 mixed-race children, of whom eighty-four were Métis and nineteen more were mulattos.

Did these Métis and mulattos go on to have more children with French Canadians? Or did they die out with the first generation, so that French Canadians today can make no claim to having slave ancestry? Genealogists will have to investigate the matter. As a first step, we drew out of our inventory those French Canadians with Métis or mulatto children who themselves later married, or at least seem not to have died in infancy. We only identified those Métis and mulatto children who married or who did not die young. But it remains to be determined whether other children were born, and above all whether these Métis and mulatto lineages have survived up to the present time. It should be noted that it was beyond the scope of our research to consider whether the current population may still have some trace of slave ancestry. However, it is conceivable that all these people may have descendants alive today, because we know their own children and grandchildren got married.

It is quite possible that among the following families, French Canadians can today be found who are descended from Amerindian or black slaves:

Beauchamps	Guibeau	Provençal
Beauchemin	Jasmin	Racicot
Beaumuny	Jolibois	Rapin
Bellerose	Jollivet	Raymond
Blanchetière *dit* Saint-Georges	Lafleur	Regereau
Bourassa	Laframboise	Riberville
Bourdon	Lagerne	Rigal
Boyer	Lalonde	Riquier
Brunet	Lamothe	Sabourin
Calmet *dit* Jolibois	Landry	Saint-Georges
Champagne	Langevin	Saint-Maurice
Chatel	Langlade	Sainton *dit* Carterel
Chauvet *dit* Lagerne	Le Renard	Sanscrainte
Chevalier-Lullier	Lespérance	Sansregret
Content *dit* Bourdon	Léveillé	Scayanis
Courchaîne	Longueuil	Sincerni
Cuillerier	Lorain	Véronneau
De Raby	Macchabé	Villeneueve
Desforges *dit* Saint-Maurice	Mervillon	Williams
Dion	Monplaisir	Wright
Doyon *dit* Laframboise	Morand	Xandre
Duchesne	Mouet de Laglade	
Dumas	Parant	

By following the various branches of their family tree, people in Quebec today may suddenly locate a great-great-aunt or distant cousin who lived in a union with a slave or the descendant of a slave, which may be the case in the following families (this is certainly the case for families which are not now extinct, such as the Trudels):

Beaugis	Lafond	Olivier
Bouchette	Laisné	Philippon
Bourdeau	Lalonde	Raymond
Casse	Lamontagne	Renaud
Chalifour	Langevin	Rivet-Lavigne
Demers	Laspron	Robidoux
Gareau	Lavigne	Sabourin
Gélineau	Lemaire	Saint Jean
Gourdon *dit* Lachasse	Lemire	Talon or Tanon
Grenier	Lepage	Terrien
Guertin	Lereau	Trottier
Guiot	Marois	Trudel
Hubou	Martin *dit* St-Jean	Vaudry
Jourdain	Mondina *dit* Olivier	
Lachasse	Morisset	

Some people in Quebec utterly reject the idea of mixed-race marriages, whereas such unions turn up in the family trees of prominent people throughout the history of Quebec. For example, Louis-François Laflèche, bishop of Trois-Rivières, was a Métis although not descended from an Amerindian slave; we are almost certain that Maurice Duplessis, premier of Quebec from 1936-1939 and again from 1944-1959, was descended from the Mascouten Jean-Baptiste *dit* Duplessis, originally from the Great Lakes region, who had been the slave of the fur trader Gastineau *dit* Duplessis: this Mascouten was thus the grandfather of the great-grandfather of Maurice Duplessis.

Another challenge facing genealogists is the fact that some slaves turn up in Quebec family trees at the origin of new branches that are related to an elder branch by name alone. People interested in tracing the history of the Léveillé, Rapin, Monplaisir, Leduc, Bourdon, Riberville, and Doyon *dit* Laframboise families should forget about identifying the French founder of such families, since all are descended from Amerindian slaves who took French names when they married Canadians. And while some names such as Angélique de Berey or Paul-Joseph Longueuil may appear to be aristocratic, Angélique was actually a slave belonging to her master Berey des Essarts. For his part, Paul-Joseph Longueuil was a slave belonging to the Lemoyne de Longueuil family, who assumed their name and perpetuated it through his children. It is important not to confuse the descendants of slaves with their masters!

TREATING AN IRRITATING PROBLEM IN JEST

Quebec francophones do not seem to relish speaking about the mixed-race unions that were so obviously a feature of life in New France. People who claim that the Québécois have native Amerindian blood are usually met with denial, even when no one has taken the trouble to investigate the matter thoroughly and establish the facts. A century ago, the historian Benjamin Sulte wrote: "we might say that every year a few drops of Missouri water fell into the St. Lawrence River."[185] It is true that the number of marriages between Canadians and Panis or blacks was not particularly high – we only traced forty-five of them. However, the number of such marriages matters less than the number of resulting Métis and mulattos: one has only to consider the fact that more than 20,000 people alive today descend from a single seventeenth-century French immigrant who only married once. It remains to be determined how many people also descended from these mixed-race unions, a question which should interest the Léveillé, Leduc, Doyon and other families.

Adolphe-Basile Routhier ventured onto this dangerous territory in the nineteenth century when he made fun of Father Henri-Raymond Casgrain, who proudly claimed to be descended from the historic Casgrain d'Airvault and Montmorency families. Routhier took pleasure in bursting Father Casgrain's pseudo-aristocratic bubble. Routhier wrote:

> Alas! This golden page of [Casgrain family history], prob-
> ably has no basis in fact. Because before including Father

Casgrain in some *Gotha* of the French nobility, we should first do some digging in the civil registry of Quebec, and in the registers of baptisms and burials in the parishes of Quebec City and Beaumont, where various deeds state that Jean Casgrain was a caterer in the Lower Town, in other words he prepared and served food and drink for travelers and pleasure-seekers of the time, and he married at Quebec one Miss Duchesne *dite* LeRoide, daughter of André LeRoide of the Panis nation. These acts establish that Jean Casgrain was by no means a native of the Vendée region of France, but came from the old province of Aunis, and instead of being a sergeant leading troops in battle he was simply a cook leading his dishes; and if he spilled blood then it was only the blood of a chicken, and if he suffered injuries it was probably burns in the kitchen. So, if [Father Casgrain's alleged ancestor], Jean-Baptiste Casgrain actually existed – this man of the Vendée, born in Airvault, this sergeant who fought at the head of the troops of France and Navarre, this Turk-slayer not to mention Turk-eater, if this peg-legged, scarred, battle-hardened Casgrain actually existed, which nobody can actually believe, then it cannot be the same person as Jean Casgrain the cook, who in the year of grace 1750, tossed crêpes in his cheap little eating joint in the Lower City, and led Miss LeRoide of the Panis nation to the altar.

Routhier was sure about his facts. What he wrote about Jean Casgrain was literally true: Jean Casgrain first married the Panis's daughter, then married a Canadian woman. Routhier could have added, however, that the Canadian Casgrain family descends from Jean Casgrain's second marriage with the Canadian Marguerite Cazeau, but this would have weakened the delicious effect of his satire... Routhier generously showed his respect for the Métis people: "Do not think I am deriding the Panis, or any other savage tribe. Quite the contrary. And if someone were to tell me that I had

Amerindian blood, I would not feel humiliated in the least. All I want to establish is that Father Casgrain does not descend directly from the Montmorency family or the Caniac family of Périgord."[186]

Routhier and Sulte both considered mixed-race unions between the French and slaves something to joke about, and the same goes for Québécois today when they address this issue. An elegant way to dismiss irritating little problems is to poke fun at them.

CHAPTER TWELVE

Slaves Disappeared One by One

The Anti-Slavery Campaign

Slave-owners were getting anxious about the gains of the anti-slavery movement. Evidence of this anxiety is contained in a sales contract from November 1787. Pierre Joinville, a resident of Île Dupas, represented by the merchant Louis Olivier, bought Cynda, a ten-year-old black slave from John Lagord for the sum of 750 livres. Joinville added an important clause to the contract: "Should any law be adopted by the Legislative Council currently in session or by any other authority, emancipating slaves and giving them their freedom," the seller, Lagord, would have to take his black slave back and reimburse the entire sum he had received from Joinville.[187] Already by 1787, it was clear owners feared the more or less imminent abolition of slavery. Was the Legislative Council of Quebec serious about abolishing slavery or was it only rumoured to be concerned about the matter? We found no documentary evidence either in or before 1787 that would help answer this question. On the one hand, Pierre Joinville did not want to pay a hefty price for a slave he might have to give up soon afterwards, whereas on the other hand, John Lagord may have agreed to reimburse the entire sale price in the event of abolition because he was not that worried it would happen anytime soon. By 1787, there had been no public campaign in Quebec against slavery: newspapers were silent on this issue.

It was only in July 1790 that newspapers began to publish anything on slavery. On July 22, 1790, the *Quebec Herald* printed a 48-verse poem, "*Domestic Slavery; or Lines occasioned by the Efforts to emancipate the African Negroes.*" The poem is attributed to one Quoilus and we cannot say whether the author was Canadian or whether the piece had previously appeared in the British or American press. This poem is a rather innocuous satire aimed at zealots clamouring for the emancipation of blacks: the gist of the poem is that thousands of people are pushing for the liberty of blacks, which means everyone is a slave, whether of the countryside, of the Court, or of boredom: people should therefore advocate liberty for all humanity. This poem was the first literary piece in this country on the subject of slavery. The following December a second piece appeared in the *Quebec Gazette*: "The Negro's Recital" made a plea for blacks, and ended with the lines:

"For though no Briton, Mongo is – a man*!"*

In other words, although the slave Mongo was not a Brit, he was nonetheless a human being! The author (of unknown nationality) underscored both *Mongo* and *a man* to make his point, following the poem up with a brief article on slavery.[188]

The anti-slavery campaign gathered steam during the summer of 1791. In April that year opponents of slavery engaged in a passionate debate in the British House of Commons, describing scenes of torture and everything they held to be heinous about slavery, but in the end a majority of MPs voted against abolition: every week between July 21 and September 8 the *Quebec Gazette* gave a full account of the debate. On September 15, the *Gazette* published the resolutions of an anti-slavery committee in London, which regretted Parliament's continuing support for the slave trade, and hoped that the cause of freedom would ultimately prevail.[189]

On March 12, 1792, the *Quebec Herald* published a 56-verse poem: "*The Negro's Complaint.*" In this anti-slavery diatribe, a Negro woman recounts her woes, and addresses her masters sharply, calling on God as her witness. The following month, on April 16, the same newspaper reprinted reports from the British press about a four-part plan to free the slaves of the British West Indies; this report was accompanied by commentaries from British newspapers. On June 7, the *Quebec Gazette* reprinted reports from the British press about the historic meeting of the House of Commons on April 2, when MPs voted for a gradual abolition of the slave trade by a margin of 230 to 85. However, Quebec journalists reported this first step in the long march towards slave emancipation as straight news, without making any direct comment. On June 21, the same newspaper reported the story of a black woman who had given birth to a child, then jumped into the sea to escape a life of servitude: but this story had been translated from French, was set outside of Canada, and could actually have been made up, since literary works could help in the struggle against slavery.[190] The *Quebec Herald* then began reporting on the debates of the previous April, that had led the British House of Commons to call for the gradual abolition of slavery: on July 16 the *Herald*, a weekly newspaper, devoted a column and a half to the historic debate, boosting its coverage the following week to five and a half columns! The abolition of the slave trade had unquestionably become the great question of the day. Finally, on August 30, the *Quebec Gazette* published a report on the abolition of black slave trafficking, which had been tabled in the French National Assembly.

There is not much point in trying to detect any coherent and orchestrated anti-slavery campaign in these writings: after two initial poems were printed in 1790, more material came out in the summer of 1791, but the Canadian press campaign was of an episodic character. Coverage depended on events taking place in Europe: the subject of slavery could disappear from the press for months, then suddenly regain importance before retreating from public view once again. We should note there was nothing original about the anti-slavery press campaign, nothing relating explicitly to slavery in Canada: newspapers reprinted the text of debates taking place in London as foreign news, without any accompanying comment relating these debates to the practice of slavery in Canada itself. Reading this anti-slavery coverage one could easily conclude there were no slaves in Lower Canada.

And yet there were still slaves: according to the 1784 census there were at least 304 slaves remaining in Canada. Some of them died before 1790, although others came to take their place. Newspapers continued reporting slave sales or descriptions of fugitive slaves. Between 1790 and 1792, fifteen Amerindian and eleven black slaves appear in the baptismal and burial registries. Slaves were not numerous, but slavery still existed.

AN ANTI-SLAVERY BILL

The anti-slavery campaign waged by Canadian newspapers was modest, but with England, France and even some American states seeking to improve the lot of slaves, the Legislative Assemblies of Upper Canada or Lower Canada could be expected to address the issue during the 1792 session. The House of Assembly of Upper Canada sat from September 17 to October 15. During this very short session, no measure relating to slavery was considered. On December 17, the House of Assembly of Lower Canada began a session which would last four and a half months.

On January 28, 1793, the fifty members of the House of Assembly, meeting in the former bishop's chapel of Quebec, began considering the issue of slavery. That day, according to the *Journal*, a member of the House, Pierre-Louis Panet, "asked leave to bring in *A bill tending to abolish slavery in the Province of Lower Canada*." Mr. Dunière seconded the motion, which was unanimously adopted, and the bill was tabled. The question before the House of Assembly was whether slavery should be abolished or retained. It was not until March 8, however, that another member, Bonaventure Panet, moved the first reading of the bill proposing to abolish slavery; the member for Quebec, Amable Berthelot, seconded Panet's motion and the House began the first reading of the bill.

The members of the House faced more pressing matters at the time, however, and the subject of slavery only came up again a month later. On April 10, Pierre-Louis Panet, seconded by Amable Berthelot, moved the second reading of the bill for the following day, but while this motion was unanimously adopted, nothing happened the next day. The second reading only took place on April 19. After the bill was read Pierre-Louis Panet moved "That this House resolve itself into a Committee of the Whole House to consider the Bill tending to abolish slavery, next Thursday," that is, the 25th. So far, Panet's plan of emancipation seemed to be on track, but moving debate to a Committee of the Whole was a decisive part of the plan, and proved to be controversial. Pierre-Amable Debonne, the member for York, proposed a destructive amendment that would involve adjourning debate on the subject. Debonne was seconded by George McBeath who represented the same riding as Bonaventure Panet. The House voted and Debonne's amendment passed by a margin of 31 to just 3. The bill was now dead, and by the will of the House of Assembly slavery would be maintained in Lower Canada.

The failure of this first bill introduces us to four opponents of slavery: Pierre-Louis Panet, Louis Dunière, Bonaventure Panet and Amable Berthelot. Oddly enough, one of the four men had already owned a slave: in 1751, Louis Dunière had bought the black Jean Monsaige, and his brother, the parish priest of Saint-Augustin, had owned the black Daniel-Télémaque.

The vote on April 19, 1793 showed that a large majority of members of the House of Assembly favoured maintaining slavery. Of these proponents of slavery, we know that at least twelve were then, or were about to become, slave owners: Michel Chartier de Lotbinière, William Grant, Pierre-Guillaume Guérout, Antoine Juchereau-Duchesnay, Hippolyte-Saint-Georges Lecompte-Dupré, John Lees, Robert Lester, David Lynd, James McGill, Mathew McNider, Louis Olivier and John Young.

Indeed, Chartier de Lotbinière had at least two blacks. William Grant, who had a black woman in 1772 and lost a black man in 1776, had seen his slave Jack escape in early 1792. In 1783, Pierre-Guillaume Guérout had a black man named Charles, who fled servitude. Antoine Juchereau-Duchesnay had a black slave at his manor at Beauport who had married a French Canadian, and was the father of four more slaves. We know Hippolyte-Saint-Georges Lecompte-Dupré had a black in 1774. John Lees owned two married black slaves and their young son. Robert Lester, an English Catholic, had lost a black in 1783, but that same year he baptized another black and probably still owned him. In 1798, David Lynd would baptize a seventeen-year-old black slave. James McGill had lost a Panis man in 1778, a Panis woman in 1783, and a black woman in 1789: he may have been the owner of the black Jacques, baptized in 1806 at the age of about forty. Mathew McNider owned a black man who fled in 1788 and another slave who was treated the same year at the Hôtel-Dieu de Québec. Louis Olivier had received the black Marie Bulkley from his father-in-law Pierre Joinville – this woman gave birth to a child in 1792 and the child was sold as a slave in 1797. John Young would buy a black in 1795 and is known to have owned another black slave in 1798.

Twelve of the fifty members of the House of Assembly of Lower Canada in 1793 were, or would become, slave-owners, while one member, Louis Dunière, spoke out against slavery. The other members appear to have favoured the status quo. The fact twelve of the fifty Assembly members were slave-owners did not necessarily guarantee that slavery would continue. But these slave-owners – William Grant, Antoine Juchereau-Duschesnay, Hippolyte-Saint-Georges Lecompte-Dupré, John Lees, James McGill, Mathew McNider and John Young among them – were influential men. However, we would need to know exactly what was said during the debates in order to form a reasonable judgment of what happened. Unfortunately, the *Journal* of the House of Assembly provides few details.

Upper Canada Banned the Importation of Slaves

The *Constitutional Act of 1791* divided Canada into two distinct provinces: Upper and Lower Canada. Upper Canada, which eventually became Ontario, was the first of these provinces to adopt legislation specifically on slavery. The Legislative Assembly of Upper Canada did not address the issue of slavery during its first session, which lasted one month, but it raised slavery during its second session, which opened in spring 1793, by adopting a bill to prevent the importation of slaves to the province and to determine the conditions needed to bring an end to slavery. The *Act Against Slavery* prohibited the future introduction of black slaves or any other person into Upper Canada with a view to subjecting them to slavery; slaves already present in the province would continue to live in bondage and any child born of a slave mother would also be a slave, but only until the age of twenty-five.

The 1793 *Act Against Slavery* of Upper Canada did not abolish slavery, it only prohibited the introduction of new slaves into the province and provided that children born to a slave mother would gain their freedom at the age of twenty-five. As Assembly member D.W. Smith wrote to the merchant John Askin: "We have made no law to free the slaves. All those who have been brought into the Province or purchased under any authority legally exercised, are Slaves to all intents & purposes, & are secured as property by a certain Act of Parliament." Speaking of the members, Smith added: "They are determined however to have a bill about Slaves, part of which I think is well enough, part most iniquitous! I wash my hands of it. A free man who is married to a Slave, his heir is declared by this Act to be a slave. fye. fye. The laws of God and man cannot authorize it." D.W.Smith was shocked by one thing more than anything else, although it had been in the *Code Noir* since 1685: that the child of a slave was a slave like its mother, regardless of the father's condition.

As a major owner of black and Panis slaves, John Askin needed reassurances about the new legislation, but he had little to worry about, since his slaves – and even those born just before the *Act* became law – would continue as slaves indefinitely, whereas any infants born to a slave mother would remain in servitude until their twenty-fifth birthday.

The Legislative Assembly of Upper Canada had squared the circle by seizing on a formula that satisfied slave owners, respected their ownership rights and opened the way to the gradual extinction of slavery. The *Act* had one significant and immediate consequence: Upper Canadians could no longer import slaves. But the *Act* also had the longer-term effect of turning Upper Canada into a "land of liberty" for runaway slaves. Indeed, the *Act* of 1793 prohibited that any black or Indian slave entering the province of Upper Canada should be treated as a slave: as a result, any fugitive slave seeking asylum in the province would be released from bondage. And, in fact, slaves from outside Upper Canada quickly took advantage of this opportunity – from Detroit (which Britain handed over to the United States in late 1796), the slaves crossed the Detroit River, while others were spirited out of New York and Lower Canada from 1792 until the early 1860s, by a web of smuggling networks known as the Underground Railway. These smugglers traveled along secret paths and riverside wetlands.[191] Fugitive slaves reaching the province saw Upper Canada as an international place of refuge, but slaves already established there before 1793 continued to toil in servitude.

THE CHIEF JUSTICE DID NOT RECOGNIZE SLAVERY

In Lower Canada, meanwhile, the bill introduced in the House of Assembly in the spring of 1793 was still "lying on the table" and the conditions of slavery remained unchanged: slaves in the province would remain in servitude indefinitely, fresh slaves could be brought into Lower Canada, and once they got there they would in principle remain slaves as before. Civil registries continued identifying blacks and Panis in bondage as slaves, as they had done since around 1700: the historical records indicate eight such slaves in 1793, seven in 1794, two in 1795, six in 1796, four in 1797, and five in 1798. Hospital records also refer to slaves: two in 1793, one in 1794, and one in 1796. In other cases, slave owners posted notices in newspapers or other places to the effect their slaves had escaped: in 1794, Pretchard was looking for his black slave, Isaac; in 1798, Madame Sawer of Sorel, lost her black slave, Phillis; James Fraser was looking for his black slave Lydia who deserted with a four-year-old mulatto girl. In 1797, George Westphal pawned his mulatto Sedy, since he owed money to Richard Dillon. These diverse sources of information between 1793 and 1798 indicate the presence of eight Panis and thirty-three blacks, who were still held in slavery.

To this number should be added individuals put up for sale. Here are some examples of twenty advertisements from 1793 to 1798:

> 1793: Mulatto, 22 years of age, for sale in February and March: contact Jean Routhier, residing in Rivière-Duchesne, or Jean-Marie Huppé, residing in the Faubourg Saint-

Antoine (*Montreal Gazette*, published by Edwards, February 21 and 28, March 7).

1795: Judith, Negress, purchased January 27, 1795 in Albany by the merchant Elias Smith, of Montreal, for consideration of 80 pounds, New York currency (*Journal of the House of Assembly*, 1799: 126).

1796: Rose, Negress, aged 31, sold September 9, 1796 by Louis Payet, parish priest of Saint-Antoine-de-Richelieu, and Thomas Lee, for the sum of 500 livres, old currency (Michaud notarial registry).

1797: Negress, aged about 17 years: her remaining seventeen years of service being offered for sale (*Montreal Gazette*, published by Edwards, July, August and September 1797).

From 1793 to 1798 owners were still selling or trying to sell slaves, and among these sellers we even find a Catholic priest, Father Louis Payet, among the very last people trafficking in "Negroes." In the last confirmed sale we know of, the former member of the Assembly Louis Olivier sold a slave in May 1797 to the sailor Joseph Gent: this last slave sale was thus made by a French-speaking person in Lower Canada. The last offer of a slave for sale was in January 1798. These incidents mark the end of the slave trade in what is now the province of Quebec.

There had been considerable uncertainty about slavery for a number of years. We should recall that in 1793 members of the House of Assembly of Lower Canada had proposed the abolition of slavery but had failed in their attempt, while Upper Canada that same year forbade the importation of new slaves. This measure was not likely to reassure slave owners in Lower Canada, and the Courts gave them more cause for anxiety.

In 1794, a Court of Justice in Montreal set a precedent for slaves. A black man, whose name was not recorded, had fled the United States and found refuge in Montreal. He then went to work at Rivière-

Duchesne; a certain Mr. Platt of Plattsburgh (on Lake Champlain), turned up, claiming the man was his slave; Major Anctil refused to allow the black to be taken out of the country; a lawsuit was filed and the judge, stating that slavery was not "known under the Laws of England," freed the black from any further prosecution.[192]

For the judge to rule that slavery was unknown under the laws of England was a highly debatable, although commendable, step to take – slavery had actually been formally recognized in the British colonies, and the Parliament in Westminster had not yet taken a position on the gradual abolition of the slave trade. In any event, the precedent was set – a judge had just discharged a black from prosecution for being a runaway slave.

Was this judge William Osgoode? To our knowledge, the only document recording this event does not identify the judge. William Osgoode, said to be the author of the 1793 *Act Against Slavery* of Upper Canada, was promoted Chief Justice of Lower Canada in early 1794, but it was not until December 11 (i.e. after the ruling of the Court of Montreal) that he was appointed Chief Justice of the Court of King's Bench.[193]

Although we cannot tell whether Chief Justice Osgoode set this precedent of 1794, we know for certain that on three occasions in 1798, he released blacks whose only crime was to have run away from their owners. The first of these, the black Charlotte, belonging to Jane Cook of Montreal in February 1798, left the service of her mistress and was arrested under the Magistrates Warrant. When she refused to return to her mistress, she was thrown behind bars. She then obtained a writ of *Habeas Corpus*, but since the Court was now on holidays, Chief Justice Osgoode decided to discharge the black woman without requiring any future appearance before the Court. This decision immediately caused a stir, as stated in a petition to the House of Assembly: "Upon this enlargement, the Negroes in the city and district of Montreal threatened a general revolt."[194] In other words, other slaves wanted to obtain their freedom by similar means.

We do not know the details of this "general revolt," and it is possible that the petitioners were overstating their case. In any event, two slaves quickly followed Charlotte's example: the black Judith (also known as Jude) and the black Manuel. Jude had been purchased in 1795 in Albany by the merchant Elias Smith. After Charlotte's discharge, Jude fled her master and Smith had her arrested and jailed. Jude invoked her right to appear before a judge, and the judge in question was none other than William Osgoode. On March 8, 1798, he discharged the woman, declaring at the same time, in open Court, "that he would, upon *Habeas Corpus*, discharge every Negro, indented Apprentice, and Servant who should be committed to Gaol under the Magistrates Warrant in the like cases."

On another occasion, the following December, Chief Justice Osgoode refused to recognize slavery. The black Manuel had been sold in 1797 by Jervis George Turner to the innkeeper John Thomas Sullivan: the innkeeper made a first payment of eighteen pounds (Quebec currency), promising nonetheless to free the slave in five years. However on March 1, 1798, Manuel decided to flee like the previous two black slave fugitives. Sullivan refused to discharge his debt to Turner and was sued on these grounds. Sullivan defended himself, claiming that Turner had sold him a free "Negro," and demanding that the eighteen pounds be reimbursed. Manuel then declared that Turner had no right to sell him because according to Manuel the country's laws did not recognize slavery. On December 18, Chief Justice Osgoode ruled that Turner had not proved he had the right to sell the "Negro" Manuel, nor could Sullivan establish his ownership of the slave: the sale was therefore null and void, and the eighteen pounds had to be returned to Sullivan. Manuel's own intervention in Court was turned aside.[195] Turner did indeed own the black slave, since he had bought him from a man named Allen, but that was not enough for Justice Osgoode, who considered slavery to be illegal. Meanwhile, there was nothing further that Sullivan could do to establish his property rights. As for Manuel, there were no grounds for him to intervene because, according to the sentence, he had not been sold in the first place. As a result, he was now free to go.

Slave Owners Addressed the House of Assembly
Still no law in Lower Canada explicitly prohibited slavery: existing

legislation remained in force. If the Chief Justice persisted in freeing slaves on the grounds that he did not consider them legally to be slaves, then slave owners could no longer rely on the protection of the courts. Accordingly, in April 1799, a group of Montrealers had Joseph Papineau, a member of the House of Assembly, present a petition on their behalf in the House.

Presented and read to the House on April 19, the petition drew the members' attention to the legal basis of slavery: Intendant Raudot's ordinance of 1709 had established that blacks and Panis belonged to those who had bought them "as their own slaves"; the King of France had never disapproved of this ordinance, which was still in force in 1763 and, consequently, had become part of the "laws, usages and customs of Canada" in 1774; slavery was considered lawful in the British colonies; an Act of the British Parliament in 1732 for the recovery of debts in the colonies included slaves among "real states" (immovable property) which could be seized in order to satisfy debts: by virtue of the *Quebec Act*, this 1732 act was in full force in Lower Canada; the "*Act for couraging new settlers in His Majesty's Colonies and Plantations in America*," passed in 1790, ensured that subjects of the United States could lawfully bring their slaves and other property with them, and could sell them within twelve months of their arrival.

It was "upon the faith of His Majesty's Government," the petition stated, that the inhabitants of the province in general and of Montreal in particular "have purchased for a valuable consideration, a considerable number of Panis and Negro Slaves"; and it was upon the same faith that diverse persons, formerly subjects of the United States, had imported Negro slaves into the province; that these "Panis and Negro Slaves have always comported themselves in a becoming manner until lately, that they have imbibed a refractory and disobedient spirit, under pretext that no slavery exists in the Province." The petition provided two examples of this change in attitude: the Negro women Charlotte and Jude, whom Chief Justice Osgoode had released because he did not recognize slavery. "Upon this enlargement, the Negroes in the city and district of Montreal threatened a general revolt." Under these circumstances, His Majesty's Justices had no power to compel absconding Slaves to return to the owner's service, while the owners had no "power to enforce obedience"; the "Memorialists" (who had drafted the petition) foresaw "alarming consequences to this Province ... independent of the great loss which his Majesty's Subjects of this Province, owners of Negro Slaves, and the Creditors of such owners, may sustain by the disability such owners now labour under of preserving their property in their Slaves." The Montreal slave owners therefore called on the House of Assembly to enact legislation that provided for the jailing of slaves who deserted their masters, in the same way as indentured apprentices and servants were jailed in England; or that "a Law may be made declaring that there is no Slavery in the Province; or such other provision, respecting Slaves as this House in its wisdom shall think proper."

Slave owners were pushing for a clear choice: the House should either uphold their property rights over their slaves, or it should abolish slavery altogether. But the House of Assembly seems to have taken the petition in stride, ordering only "that the said Petition do lay upon the table for the consideration of the members."[196]

Slaves could continue to desert because the House of Assembly had refused to take a stand and the Chief Justice had ruled that British law did not recognize slavery. For example, when James Fraser immigrated to Quebec from the United States in 1783, he brought his slaves with him. By 1799, only one slave was left, a black man by the name of Robin (also known as Robert or Bob). According to a petition presented to the House of Assembly, this slave was "one of three, the only property [Mr. Fraser] had saved from the ravages of the late war, and his chief dependence for support in his old age"; but Robin, who had already deserted previously, disappeared once again in the spring of 1799. The master waited for him in vain, only to discover, on January 28, 1800, that Robin was now staying with the innkeeper Richard Dillon, where life was obviously more attractive; the following day, the black man was arrested and jailed. A lawyer named Perry took up the black man's defence, and on February 4 obtained a writ of *Habeas Corpus*. As a result, on February 10, the slave appeared before the Court of King's Bench, with Chief Justice

Osgoode presiding, flanked by Justices Pierre-Louis Panet and Isaac Ogden. Perry requested that the black be released, whereas a lawyer named Kerry pleaded the owner's case; the justices heard the arguments by both parties on February 13, and ruled finally on the 18th to discharge the slave unconditionally. One of the grounds the Court invoked was a law of 1797 that prevented the seizure of slaves for the payment of their master's debts: in the Court's view, this law amounted to emancipation. In any case, Chief Justice Osgoode and his colleagues refused to punish a slave whose only offence was to have run away from his master.

Slave owners did not give up the struggle. Indeed, they once again called on Joseph Papineau to present a petition in the House of Assembly: the petition was "brought up and read" on April 18, 1800. This petition was somewhat different from the previous one, in that it asked the Legislature "to vest in a more effectual manner the property in slaves in their masters, and to provide laws for the proper regulation and government of such a class of men as come within the description of slaves." The petition repeated the same arguments used in 1799, but this time, instead of merely referring to legal texts, it took the trouble to quote from them at length: the Raudot Ordinance in 1709 which "was never altered or repealed"; the law of 1790 concerning Americans leaving their country for British colonies in North America. "Many faithful and loyal subjects of His Majesty," the petition stated, "after exposing their lives in his service, and sacrificing almost the whole property they were possessed of in the late calamitous war, came into this Province with their slaves under the sacred promise held out to them in the last mentioned statute, and from an idea lately gone abroad, that slavery does not exist in this country." The petition backed up this statement by giving the example of James Fraser who had only one slave "for support in his old age" but who had suffered the indignity of having the Court deprive him of his property. The petition maintained, in defiance of the Court ruling, that the law of 1797 prohibiting the seizure of slaves for the payment of their master's debts "does not go so far as to divest such owners of their property in their slaves, nor can it be considered as tending to emancipate the slaves in His Majesty's plantations."[197]

The petitioners said they were "extremely sorry to detain the House so long on this occasion, so interesting to them, as many of the petitioners have paid considerable sums for slaves who have deserted their service, and all of them are deeply sensible that this class of men who are now let loose on society, and live an idle and profligate life, may be tempted to commit crimes, which it is the duty of every citizen to endeavour to prevent." What were the petitioners seeking? "That it may therefore please this House to frame such an Act as will declare that slavery exists under certain modifications in this Province, and will completely vest the property in Panis and Negroes in the owners thereof; and further, that this House will provide such Laws and regulations for the government of slaves as in the wisdom of the House may be thought expedient."[198]

They could have provided an additional argument – namely, the example of Upper Canada. In fact, the petitioners were seeking exactly what the Legislature of Upper Canada had established in 1793: that Parliament formally recognize slavery, ensure that slave owners would have full property rights over their slaves, and introduce restrictive measures, if necessary, on the importation of new slaves. We do not know why these Montreal petitioners failed to invoke the precedent of Upper Canada. In 1791, what was then known as the "Province of Quebec" had been divided into Upper and Lower Canada, and legislation addressing common problems ought to have been harmonized in these two jurisdictions.

THE HOUSE OF ASSEMBLY STILL REFUSED TO TAKE A STAND

The petition of April 1799 had quickly been laid on the table of the House, which amounted to dying in procedural terms, but the petition of April 1800 got a little further. On the motion of Joseph Papineau, the House agreed to refer the petition to a committee of five members "to examine the matter thereof, and report theron with all possible diligence"; sitting on the committee were Joseph Papineau, William Grant, John Craigie, James Cuthbert and Alexandre Dumas. The composition of the committee gave slave owners cause for hope, since three of the five members wanted to see a law on slavery, Joseph Papineau was advocating the position of slave owners, while William Grant and James Cuthbert had owned slaves.

The committee got to work quickly: the petition was filed on Friday, April 18, and the committee reported back to the House on the following Monday. As committee chairman, James Cuthbert presented the report, after which the Clerk of the House read out the committee's two resolutions:

> RESOLVED, that it is the opinion of this Committee, that there are reasonable grounds for passing a Law to regulate the condition of Slaves, to limit the term of Slavery, and prevent the further introduction of Slaves in this Province.

> RESOLVED, that it is the opinion of this Committee, that the Chairman move the House, that leave be given to the said Committee to bring in a Bill accordingly.

In calling for a law to regulate the conditions of slaves and at the same time limit the term of slavery, the committee was aligning itself with the law passed in Upper Canada in 1793. The House of Assembly immediately approved the committee's two resolutions. The next step was debating the bill itself.

James Cuthbert moved the first reading on April 30. The second reading was set for May 2, but the matter was deferred till Saturday, when there was no time to deal with the matter. The second reading took place on Monday, May 5, and on motion of James Cuthbert and Joseph Papineau, a Committee of the Whole House was formed to debate the bill. Discussion proceeded apace, the House proposing to continue the following, since no further debate was possible that day, for want of a quorum. Work resumed on May 7 but "several members having retired," the House was again adjourned for want of a quorum. No further mention was made of the bill during the session, which ended May 29.

The *Journal* of the House of Assembly does not provide a verbatim account of debate on the slavery bill: it would have been interesting to follow the debate, and see why several members of the House were absent, just when the bill reached a third and final reading. Was this an indication of their opposition to the bill, or of their indifference? In any event, only six of fifty members had a personal stake in the issue of slavery, whether because they still owned or had once owned slaves: Louis-Charles Foucher, William Grant, John Lees, Joseph Périnault-Lamarche, Denis Viger and John Young.

For this reason slave owners in Lower Canada failed to validate their ownership rights by means of a specific law. Once the House of Assembly was dissolved at the end of May 1800, everything was put on hold until the next session began after a general election. And the slave owners had a lot to worry about; in that same year, 1800, Nova Scotia deported a cargo of its slaves to Africa. An indication of this anxiety appeared in Chartier de Lotbinière's inventory of his property in August 1800. Writing of his black slave, Joseph-Louis *dit* Pompée, aged about 20 years, he noted: "Given that there is no way in this province to hold this kind of property, it is considered precarious and uncertain."[199]

After the general election the new session of Parliament opened on January 8, 1801. On January 17, James Cuthbert and Justice Pierre-Louis Panet presented a new bill in the House to regulate the condition of slaves and limit the term of slavery, and moved the first reading. The second reading took place on Friday, January 23. Cuthbert and Lees moved that the following Friday a Committee of the Whole House should consider the bill, and this motion was approved. But the following Friday came and went, and the bill seems to have fallen by the wayside. On February 5, James Cuthbert returned to the charge, seconded by Pierre-Louis Panet, and the House agreed to go into a Committee of the Whole on February 26. But the House did not sit on the 26th. On March 2, James Cuthbert presented his motion again, seconded by Francis Badgley, and the House agreed to sit in a Committee of the Whole on Friday, March 6; that day, Pierre-Louis Panet and Joseph-Périnault Lamarche moved to defer the matter to the following day, but no mention of it was made. Then, on March 9, the House met as a Committee of the Whole, chaired by Francis Badgley: there was a little discussion, but the member speaking returned to his seat, and the committee adjourned its work, in what proved to be its last meeting of the parliamentary session.

How can this new failure be explained? The only way for us to understand what really happened would be to examine the verbatim account of the debates, but no such account exists, and we can do no more than record yet another failure.

It was not until 1803 that slave owners made a new attempt in the House of Assembly. On March 1, James Cuthbert presented a bill "to remove all doubts about slavery in this province and other effects": the bill went through first reading in the House, while the second reading took place on March 7. Debate generally began in earnest after the second reading. James Cuthbert and Denis Viger moved that the bill be referred to a committee that would report "with all due despatch"; the committee consisted of James Cuthbert, Justice Pierre-Amable Debonne, Alexis Caron, John Craigie and John Lees. The committee got to work; on March 13, Cuthbert and Caron proposed the addition of two members, and François Huot and Jean-Baptiste Raymond were named. But this proved to be the last time the *Journals* of the House of Assembly ever mentioned a bill on slavery. Indeed, after all these unsuccessful attempts to get the House of Assembly of Lower Canada to enact legislation on slavery, nothing further was done: after 1803 the question of slavery never appeared in the agenda of the House of Assembly. Ultimately, no Act specifically addressing the condition of slaves was adopted in Lower Canada.[200]

SLAVERY DISAPPEARED BEFORE IT WAS FORMALLY ABOLISHED
While these various attempts were going on were there still that many slaves in Lower Canada? We believe the number of slaves still held in bondage had to be greatly reduced for the House of Assembly to treat the issue of slavery with such indifference, for newspapers to

maintain complete silence about the matter, and for owners such as James Fraser to be intent only on keeping whatever slaves remained to them personally. Only a handful of slaves turn up in the historical record. The last deed of sale is dated May 13, 1797 (when Louis Olivier of Berthier-en-Haut sold the black woman Marie Bulkley to the sailor Joseph Gent) and the *Montreal Gazette* was the last newspaper to print an advertisement for a slave sale, on January 29, 1798; the market in slaves had dried up. After 1799, we only find a very few blacks and Panis still living in bondage. In fact, we only know of nineteen slaves, eleven of them blacks and eight Indians:

1799	2	1806	1
1800	2	1807	2
1802	7	1808	2
1803	2	1821	1

Historical records indicate the presence of a few slaves every year until 1808, but then there is a gap of thirteen years until 1821, when the last historical document mentions an individual slave. In fact, the Panis Marie-Marguerite would have the distinction of being the last person in the catalogue of slavery, when she was donated by Grasset de Saint-Sauveur to the Hôpital-Général de Montreal on his return to France. The last time the word "slave" actually appears in the civil registries was on November 13, 1793, at the christening of the black Henry Williams in the Anglican Church in Quebec.

There may well have been other slaves than these nineteen individuals identified as such at the time of enumeration. We know that some slaves did not want to be freed. For example, the black Angélique, who lived with the Neilson family in Trois-Rivières, died a willing slave around 1808 or 1810. This was also the case of Lisette, a mulatto woman who had been bought by the grandfather of the writer Aubert de Gaspé and was attached to his family: an attempt had been made to free her but "'I don't give a fig for your freedom!' she would say, snapping her fingers. 'I've as much right to remain in the house where I was brought up as you and all your family.' If her exasperated master were to put her out by the north door, she would immediately come back in by the south, and vice versa."[201]

Former slaves also turn up in historical records, although we cannot determine whether they had been freed or not. On April 12, 1799, the Panis Marie-Joseph, aged about 100 years, was buried at the Hôpital-Général de Montréal: she had belonged to the late Madame Ruette d'Auteuil; also buried at the same place were the eighty-seven-year-old Panis Marie-Louise, formerly the property of Chevalier de Lacorne, on March 22, 1802, and the sixty-year-old black woman Marie-Louise-Jeanne "Thomme", who had belonged to Jean Orillat, on July 6, 1802. The seventy-year-old Panis Marguerite, now described as a servant, was buried at the Hôtel-Dieu de Québec, on June 8, 1810. And on October 23, 1812, the eighty-eight-year-old black Marie-Élisabeth, widow of the black Jacques-César and a former slave of the Lemoyne de Longueuil family, free since 1763, was buried in Longueuil. The sixty-year-old Panis Marie was buried at the Hôtel-Dieu de Québec on December, 25 1814. The twenty-two-year-old Panis Marie was buried in Montreal on March 22, 1819. Dr. Boucher de Labruère who was jailed in Montreal, mentioned an old black woman in December 1838 "who comes to wash our things for practically nothing." This old black woman must have been a slave, at least in her younger years.[202] We should finally mention the eighty-three-year-old black Catherine Thompson, widow of Jean-Baptiste Johnton, buried at Vaudreuil on June 30, 1840. She must also have had personal experience of slavery in former times.

It is hard to say exactly how slavery ended in French Canada. The last sale of a slave took place in 1797; the word "slave" appeared for the last time in civil registries in 1798; the subject of slavery was never again raised in the House of Assembly after 1803; and the last individual slave – a Panis woman – died in 1821. Did the history of slavery in Lower Canada end because of a law enacted in Britain? On August 28, 1833, the British government voted to put an end to slavery throughout the British Empire. The *Slavery Abolition Act* came into force in 1834, and provided "a period of apprenticeship of freedom that was to last until August 1, 1838 for urban slaves and until August 1, 1840 for rural slaves," but this learning period was soon shortened and "by 1838, to all intents and purposes, all slaves had been emancipated" on British soil.[203]

Were there any remaining slaves in Lower Canada to take advantage of this legal emancipation? Benjamin Sulte said he had known "several Negroes emancipated by the Act of 1833, but not a single Panis"; what a pity he failed to record their names![204] Given that the slave market had ceased to exist by the dawn of the nineteenth century, we are inclined to believe that whatever slaves were emancipated by the Act of 1833 must have been very old blacks or exceptional cases. One thing seems clear – no Indian slaves were left in Lower Canada to enjoy the fruits of emancipation. Suffice it to say that in Quebec, slavery withered away on its own, and no date can be assigned to its final disappearance.

Conclusion

Throughout this work we have been dealing with a historical territory which does not quite occupy the same space as present-day Canada. Our study establishes that slavery had an official, legal existence over two centuries, that is between 1632 and 1834.

It is hard to imagine why Amerindian and black slavery would not have been practised in Quebec during this period, when it was a widespread institution in all European colonies, Catholic and Protestant alike. However, slavery here remained on a relatively small scale. The black man that Guillaume Couillart received as a gift in 1632 would remain the colony's only black inhabitant for a quarter of a century. Governor Courcelle and the explorers Jolliet and Dulhut received Amerindian slaves as gifts, but it was not until the last years of the seventeenth century that slave ownership in New France, whether of Amerindians or blacks, became a regular feature of society. Indeed the word "slave" was mentioned for the first time in the civil registry on October 28, 1694.

The original French colonists of Quebec wanted to import massive numbers of black slaves into the colony. In 1688, three years after the publication of the *Code Noir* regarding the French islands of America (the Caribbean), Governor Denonville and Intendant Bochart de Champigny asked for blacks. In 1689, Ruette d'Auteuil wrote a memorandum to the king claiming that enterprises in Canada were failing because of the scarcity and high cost of labour, whereas they would succeed if "Negroes" were imported. In 1689, Louis XIV therefore allowed colonists in New France to own slaves, although he also urged caution since these blacks, acquired at great cost, might not adapt well to the climate. This first royal sanction of slavery remained a dead letter because of the outbreak of war, and a second royal sanction in 1701 also remained without effect when war resumed.

No massive importation of black slaves took place, but Canadians were able to draw off a few black slaves while warring against the Thirteen Colonies, and to exploit increasing numbers of Amerindian slaves who were brought back from the Midwest to Montreal as a result of the fur trade. The situation remained somewhat confusing since owners still lacked specific legal guarantees of their slave ownership. In 1709, Intendant Raudot ruled that people who had bought or would buy blacks and Panis as slaves did in fact own them. From that time, slavery became legal, and starting in 1709 notaries began to draw up deeds for the sale of slaves. Raudot's ordinance remained in force thereafter, and in 1730 Intendant Hocquart had it reprinted as a way of reminding French colonists that the purchase of black and "red" slaves was legal.

There was no particular problem about black slavery – unless a "Negro" had been formally emancipated, he was a slave wherever he might be, and the kings of France authorized Canadians to own such slaves. But Amerindian slavery was not so clear-cut. Could an entire "savage" tribe be enslaved, even though Intendant Raudot had only specifically mentioned the enslavement of the Panis? And what of Amerindians who had been baptized as Catholics – if baptism accorded them the same rights as French colonists, at least in principle, could they also be held as slaves? A case in point arose in 1732, when a Paducah slave who had already been baptized was seized, and then sold at auction. Once Louis XV was apprised of this case, he refused to issue a formal law on Amerindian slavery, preferring that judges in New France follow customary practice in the colony, which meant that these "savages" were indeed slaves but they could only be emancipated by a notarized act.

Was it acceptable to export Amerindian slaves? Intendant Raudot replied that it was not, because his ordinance was only valid in Canada; but actually, some "savages" were transported to the Caribbean, whether to undergo the punishment of exile or because owners no longer wanted to keep them.

Whatever the case, Raudot's ordinance definitively established the right of slave ownership; throughout the French regime this ordinance was invoked whenever the owner felt his right was under threat. Finally, Article 47 of the Articles of Capitulation in 1760 maintained the French institution of slavery under the British regime, without providing any new legal foundation for it: slave owners would still refer to Raudot's ordinance in 1800, when petitioning the House of Assembly.

In this study we counted a total of 4185 slaves from 1632 to the first third of the nineteenth century, within Quebec's traditional boundaries, as well as various other territories that depended on it from time to time. These 4185 slaves can be broken down into three groups: 2683 native Amerindians, called "red slaves"; 1443 blacks; and fifty-nine other slaves whose origin is not recorded in historical documents.

It should be noted that these 1443 blacks represented 35% of the total, and were definitely in the minority. They only began to acquire importance during the last two decades of French rule, especially as war booty and fugitive slaves, although some Canadian merchants managed to import small numbers of ebony slaves from the Caribbean. But after 1760, the number of blacks rose rapidly, especially as Loyalists fleeing America brought their slaves with them. Black slavery became more generalized under the British regime.

The largest single group among Canadian slaves were aboriginal people, who accounted for 2683 individuals or 65.1% of the total slave population. Nearly two-thirds of these slaves were identified as Panis, a nation living in the Upper Missouri and Kansas regions. However, not all slaves described as Panis were actually from the "Pawnee" nation. The term "Panis" came over time to be applied generically to any Amerindian slave. The origin of some Amerindians was specifically entered in registers: from the Mississippi Basin came Amerindians of the Iowa ("Aiouois"), Missouri, Kansas, Arkansas, Ouacha, Natchez, Choctaw, Chickasaw, Shawnee, Cahokia, Tamaroa and Illinois nations; from western Canada came Amerindians of the Sioux, Brochet, Assiniboine, Cree and Mandan nations; from the Great Lakes region came Amerindians of the Ojibwa, Fox, Menominee, Mascouten, Potawatomi, Ottawa, Iroquois and Mohican nations; and from the northern reaches of the colony came natives from the Gens de terre, Têtes de boule, Montagnais and even Eskimo nations.

Slavery seems to have been on a modest scale, if we consider there were 4200 slaves in Canada over two centuries, but 5000 slaves in Louisiana in the year 1746 alone. Slavery was an economic imperative in colonies where sugar and tobacco were grown, whereas in French Canada no economic activity required the presence of slave labour; agriculture was only practised on a small scale, any colonial activity that could compete with metropolitan French activity was strictly forbidden, and the main commercial activity, the fur trade, involved transiting goods from one place to the other. True, domestic servants were hard to find under French rule, which could lead us to assume that Canadians imitated other slave-owning colonies. But actually, the scale of slave ownership here was nowhere near the same.

Slaves were distributed throughout Quebec, but were mostly held in bondage in the cities of Montreal and Quebec. Montreal accounted for 1525 or 36.4% of all slaves, ahead of Quebec with 970 slaves or 23.2%. Montreal was also the terminus of the fur trade – a long canoe voyage away from the *pays d'en haut* – so it was in Montreal that the greatest numbers of Amerindian slaves were to be found: 1007 or 37.5%, whereas Quebec City's 400 Amerindian slaves (14.9% of the total) were a distant second. These two cities had more even shares of black slaves: 39.5% in Quebec, and 35.9% in Montreal.

In the *Dictionnaire des esclaves et de leurs propriétaires*, we tracked 1574 masters: of this group, 1535 were specifically identified as slave owners, 1312 or 80% were francophones and 223 or 20% were anglophones. Francophones had a total of 2858 slaves (86.8% of all slaves identified), including 2262 Amerindians, while anglophones only held 132; francophones were mainly responsible for Amerindian slavery. Furthermore, blacks made up just 20.9% of all slaves held by francophones, whereas they represented 69.5% of slaves held by English-speaking owners.

These 1574 slave owners belonged to all ranks of society and practised many different professions. They were found among the highest
officials (governors general, intendants, etc.), among members of
the Conseil supérieur, the legislative and executive councils, judges,
military officers, doctors, surgeons, notaries, surveyors, interpreters,
printers, tradesmen and even a sculptor; slave ownership was common among persons engaged in trade (a third of all slaves were held
by the merchant class), and there again, even after the Conquest,
French-Canadian merchants owned more slaves than their English-
speaking counterparts. Seigneurs held a combined total of 442
slaves, which leads us to conclude slaves were a regular feature of life
in seigneurial manors.

The clergy had slaves: three bishops, four secular priests (including Louis Payet, who owned five slaves and was one of the last
people in French Canada to buy a slave), two Sulpicians, a Récollet
Father and four Jesuits. Religious communities also owned slaves:
the Jesuits in Quebec, Saint-François-du-Lac, Sault-Saint-Louis, the
Detroit (Pointe-de-Montréal) and Michilimackinac missions; the
Brothers of Charity in Louisbourg; the Hôpital-Général de Québec,
the Hôtel-Dieu de Montréal, the Congregation of Notre Dame
and especially the Hôpital-Général in Montreal where a number
of slaves lived – both the slaves Mother d'Youville had inherited
from her husband, and those slaves donated to the hospital by
French colonists returning to France after the Conquest, as a way
of supporting the hospital's good works, or of ensuring the welfare
of slaves who could not be taken back to France. Although neither
the Séminaire de Québec nor the Ursulines seem to have owned
slaves in Quebec itself, some religious communities held slaves in
far-flung parts of the colony: both the Séminaire de Québec and
the Jesuits had slaves in their Kaskaskia missions, and the Ursulines
had slaves in New Orleans. Within present-day Quebec, the clergy
and religious communities had a combined total of at least forty
slaves. We should recall than in 1720, religious communities joined
the rest of the population in petitioning Intendant Bégon to allow
them to import hundreds of blacks. Such practices were considered

normal. Slavery was a socially accepted practice, and there seemed to be nothing untoward about owning slaves at the time.

Major slave owners were few and far between, and by "major" we mean people holding at least a dozen slaves: we know of only twenty-nine owners in this category. When these major owners are grouped into families, we find the Campeau family (most of whom were closely related) leading with fifty-seven slaves, with the Lacorne and Lemoyne de Longueuil families ranking second. The Campeau family were only small-scale fur traders, people of modest means, whose extravagant taste for slave ownership actually surpassed that of the wealthiest seigneurs.

No code in this society set out the relations of masters with their slaves, nor even the general condition of slaves. However, slave owners complied strictly with the *Code Noir*, even going beyond it at times, and in so doing they gave something of a family character to slavery, sometimes considering the slave as an adopted child.

We should not forget however that the slave was a form of personal property: newspapers advertised slaves as commodities (over a thirty-year period, we found 137 slave ads in newspapers), sometimes offering them for sale alongside livestock; slaves were listed in inventories of property along with animals, and were sometimes exchanged for horses, even when the slave had been baptized. There does not seem to have been any public market specially designated for slave sales, although we know for certain that some slaves were sold at auction or on the market square. It was rare for batches of slaves to be sold together, and the largest batch was only five slaves.

Slaves were bought and sold under the same conditions as any other merchandise – they were carefully examined; young, and even very young slaves were preferred; slaves were bought at twenty and even fifteen years of age, and often much younger than that; slaves had to be trained, and brought to identify with the slave-owning family before adulthood, when the temptation to run away (especially for Amerindian slaves) grew stronger.

The slave was an expensive item because he was not really essential in economic terms. The average "savage" slave cost 400 livres while the average black slave cost 900 livres, but then there was a ready supply of Amerindian slaves whereas black slaves were harder to get and bring into the colony by sea. Some prospective slave owners were prepared to buy slaves on credit, even going so far as to mortgage their property in order to acquire this luxury item.

No law compelled owners to baptize their slaves and they were in no hurry to do so: some owners waited several years, sometimes (although rarely) letting the slave reach an advanced age before being baptized on their deathbed. Under French rule, baptisms could be important social events, drawing the most prominent citizens: when the ten-year-old black slave Pierre-Louis Scipion was baptized in 1717, thirteen people signed the baptismal registry. Sponsors at slave baptisms included Governor Beauharnois, Intendants Dupuy and Hocquart, other senior officials and members of the clergy. The owner often reserved the honour of serving as godfather to his own slave, although this practice was only found in French and Catholic society.

Even when they were baptized, many slaves were entered in the baptismal registry without either first name or surname. For this reason, 25.3% of Amerindians and 17.3% black slaves appearing in historical records remain anonymous. The first name was recorded for 68.6% of Amerindian slaves, and 50.2% for black slaves. When slaves acquired a first name, they were often given the same name as their sponsor or master. Some slaves acquired celebrated names such as the slave Versailles owned by Vergor in 1749, or Louis Quatorze who was buried at Saint-Vallier in 1773.

Finally, slaves were allowed to marry if they first obtained the consent of their master. The marriage ceremony followed the usual ritual, with masters, family members or friends – and even sometimes slaves themselves – serving as witnesses. Even when married, slaves continued living in bondage unless their master formally emancipated them; the legitimate children of slaves remaining in bondage belonged in full ownership to the mother's master. We tracked seventy-three marriages between slaves in historical records.

Slaves were generally illiterate and only one Amerindian slave could sign his name: the Fox Michel-Louis, also called Michel

Ouysconsin, who had belonged to one Lanouillier. Eight black slaves were able to sign their name, including Pierre-Dominique Lafleur, a black slave belonging to Philibert du Chien d'Or. When he married a Canadian in 1749, he signed the registry of civil status, although his wife was not competent to do so.

Amerindians do not seem to have practised trades, apart from the English-speaking Amerindians that Madame Legardeur de Repentigny had purchased for her Montreal factory; they generally served as domestic servants; a handful of them (just eight) had gained enough of their master's trust to be sent into the *pays d'en haut* to trade in furs. Most blacks had a trade, the most popular ones being cooks and hairdressers.

Although slaves were not protected by any code, they nevertheless enjoyed some of the same privileges as people of a free condition: they could serve as witnesses in religious ceremonies (baptism, marriage, burial) and their names could be entered as witnesses in civil registries. A slave was even a plaintiff in a case against a free person: in 1727 the Panis Catherine, slave of Lachauvignerie, brought a lawsuit against Benoist the surgeon, and won. Slaves fought for their freedom in the courts, where judges allowed them to use any legal means at the disposal of ordinary citizens. This was the case when the Panis Marie-Marguerite Duplessis *dite* Radisson took Chevalier Dormicourt to court to avoid being exported to the Caribbean. In criminal cases a slave was treated the same way as a citizen. The slave easily obtained permission to appear before a judge and then to appeal before the Conseil supérieur, while under British rule the slave enjoyed *Habeas Corpus* and could request a trial by jury. Such privileges meant the slave here had far greater rights than slaves in other colonies.

Moreover, slaves were not punished any more severely than free persons, as we established in studying documents relating to eighteen slaves punished for crimes. Slaves and free persons were led to the gallows for petty thievery, burglary occurring at night, violence, arson and murder. Some slaves faced less severe punishment, for example when they were deported, while a Canadian found guilty of the same crimes would be hanged: this can no doubt be explained by the fact that rebellious slaves were not as dangerous here as they would have been in the Caribbean. The crimes committed by slaves here were rare and isolated acts, bearing no resemblance whatever to some class revolt against slave-owning society.

Another privilege of the slave was acquiring a family name: it was common practice under French rule for the slave to bear the same name as his master, and if the slave had already been given the master's first name, then both slave and master had identical names, which can be confusing for genealogists today. We counted 158 Amerindian slaves or 5.9% of the total with a Québécois family name, whereas 32.5% of black slaves had their master's name. This suggests that slavery here had a more humane and family character.

When the slaves became ill thy were generally sent to the hospital. Between 1690 and 1800, at least 525 slaves were hospitalized, and we would definitely have found more if the records of the Hôtel-Dieu de Montréal had been preserved – Montreal had the largest slave population in all of Quebec. It sometimes happened that once a slave became "worn out," the owner's family placed him at the Hôpital-Général where he remained comfortably until the end of his days.

It is astonishing to discover how young slaves were when they died – on average 19.3 years of age. In other words, slaves generally did not reach twenty. Amerindian slaves, on average, died younger (17.7 years), though black slaves lived longer (dying on average at 25.2 years). On the other hand, blacks had a higher rate of infant mortality: while 25% of Amerindian infants died in their first year, 29.1% of black infants died over the same period. Under these conditions, few slaves reached an advanced age. No male Amerindian slave reached 70 years. Only twenty-three slaves lived to their eightieth year, and only two blacks to their ninetieth. Finally, only two slaves, both women, lived to their hundredth year: the Panis Marie-Joseph, former slave of Ruette d'Auteuil, was placed at the Hôpital-Général de Montréal, and died there in 1799, aged 100 years, while the black Mary Young died in Montreal in 1813 at the age of 106 years!

Slaves were buried roughly along the same lines as in free society. Some were buried on the day of death, although most were buried the following day, as in free society; the burial act was written in exactly the same ritual terms, before witnesses, who were sometimes slave owners (none of them English-speaking, however), other slaves or simply the beadle, a parish officer. In most cases slaves were buried in the paupers' cemetery, but one female slave was buried in a church next to her mistress.

As in other colonies the slave could obtain his freedom if his master were willing to emancipate him. Until 1709, it appears from Intendant Raudot's ordinance that several slaves had been emancipated on the basis of a simple verbal declaration; from 1709 on the only way for a slave to be emancipated was in a notarized act. We found very few of these acts, although documents often identified freedmen or free Panis (which amounted to the same). Once freed, the slave was left to his own devices; freed Amerindians only seem to have known the trade of canoeing, but freed blacks had knowledge of more trades and were better prepared than Amerindians to enjoy their freedom.

The presence in our society of nearly 4200 slaves naturally led to "métissage" or interbreeding, resulting in children of mixed race. These slaves lived in family settings, Canadian men had a penchant for "savage" women, and most slaves were actually Amerindian women.

Many love affairs resulted, as well as children born out of wedlock. Of 573 children of slaves 59.5% were born out of wedlock. Amerindian women were the most likely slaves to have illegitimate children: indeed, we calculated that 75.9% or three-fourths of children born to such Amerindian woman were illegitimate, whereas the proportion of illegitimate children born to black slaves was 32.1% (which was still high). Who were the fathers? Historical records do not provide much information about this: the father was generally given as "unknown," only nineteen fathers being identified by name. Whoever the father may have been, these illegitimate children were born into bondage and belonged to the mother's master.

White masters sometimes married their slaves. This should not be considered particularly surprising, since Colbert and Talon had hoped the French and Amerindians "would form only one people and one blood." The first such marriage took place in 1705. We tracked forty-five marriages between masters and slaves, thirty-four of them between whites and Amerindians, and eleven more between whites and blacks. There were almost as many white men marrying Amerindian women as Amerindian men marrying white women. Strangely enough, no white masters married black women, although some white women married black men.

A total of 103 children were born of these hybrid unions: eighty-four Métis and nineteen mulattos. Many of these children married in turn, and left descendants of their own. Was Benjamin Sulte right in thinking that the mixture of slave and French blood amounted to a single drop of Missouri water falling into the St. Lawrence? But Sulte did not base this remark on statistics. The statistics provided in our own work should only be considered as a starting point for research; historical records would have to be examined carefully, to identify the descendants these slaves may have left among us, if we were ever to attempt to determine the extent of slave ancestry among ethnic French Canadians alive today.

Nor is it that straight-forward to determine exactly when slavery ended in our society. In 1787, owners began to express initial concerns about their rights as slave owners. Starting in 1790, newspapers campaigned against slavery, although this campaign was only occasional, and consisted mainly in reprinting news and literary pieces drawn from foreign newspapers: at no time was the system of slavery in Lower Canada attacked head-on. Then on January 28, 1793, Pierre-Louis Panet submitted a first bill for the abolition of slavery to the House of Assembly of Lower Canada. Panet's bill died on the order paper, perhaps because twelve of the House of Assembly's fifty members were slave owners themselves. In neighbouring colonies, however, concrete steps were being taken against slavery: Nova Scotia sent a first shipment of black slaves to Africa, and in the spring of 1793, Upper Canada passed a law prohibiting the introduction of new slaves into the province, although slaves already there would remain in that condition, and their children would gain their freedom on reaching the age of twenty-five. It followed that any slave moving to Upper Canada automatically became free, and from 1793 on, the province became a haven of liberty for slaves fleeing neighbouring colonies.

In Lower Canada slave ownership continued, although owners were increasingly concerned about the situation. In 1794, a Montreal judge refused to recognize the condition of slavery, and freed a slave whose only crime was to have run away. In 1798, Chief Justice William Osgoode, based in Montreal, refused in principle to convict a slave charged as a runaway, ruling that in future he would free every slave brought before his court. As a result, slaves began deserting their masters with all impunity. Masters had one last recourse – Parliament. In April 1799, Montreal slave owners working through Joseph Papineau, a member of the Lower Canada House of Assembly, asked the House to rule on the status of slaves, although the House paid scant regard to this initial request. In April 1800, slave owners renewed their request, and this time the House of Assembly set to work drafting a bill, which died on the order paper after two readings.

Slave owners continued to feel alarmed. The courts of Lower Canada no longer recognized the condition of slavery, Upper Canada had become a haven for runaways, and in 1800 Nova Scotia transported a second shipment of slaves back to Africa (since 1755, deportation had become truly fashionable in this province!). During the January 1801 session, James Cuthbert introduced a bill on slavery, which went through two readings, but the House of Assembly let the matter drop. In March 1803, James Cuthbert tried once again to get fellow members to rule on the status of slaves, but his bill died on the order paper after two readings, and the matter of slavery would never again be raised in the House of Assembly.

At the same time, the practice of slavery was gradually dying out. The last slave sale in Lower Canada was contracted on May 13, 1797; the last newspaper advertisement for a slave sale appeared on January 29, 1798; the word "slave" appeared for the last time in civil registries on November 18, 1798. In the years to follow, only a very few slaves appeared in historical records: the last slave we were able to document was the Panis, Marie-Marguerite, donated by André

Grasset de Saint-Sauveur to the Hôpital-Général de Montréal in 1764, who belonged to the same hospital in 1772, dying there on April 6, 1821 at the age of seventy-eight, although it is impossible to say whether she was still a slave at death or had been freed by then. By 1833, when Britain abolished slavery in the colonies (the law took effect in 1834), there were no longer any Amerindian slaves in Lower Canada, although a handful of black slaves may have benefitted from this imperial legislation. In Lower Canada, slavery disappeared as mysteriously as it had begun.

Even more surprising than this silent withering-away of slavery is the fact that it has left so few traces in the collective memory and literature of Quebec. In the 1863 romance *Les Anciens Canadiens* (*Canadians of Old*), Philippe Aubert de Gaspé gave a minor role to a mulatto woman his grandfather Ignace-Philippe Aubert de Gaspé had bought around 1787[205]; the same writer wrote *Femme de la tribu des Renards* (Woman of the Foxes) providing biographical details about Marie-Geneviève, a Fox slave held by the Couillart family of Saint-Thomas-de-Montmagny.[206] Around 1881, when Father Raymond Casgrain waxed poetic about his own supposed descent from Crusader ancestors, Adolphe-Basile Routhier playfully tore this claim to shreds, establishing somewhat mischievously that the earliest Casgrain to reach Canada had first of all married the daughter of a Panis.[207] In 1891, Father Casgrain wrote of the mulatto Thérèse, former slave of the Duperron-Bâby family,[208] and in 1898, P.-B. Casgrain devoted a few lines to two other slaves held by this same family: the mulatto Rosalie or Rose Lontin and the Panis Catherine.[209] These scattered references are the only ones to appear in nineteenth-century literature.

And yet, French Canadian writers regularly exploited the grand themes of Canadian history! Prominent literary figures such as Octave Crémazie, Louis-Honoré Fréchette and Pamphile Le May were forever writing about heroes in the epic mode, although they never mentioned a single episode or victim of slavery here. Our novelists based their work, above all, in historical personalities and events, but they never noticed the presence of slaves. At a time when novelists relished in historical re-enactments, none, apart from Aubert de Gaspé, ever bothered to mention slaves. The strangest case was surely that of William Kirby, author in 1877 of *The Golden Dog*. The work contains meticulous descriptions of the final years of French rule; the main character is Philibert, a bourgeois and master of at least five slaves, one of whose black slaves married a Canadian woman. Other characters in this work own slaves; but when Kirby describes family life and mentions domestic servants several times, no slaves make an appearance. Nineteenth-century Canadian literature simply omitted the theme of slavery.

Another trace of slavery turned up in the autobiographical account of an Oblate Father, Damase Dandurand, who died in 1921 aged 102. Born in Laprairie, where he spent his early childhood, Dandurand remembered going to Montreal as a child with his mother. There they met a black slave who was being offered for sale, in the last years of slavery. According to Father Dandurand, the slave pleaded to be bought.[210] By the time the Oblate wrote up this experience, were his memories accurate, or did he combine the facts with details he had gleaned somewhere else? Whatever the case, this seems to have been an authentic eye-witness account of an institution quickly forgotten.

The next mention of slavery we found was in 1951. In *Testament de mon enfance* (*Testament of My Childhood*), Robert de Roquebrune dwelled at length on the memory of a black man, Sambo, who long before the author's birth "had turned up one evening at Christmas-time, like one of the Wise Men of the East who had lost his way in the snow." Sambo had been a slave in Virginia before the Civil War, and was taken in at the manor of Saint-Ours in L'Assomption,[211] and as such was neither a survivor of Canada's own slave population, nor a vestige of this slavery in our own literature. The next time slavery featured in a Canadian literary work was not until 1999, with the publication of Micheline Bail's historical novel *L'Esclave* (*The Slave*), which rigorously reconstructed the life of a female slave of the eighteenth century.

So much for literature. Has language in Quebec retained some trace of an institution that existed here for two centuries? By 1881,

Adolphe-Basile Routhier preferred the English spelling "Pawnee" to the French spelling "Panis" – even though this latter spelling had regularly turned up in the civil registry and countless historical documents, in both languages. Although the last Panis slaves disappeared from the historical record in the early nineteenth century, we find it astonishing that just fifty years later, a leading judge and author (who penned the words to *O Canada*) was no longer capable of spelling the term properly. Indeed, each time we have spoken about Panis, we have been met with a dazed look and the question "But what's a Panis?"

According to an old Quebec folk tradition, whenever children asked where babies came from, the answer was: "Well, 'savages' passed by, and left a baby behind"; according to another version, babies turned up in cabbage patches... Why all this discretion about "savages" in Quebec? It could have resulted from the proximity of aboriginals; but if we recall how many times fur traders of the eighteenth century returned from the *pays d'en haut* with very young Panis obtained from "savages," it is conceivable that the folk tradition of Amerindians leaving a baby in a cradle actually goes back to the era of slavery.

How can slavery in Canada have been virtually forgotten? Historians are surely to blame, whether because they did not examine slavery or because they failed even to notice it. Despite the fact that the historian François-Xavier Garneau was born in 1809, when slavery still existed in Lower Canada, he completed misinformed his readers about slavery:

> We feel it is our duty to cite a decision here, which greatly honours the French government, the decision consisting namely in prohibiting the entry of slaves into Canada, a colony which Louis XIV preferred to any other because of the warlike character of its inhabitants; a colony which he seems to have wanted to model on the image of France, to infuse with courageous nobility, and to colonize with a truly national, Catholic and French population without any admixture of races. In 1688, it had been proposed that Blacks be resorted

to, for the purposes of agriculture. The ministry replied that it feared these Blacks could perish in experiencing the change in climate, and that the project was therefore not worth pursuing. This decision effectively prevented the introduction of a great and terrible plague into our society. It is true the Code Noir conceived for the Caribbean was extended to Louisiana; it is true that there were ordinances about slavery; nonetheless, slavery was not prevalent in Canada; there were scarcely a handful of slaves by the time of the Conquest. Indeed, their number increased as a result of the Conquest, after which they completely disappeared.

Garneau dug himself even deeper into a hole by claiming that "the government and Canadian clergy should be honoured for consistently opposing the introduction of Blacks into Canada."[212]

What an extraordinary distortion of historical truth! Jacques Viger and Louis-Hippolyte LaFontaine would rightly blame Garneau for removing from his *History* "the most important aspect of this problem: that the king authorized the purchase of slaves."[213] In fact, at the urging of Ruette d'Auteuil and Intendant Bégon, the King of France explicitly authorized Canadians to buy black slaves. He approved ordinances on slavery issued by his intendants, and the mixing of races was strongly recommended by Colbert and Talon. Contrary to Garneau's claims, slave ownership was just as prevalent under the French regime as it would later be under the British regime; and while Garneau claimed the clergy had consistently opposed slavery, the Catholic Church of Canada actually never took a position on slavery; in fact, we have established that senior ecclesiastics, bishops, priests, religious and members of religious communities all owned slaves. Finally, Garneau left out all mention of "savage" slaves, who actually far outnumbered black slaves. Coming from a historian who had such a profound impact, this erroneous description of slavery could only have one result – helping society forget the institution had ever existed here.

Jacques Viger and Louis-Hippolyte LaFontaine refuted Garneau in 1859 when they published a work on the legal foundations of slavery in French Canada. Their pioneering work was not followed up for two decades, however.

In the last quarter of the nineteenth century, Cyprien Tanguay brought out his multi-volume *Dictionnaire généalogique des familles canadiennes*, which included approximately 200 Amerindian and black slaves under the French regime.[214] The question only came up again in 1906 when Colonel Hubert Neilson (whose grandfather, the printer John Neilson, had owned slaves) devoted twenty pages to slavery and accused Canadian historians of studiously ignoring the subject.[215] Historians gradually began to mention slavery more often: in 1911 Benjamin Sulte wrote the first really interesting study, although it was only fifteen pages long and had no statistics.[216] In 1913 Mgr. L.-A. Pâquet lamented that "the stain of slavery" had been legally sanctioned in Canada,[217] and two years later, O.-M. H.-Lapalice pieced together an incomplete inventory of blacks living in Montreal under French rule.[218] Seven years later Pierre-Georges Roy published a series of sales contracts, showing once again that slave trading had been well-established here.[219] Nothing new on the subject was published for another quarter century. Then, in 1949 and 1956, Robert-Lionel Séguin focused renewed attention on the problem of slavery, although limiting himself to the area around Vaudreuil-Soulanges.[220] Finally, in 1960, we published a 400-page work, *Histoire de l'esclavage au Canada français*, following it up with a comprehensive study of all slaves and masters in our 1990 *Dictionnaire des esclaves et de leurs propriétaires au Canada français*, a second edition of which appeared in 1994. We have also given lectures and speeches in various parts of Quebec about the practice of slavery here.

And yet, at the beginning of the twenty-first century, the phenomenon of Quebec slavery seems still relatively unknown. Who knows, for example, of the old slave cemetery in Saint-Armand, near the Vermont border? It seems that in 1794 the Lukes, a Loyalist family fleeing the American Revolution, settled in this village with their slaves, who worked at clearing the land and making potash. These slaves were buried near a place now called Nigger Rock.

Although we have put a lot of energy into establishing rigorous historical facts about slavery, we are still met with surprise and especially disbelief: "What! Do you mean slavery actually existed in Quebec?" The version of Quebec history we have long been told was all about missionaries and spiritualists, whereas in point of fact, our colonial past can be likened to the Thirteen Colonies of America. And as for our supposed "ethnic purity" … it has actually been "corrupted" by Amerindian and Afro-American blood! As the *Bible* says: "The fathers have eaten sour grapes, and the children's teeth are set on edge."

End Notes

INTRODUCTION

[1] In this work, we use the term "savage" in reference to native Amerindians, when quoting from, or paraphrasing, historical documents of the period in question, since this term was frequently used at the time. Likewise, during the slave era, the word "Negro" meant a black slave working in the colony. The Negro was considered to be a form of merchandise or personal property. Over time, the word "Negro" took on a pejorative meaning. In this work, we will use the terms "black, black man, black woman, black person," etc. rather than "Negro," except in historical quotations and contexts where individuals are clearly identified as objects for sale.

[2] *Relations des Jésuites*, Thwaites edition (hereafter referred to as *RJ*), V, pp. 62and 196; doc. August 20, 1638 in the Archives du Séminaire de Québec (hereafter referred to as ASQ), *Documents Faribault*, p. 17; burial act, May 10, 1654, registry at Notre-Dame-de-Québec.

[3] Letter in *RJ*, II, p. 43.

[4] Lafitau, *Moeurs des sauvages américains* (1724 edition), IV, pp. 1-33; Lahontan, *Voyages*, I, p. 148.

[5] To the Jesuit Bonin, October 2, 1735 contained in the *Rapport de l'archiviste de la province de Québec* (hereafter referred to as *RAPQ*) for 1926-1927, p. 285.

[6] Bossu, *Nouveaux voyages aux Indes occidentales* (1768 edition), I, pp. 136-140.

[7] Readers should consult Benjamin Sulte's erroneous interprestion in *Histoire des Canadiens-Français*, I, p. 66; and our own interpretation in *Histoire de la Nouvelle-France*, II, p. 480.

[8] Sagard, *Histoire du Canada* (1866 edition), IV, pp. 829 et seq.; *The Works of Samuel de Champlain* (Champlain Society edition), V, p. 428; VI, pp. 51 et seq.

[9] Dollier de Casson, *A History of Montreal* (bilingual edition), pp. 353 and 355.

[10] Dollier de Casson, *op. cit.*, p. 339.

[11] Jolliet to Mgr. de Laval, October 10, 1674, in Delanglez, *Louis Jolliet*, p. 403; also p. 194.

¹²Buade de Frontenac to Colbert, November 14, 1674, *RAPQ*, 1926-1927, p. 77.

¹³Memorandum by Dulhut for the minister, in Margry, *Origines françaises des pays d'outre-mer*, VI, p. 21.

¹⁴Archives des Ursulines de Québec, *Livre des entrées et sorties des filles françaises et séminaristes*, for the years 1679 and 1680.

¹⁵Strictly speaking, the term "Panis" refers to an Amerindian nation in the Missouri region, the "Pawnees"; but because they formed such a large proportion of the slave population, the name "Panis" came to refer to any Amerindian in a state of bondage. Any Panis was thus naturally considered a slave: every Panis referred to in this work was either already a slave or became a slave on reaching Quebec.

¹⁶Details found in the civil registry.

¹⁷Archives de l'Hôtel-Dieu de Québec (hereafter referred to as AHDQ), patient and burial registries.

¹⁸This information was gleaned in the civil registry as well as patient and burial registries at the Hôtel-Dieu de Québec.

¹⁹Lahontan, *Voyages*, I, pp. 152, 170, 186, 295 et seq. (letters of May 26 and September 18, 1688 and of September 28, 1689).

²⁰*Ibid.*, I, pp. 216, 225, 228, 233, 235, 248-250.

CHAPTER ONE

²¹*Édit du Roi Touchant la Police des Isles de l'Amérique Françoise*, in the *Code Noir ou Recueil des Règlements* (1767 edition), pp. 20 et seq. We will deal more fully with the various dispositions of the *Code Noir* later in this work.

²²Excerpts from letters of August 10, October 31 and November 6, 1688. Excerpts prepared for the government, in *Documents Relating to the Colonial History of New York. Paris Documents*, IX, p. 398.

²³Memorandum to Denonville and Champigny, May 1, 1689, in Archives nationales du Québec (hereafter ANQ), *Ordres du roi*, series B, vol. 15, pp. 108 et seq.

²⁴Instructions to Buade de Frontenac, June 7, 1689, in *RAPQ*, 1927-1928, p. 11.

²⁵Register of Notre-Dame-de-Montréal, May 24, 1692. The black Louis was confirmed in 1693, and seems to have been of a free condition in 1696, because on August 13 that year he willingly hired himself out to Jean Cailhout *dit* Baron for three years of salaried farm labour (Adhémar registry). He was then called Louis Marié.

[26]Letter of May 31, 1701, in ANQ, *Ordres du roi*, Series B, vol. 22, II, pp. 74 et seq.

[27]For more information about this black person, see our *Dictionnaire des esclaves et de leurs propriétaires*.

[28]AHDQ, patient registry, for the years 1704 and 1706; his age was variously given as nineteen and twenty-three.

[29]A black from New England who featured on a list Vaudreuil gave to Dudley, in Coleman, *New England Captives Carried to Canada*, I, p. 92.

[30]Ordinance of April 13, 1709, in *Édits, ordonnances royaux*, II, pp. 271 et seq. We will deal more fully with this ordinance in the next chapter.

[31]Lemoyne de Bienville, July 28, 1706 and October 12, 1708, in *Rapport sur les archives du Canada* (hereafter *RAC*), for 1905, I, pages 6 and 525.

[32]*Édits, Ordonnances royaux*, I, p. 330.

[33]Memorandum to the minister, October 14, 1716, in *Documents relatifs à la Nouvelle-France*, III, pp. 21 et seq.

[34]The king to Vaudreuil and Bégon, June 26, 1717, in ANQ, *Ordres du roi*, Series B, vol. 39, p. 701.

[35]The Conseil de la Marine to Bégon, June 1, 1720, in APC, C11A, 43, p. 11.

[36]Bégon to the Conseil de la Marine, October 26, 1720, letter summarized in *Délibérations du Conseil de la Marine*, January and June 1721, APC, C11A, 43, pp. 11 et seq. and 41

[37]Memorandum drafted by Bégon in *Délibérations du Conseil de la Marine*, January 13, 1721, APC, C11A, 43, pp. 11-19.

[38]The Conseil de la Marine to Bégon, June 14, 1721, APC, B, 44, II, pp. 347 et seq.

CHAPTER TWO

[39]*Édit du Roi Touchant la Police des Isles de l'Amérique Françoise*, March 1685, in *Le Code Noir ou Recueil des Réglemens* (1767 edition), pp. 29 et seq.

[40]In *Collection des documents relatifs à l'histoire de la Nouvelle-France*, I, p. 377.

[41]*Catéchisme du diocèse de Québec* (1702 edition), p. 298.

[42]Saint-Vallier, *Rituel du diocèse de Québec* (1703 edition), p. 326.

[43]Ordinance of April 13, 1709, in *Édits, ordonnances royaux*, II, pp. 271 et seq.

[44]Ordinance cited above.

[45]*Journal of the House of Assembly of Lower Canada*, p. 122.

[46]Notarized deed of sale in the Adhémar registry, held by the Archives judiciaires de Montréal. Neither the name nor the age of the Panis is indicated, but we believe it must have been Pascal, who was baptized in Montreal on May 10, 1704, and whose master was You d'Youville de Ladécouverte.

[47]Royal ordinance of May 23, 1733, in ANQ, *Ordonnances des intendants*, 21, pp. 77-82.

[48]The King to Governor Beauharnois and Intendant Hocquart, April 20, 1734, ANQ, *Ordres du roi*, 1-2-3, Series B, vol. 61, p. 69.

[49]The King to Governor Beauharnois and Intendant Hocquart, April 11, 1735 and May 15, 1736, *ibid.*, vol. 63, p. 64.

[50]Document of October 25, 1720, in Margry, *Origines françaises des pays d'outre-mer*, VI, p. 316.

[51]Quoted by Governor Beauharnois in a letter to Maurepas, September 24, 1742, *Journals and Letters of Pierre Gaultier de La Vérendrye and His Sons*, p. 371.

[52]Colbert to Intendant Talon, April 5, 1667, in *RAPQ*, 1930-1931, p. 72.

[53]Ordinance in *Édits, ordonnances royaux*, II, p. 371.

[54]Ordinance of March 23, 1710 in ANQ, *Ordonnances des intendants*, vol. IV, 34r.-35r.

[55]For more information about this trial, see our *Dictionnaire des esclaves et de leurs propriétaires*, and in particular the article on the Panis Marie-Marguerite in the chapter on Quebec.

[56]Severance, *An Old Frontier of France*, I, pp. 288-290; Gosselin, *L'Église du Canada*, II, pp. 158 et seq.

[57]The King to Beauharnois and Hocquart, April 27, 1734; the same to Champigny and d'Orgeville, May 6, 1734; Beauharnois and Hocquart to the King, December 21, 1734, in ANQ, *Ordres du roi*, Series B, vol. 60, pp. 124, 279, 271 et seq.

[58]*Documents Relating to the Colonal History of New York*, vol. X, pp. 131 and 138.

[59]Archives judiciaires du Québec, *Collection de pièces judiciaires et notariales*, file 1230. We will provide more details on this subject in the next chapter.

[60]Letter to the president of the Conseil de la Marine, May 4, 1749, in *RAC* for 1905, I, pp. 6 and 116. This letter summarized La Galissonnière's request of 1747.

[61]Edict of October 1716, article 5, 7, 14, 15 in the previously mentioned *Code Noir*, pp. 169-181.

[62]*Ibid.*, p. 436.

[63]Documents of March 31 and April 5, 1762, *ibid.*, pp. 427-444.

[64]Letter of the president of the Conseil de la marine, March 19, 1721, in *BRH*, 41,1935, p. 128; Charlevoix, *Histoire* (1744 edition), I, pp. 26-28; *Aventures du Sr LeBeau* (1738 edition), pp. 172 et seq.; *Histoire de la paroisse de Champlain*, II, pp. 120 et seq.; ANQ, *Registre du Conseil supérieur*, 4, pp. 169-170; document of 1762, in *RAC* for 1911, p. 867.

[65]*Déclaration du roi*, December 15, 1721, ASQ, *Polygraphie*, IV: 82; *Édits, ordonnances royaux*, I: pp. 438-441.

[66]Registry of Notre-Dame-de-Québec; Sulte, "L'esclavage au Canada," in the *Revue canadienne*, 61, 1911, p. 324.

[67]La Jonquière to the minister, July 16, 1750, in *BRH*, 2, 1896.

[68]*Documents relatifs à l'histoire constitutionnelle du Canada*, 1759-1791, I, p. 19.

CHAPTER THREE

[69]*Journals and Letters of Pierre Gaultier de Lavérendrye and His Sons* (Burpee edition), pp. 451 et seq.

[70]*Ibid.*, pp. 451 et seq.

[71]Some of Bougainville's memoir has appeared in English, on p. 83 of *Statues, Documents and Papers bearing on the Discussion respecting the Northern and Western Boundaries of the Province of Ontario*, Toronto, 1878.

[72]On the Panis, see J.R. Swanton, *The Amerindian Tribes of North America*, pp. 289 et seq.

[73]Letter from Charlevoix, written December 1722 on the Arkansas, in his "Journal", vol. VI of his *Histoire*, p. 163.

[74]*Journals and Letters of Pierre Gaultier de Lavérendrye and His Sons*, p. 381.

[75]Louis XIV to Denonville, March 8, 1688; the Minister to the Intenant of Galleys, 1688; letter of 1689 from Monseignat in *Documents relatifs à l'histoire de la Nouvelle-France*, vol. I, pp. 418, 426 and 485.

[76]Bougainville's *Memoir* of 1757, cited above, p. 52; Franquet, *Voyages et memoires sur le Canada*, pp. 23 et seq.

[77]Franquet, *op. cit.*, p. 181.

[78]Civil registry; Coleman, *Captives Carried to Canada*, vol. I, p. 92; *Revue canadienne*, vol. 61, 1911, p. 324.

[79]*Documents relatifs à l'histoire de la Nouvelle-France*, III, p. 219.

[80]*Documents Relating to the Colonial History of the State of New York*, X, pp. 131, 138.

[81]*Documents Relating to the Colonial History of the State of New York*, X, p. 172; Coleman, *op. cit.*, II, pp. 294-296; AHDQ, registre des malades, 1750-1751; register d'état civil de Notre-Dame de Québec.

[82]Registre de Notre-Dame de Québec, 1722, 1729; AHDQ, registre des maladies, 1731, 1737, 1745; archives du Séminaire de Montréal, acte de Panet, 1761.

CHAPTER FOUR

[83]Adhémar registry, June 15 and October 19, 1709; LeMoine, *Picturesque Quebec*, pp. 505 et seq.,; Lukin registry, September 13, 1796.

[84]Raudot Ordinance in *Édits, ordonnances royaux*, II, pp. 271 et seq.; article 44 in the 1685 edition and article 40 in the 1724 edition of *Le Code Noir ou Recueil des Règlements* (1767 edition), pp. 49 and 304 et seq.

[85]Inventory of April 1731, in Ferland-Angers, *Mère d'Youville*, pp. 286 et seq.

[86]*Quebec Gazette*, November 6, 13, 20 and 27, December 4, 1783.

[87]Faribault registry, November 18, 1784.

[88]*Édits, ordonnances royaux*, I, 10; ANQ, *Ordonnances des intendants*, 21, pp. 77-82; *Ordres du roi*, 1-2-3, Series B, 61, 69

[89]Registry of Sainte-Anne-de-Détroit, April 1739.

[90]ANQ, *Chambre des Milices de Montréal [Militia Court of Montreal]*, 1760-1764, IV, pp. 35 et seq.; city register, October 1759.

[91]*The John Askin Papers*, I, pp. 284 et seq.

[92]Statement by the priest in the civil registry of Sainte-Anne-de-Détroit, October 15, 1769.

[93]Letter of June 17, 1778 from Askin to Patterson, in the *John Askin Papers*, I, p. 135.

[94]Letters to and from William Dunlap, 1766 and 1768, ANC, *Neilson Collection*.

[95]In *BRH*, 3 (1897), p. 6.

[96]*RAPQ*, 1921-1922, p. 120.

[97]*Quebec Gazette*, October 3, 1782 and May 14, 1784.

[98]*Quebec Herald*, April 14 and 25.

[99]On the endless antics of this slave, see the article on "Joe" in our *Dictionnaire des esclaves*.

[100]This story was told me my Émilien Lamirande, in a letter of June 17, 1993 from Rock Forest. Widow of a notary, this mother of Father Dandurand married another notary: she lived in Laprairie, later moving to Saint-Jean-sur-Richelieu.

[101]Deed of sale in *RAPQ*, 1921-1922, p. 113.

[102]See the article on "Toby" in our *Dictionnaire des esclaves*, p. 120.

[103]F.-J.Audet, *Les Députés de Montréal, 1792-1867*, p. 136.

[104]Ducasse, *Les Négriers ou le traffic des esclaves*, p. 106.

[105]Deeds of sale in *RAPQ*, 1921-1922, pp. 111 et seq., and in the Archives du Séminaire des Trois-Rivières.

[106]See articles on "Nègre," 1775; "Andrew, mulâtre"; "Bruce, nègre"; and "Ismaël, nègre" in our *Dictionnaire des esclaves*.

[107]Deeds of sale in *RAPQ*, 1921-1922, pp. 112, 116 et seq.; in *RAC*, 1905, I, lxix; in *BRH*, 24, 1918, p. 345.

[108]Adhémar registry, June 15, 1799; *RAPQ*, 1921-1922, pp. 119 et seq.; Fairbault (March 29, 1787) and J.A. Gray (August 25, 1797) registries.

[109]Ferland-Angers, *Mère d'Youville*, 203. The outcome of this trial is not recorded. ANQ, Registre de Cour militaire, IV, 118v.

[110] Letter of John Askin, 1778, in The John Askin Papers, I, p. 119.

[111]Viger-LaFontaine, "De l'esclavage en Canada," in *Mémoires de la société historique de Montréal*, I, p. 43.

[112]*Documents Relating to the Colonial History of the State of New York*, X, p. 213.

[113] ANQ, *Chambre des Milices de Montréal [Militia Court of Montreal]*, 1760-1764, IV, 35v, 39v-40.

CHAPTER FIVE

[114]Deed of sale of November 5, 1763, in ASQ, *Missions*, 25, 40.

[115]Frégault, *Le Grand Marquis*, p. 130.

[116]Letter of May 9, 1750, in *RAC*, 1905, I, 6, p. 136.

[117]Letter to Bishop Pontbriand, in *RAPQ*, 1935-1936, p. 279.

CHAPTER SIX

[118]*Édit du Roi Touchant la Police des Isles de l'Amérique Françoise Du mois de Mars 1685*, in *Le Code Noir ou Recueil des Règlements*, (1767 edition), pp. 29-56.

[119]The *Code Noir* ou *Édit du Roi*, 1724, in *Le Code Noir ou Recueil des Règlements* (1767 edition), pp. 281-315.

[120]In *BRH*, 3, 1897, p. 6.

[121]*Quebec Gazette*, July 29, 1779, p. 3; Dollier de Casson, *Histoire de Montréal*, pp. 113 et seq.; *Mémoires de la Société généalogique canadienne-française*, vol. III, p. 225.

[122]APQ, *Pièces judiciaires et notariales*, p. 782.

[123]Adhémar, Lepallieur, Porlier, Danré de Blanzy and Simonet notarial registries.

[124]The canoeing positions were lead paddler, middle paddler and helmsman.

[125]P.-B. Casgrain, *Mémoiral des familles Casgrain, Bâby et Perrault du Canada*, p. 95.

[126]Contract of engagement, in *RAPQ*, 1931-1932, p. 273.

[127]APQ, *Pièces judiciaires et notariales*, p. 782.

[128]One English pound, Quebec currency, was equivalent to twenty shillings or four dollars of the time.

[129]The King to Denonville et Champigny, May 1, 1689, in APQ, *Ordres du Roi*, series B, vol. 15, 1688-1690, pp. 108 et seq.

[130]Henripin, *La Population canadienne au début du dix-huitième siécle*, p. 106.

[131]Registre de Notre-Dame-de-Montréal, December 14, 1791; *Gazette de Montréal* (published by Mesplet), supplement on December 15, 1791, p. 1.

[132]Between forty and forty-nine years: forty-six Amerindians (eight men and thirty-eight women); twenty-five blacks (thirteen men and twelve women). Between fifty and fifty-nine years: twenty-two Amerindians (six men and sixteen women); seventeen blacks (thirteen men and four women).

[133]See the article "Joe" in the *Dictionnaire des esclaves*.

[134]Letter of October 14, 1736 from Governor Beauharnois, in *Journals and Letters of Pierre Gaultier de La Vérendrye and His Sons* (Burpee edition), pp. 211 et seq.

[135]P.-B. Casgrain, "Madame C.-E. Casgrain" in Mémoires de famille, pp. 196 et seq.; P.-B. Casgrain, *Mémoiral des familles Casgrain, Bâby et Perrault du Canada*, p. 95.

[136]Aubert de Gaspé, *Canadians of Old*, translated by Jane Brierley, pp. 210-211.

[137]Aubert de Gaspé, *Yellow-Wolf & Other Tales of the Saint Lawrence*, translated by Jane Brierley, pp. 74-78.

CHAPTER SEVEN

[138]According to the 1685 *Code Noir* for the French West Indies and the 1724 *Code Noir* for Louisiana, only Catholics could own slaves, and these slaves had to be raised in the Catholic faith, but neither of these codes ever came into effect in Canada.

[139]Aubert de Gaspé, *Yellow-Wolf & Other Tales of the Saint Lawrence*, p. 49.

[140]APQ, *Collection de pièces judiciaires et notariales*, p. 502; *Plumitif du Conseil supérieur*, September 20, 1714 to March 9, 1716.

[141]Document of August 20, 1638, ASQ, *Documents Faribault*, p. 17.

[142]Severance, *An Old Frontier of France*, vol. I, pp. 288-280; Gosselin, *L'Église du Canada*, vol. II, pp. 158 et seq.

[143]Inventory of 1800, in *RAPQ*, pp. 195-513, 390.

[144]*Inventaire des jugements et délibérations du Conseil supérieur*, 1716 to 1760, vol. II, p. 211.

[145]*Gazette de Montréal* (published by Roy), March 14, 1796, p. 2.

[146]*Quebec Gazette*, supplement no. 1034, p. 2, news of June 16.

[147]*Ibid.*, March 26, 1795, p. 3; May 7, p. 2.

[148]APQ, *Registre criminel*, vol. IV, pp. 28v.-32v.

[149]*Inventaire des jugements et délibérations du Conseil supérieur*, vol. II, pp. 202 et seq.

[150]Trial evidence in Riddell, *Michigan Under British Rule*, pp. 347-355, 456 et seq.; see also *The John Askin Papers*, vol. I, pp. 410 et seq.

[151]*Quebec Gazette*, April 23, 1827, p. 2.

[152]*Ibid.*, supplement of May 22, 1794, p. 1; supplement of May 29, p. 2; June 5, p. 4.

[153]APQ, *Procédures judiciaires. Matières criminelles*, 1730-1751, vol. IV, pp. 213-216v., 221v.-223r., 229r., 233, 238r., 241.

[154]APQ, *Procédures judiciaires. Matières criminelles*, 1752-1759, vol. VI, pp. 337-397v.

[155]APQ, *Collection de pièces judiciaires et notariales*, file 447; *Procédures judiciaires. Matières criminelles*, 1706-1730, vol. III, pp. 191 et seq., 238-251.

[156]W. R. Riddell, *Michigan Under British Rule*, pp. 29-31.

[157]APQ, *Registre criminel*, vol. IV, pp. 24-26; *Procédures judiciaires. Matières criminelles*, vol. IV, sheet 237.

[158]Inventaire des ordonnances de l'intendant, II, p. 161; lettre to Beauharnois and Hocquart, April 19, 1735, in APQ, Ordres du Roi, 3-4, series B, v. 64 (1736), p. 542. In 1981, Paul Fehmiu Brown brought out an account of this incident, under the title *Ces Canadiens oubliés*, volume 1 (published by Aquarius); and Micheline Bail brought out a novel about it, *L'Esclave* (*The Slave*), published by Libre Expession in 1999.

[159]Charlevoix, *Histoire*, IV, pp. 294 et seq.

[160]*Journal of the House of Assembly of Lower Canada*, 1799, p. 126.

Chapter Nine

[161]File 1230 of the *Collection des pièces judiciaires et notariales,* held in the Archives judiciaires du Québec.

[162]Article 47 of the Capitulation of 1760, in *Documents constitutionnels, 1759-1791,* I, p. 19.

[163]Ordinance issued by Governor Gage, May 13, 1761, in *RPA,* 1918, pp. 121 et seq.

[164]Ordinance issued by Governor Burton and letter to the captains of militia, May 31, 1761, *ibid.,* pp. 239 et seq.

[165]APQ, *Chambre des Milices de Montréal,* 1760-1764, p. 77.

[166]Articles 31 and 32 of the edict of 1685 and Articles 25, 26 and 33 of the edict of 1724, in the *Code Noir* or *Recueil des Règlements* (1767 edition), pp. 44 et seq., 298 et seq., and 301.

[167]Sale of October 27, 1768 (with the petition of 1785), in the notarial registry of Jean-Claude Panet. In the petition, the black was referred to variously as Joseph Bominique and Joseph Dominique.

[168]*Édits, ordonnances royaux,* II, p. 371.

[169]J.G. Beek notarial registry.

[170]J.A. Gray notarial registry.

[171]Documents reproduced in *RAPQ,* 1921-1922, pp. 122 et seq.

[172]Racicot notarial registry.

[173]Will quoted in Audet and Fabre-Surveyer, *Les Députés au premier Parlement du Bas-Canada,* p. 168.

[174]Petition published in the *Journal of the House of Assembly of Lower Canada,* 1800, pp. 154.

Chapter Ten

[175]Journal, March 1712, Charlevoix, *Histoire,* V, p. 210.

[176]Letter from Montreal dated January 14, 1771, in the *Quebec Gazette,* January 24, 1771, p. 3.

[177]*Visite générale,* in *RAPQ,* 1948-1949, p. 140.

[178]APQ, *Collection de pièces judiciaires et notariales,* file 1230.

[179]APQ, *Ordres du Roi,* series B, vol. 78, 1744, p. 145.

Chapter Eleven

[180]Memorandum reproduced in *Nova Francia,* IV, 1929, pp. 143-145.

[181]Colbert to Talon, April 5, 1667, February 20, 1668, in *RAPQ,* 1939-1940, pp. 72 and 94 et seq.

[182]Dollier de Casson, *Histoire de Montréal,* pp. 113 et seq.

[183] Permission granted by Jean Dudouyt, cited in *RAPQ,* 1939-1940, p. 219.

[184]Vaudreuil and Raudot to the minister, November 14, 1709, in *RAPQ*, 1942-1943, p. 420.

[185]Sulte, "L'esclavage au Canada," in the *Revue canadienne*, 61, 1911, p. 324.

[186]Jean de Piquefort (Routhier's pseudonym), "Portraits et pastels littéraires," in *Les Guêpes canadiennes* (Laperrière edition), pp. 290 et seq.

CHAPTER TWELVE

[187]Jean de Piquefort (Routhier's pseudonym), "Portraits et pastels littéraires," in *Les Guêpes canadiennes* (Laperrière edition), pp. 290 et seq.

[188]*Quebec Herald*, July 22, 1790, p. 8; *Quebec Gazette*, December 16, 1790, p. 4.

[189]*Quebec Gazette*, July 21, 1791, pp. 1 et seq.; July 28, pp. 1 et seq.; August 4, pp. 1 et seq.; August 18, pp. 1 et seq.; September 1, pp. 1 et seq.; September 8, pp. 1 et seq.; September 15, pp. 1 et seq.

[190]*Quebec Herald*, March 12, 1792, p. 8; April 16, 1792, p. 5; *Quebec Gazette*, June 7, 1792, p. 2; June 21, 1792, p. 2.

[191]W.H. Withrow, "The Underground Railway, " in *TRSC*, VIII, 1902, 2, pp. 49-77.

[192]*Cours du Temps*, October 20, 1794, p. 93.

[193]Audet and Fabre-Surveyer, *Les Députés au premier Parlement du Bas-Canada*, p. 130; P.-G. Roy, *Les Juges de la Province de Québec*, p. 401.

[194]Petition of 1799, in *Journal of the House of Assembly of Lower Canada*, 1799, p. 126.

[195]According to evidence presented and summarized by Viger-LaFontaine, "De l'esclavage au Canada," in *Mémoires de la Société histor-ique de Montréal*, I, pp. 52-55.

[196]Petition dated April 1, 1799 and read in the House on the 19th, in *Journal of the House of Assembly of Lower Canada*, 1799, pp. 122-128.

[197]Petition presented to the House of Assembly in April 1800, in *Jour-nal of the House of Assembly of Lower Canada*, 1800, p. 154. Testimony and affidavits cited by Viger-LaFontaine, "De l'esclavage au Canada," in *Mémoires de la Société historique de Montréal*, I, pp. 62 et seq.

[198]Petition printed in the *Journal of the House of Assembly of Lower Canada*, 1800, pp. 150-158.

[199]Inventory published in *RAPQ*, 1951-1953, p. 390.

[200]Sulte claimed that "the Quebec Legislature regulated the condition of slaves in 1833, a precedent imitated by the British Parliament in 1834," ("L'esclavage en Canada," in *Revue canadienne*, 1911, 61, p. 333): actually, the Quebec legislature never adopted a single law on slavery.

[201]Aubert de Gaspé, *Canadians of Old*, pp. 210-1
[202]Letter to his wife, dated December 12, 1838: this letter was transmitted to us by Fernand Ouellet, assistant archivist of the Province of Quebec.
[203]Gaston Martin, *Histoire de l'esclavage dans les colonies françaises*, p. 280.
[204]Sulte, "L'esclavage en Canada," in *Revue canadienne*, 1911, 61, p. 333.

CONCLUSION

[205]Aubert de Gaspé, *Canadians of Old*, pp. 210-211.
[206]Aubert de Gaspé, *Yellow Wolf & Other Tales of the Saint Lawrence*, pp. 45-78.
[207]Piquefort, "Portraits et pastels littéraires," in *Les Guêpes canadiennes*, pp. 290 et seq.
[208]H.-R. Casgrain, "Madame C.-E. Casgrain," in *Mémoires de famille*, pp. 196 et seq.
[209]P.-B. Casgrain, *Mémorial des familles Casgrain, Bâby et Perrault*, 95, 145, n. 1.
[210]Letter sent to the author by Émilien Lamirande on June 17, 1993.
[211]Robert de Roquebrune, *Testament de mon enfance*, Fidès, 1979.
[212]F.-X. Garneau, *Histoire du Canada* (4th edition), II, 167; III, 90n.
[213]Viger-LaFontaine, "De l'esclavage en Canada," in *Mémoires de la société historique de Montréal*, I, 1859, pp. 1-63
[214]Cyprien Tanguay, *Dictionnaire généalogique des familles canadiennes*, 7 vols., published between 1871 and 1890.
[215]Hubert Neilson, "Slaves in Old Canada. Before and After the Conquest," in *Transactions of the Literary and Historical Society of Quebec*, XXVI, 1906, pp. 19-45.
[216]Benjamin Sulte, "L'esclavage en Canada," in the *Revue canadienne*, 61, 1911, pp. 315-334.
[217]Mgr. L.-A.Pâquet, "L'esclavage au Canada," in *TRSC*, VII, 1913, pp. 139-149.
[218]O.-M. H.-Lapalice, "Les esclaves noirs à Montréal sous l'ancien regime," in the *Canadian Antiquarian and Numismatic Journal*, 3rd series, XII, January 1, 1915, pp. 136 and 158.
[219]"Vente des esclaves par actes notariés sous les regimes français et anglais," in *RAPQ*, 1921-1922, pp. 109-123.
[220]Robert-Lionel Séguin, "L'esclavage dans la Presqu'Île," in *BRH*, 55, 1949, pp. 91-94, 168.

Bibliography

ACRONYMS

ASQ   Archives du Séminaire de Québec
BRH   Bulletin de recherches historiques
MSG   Mémoires de la Société généalogique
RPA   Report of the Public Archives of Canada
RAPQ   Rapport de l'archiviste de la province de Québec
RHAF   Revue d'histoire de l'Amérique française
RJ   Relations des Jésuites
TRSC   Transactions of the Royal Society of Canada

SOURCES

MANUSCRIPTS

Public archives
Scant references can be found here and there in official correspondence revealing the attitude of colonial authorities towards
slavery or the existence of slaves; correspondence in series B brings
together orders and dispatches from the French Ministry of the
Navy and in series C11A, *General Correspondence*. The *Moreau de
Saint-Méry* collection also provides some information about these
subjects.

We have undertaken research in the official archives of the
Federal and Quebec governments, examining all administrative
documents that could list individuals: the rulings of governors
and *intendants*, the registries of the Superior Council or Executive
Council, the registries of the Chambre des Milices or Militia Court
(under the military regime), census information, transcripts of the
Courts of Civil and Criminal Justice.

In researching legal archives, we have examined not only notarial documents from the early 17th century up to the abolition of slavery, but also the related series at the Archives nationales du Québec, *Collection des pièces judiciaires et notariales*.

At the National Archives of Canada we also consulted the Neilson Collection, which contains the papers and account books of the printers Brown and Gilmore.

The richest documents on slavery are official documents relating to civil status (baptisms, marriages and burials). Slavery lasted in Quebec for two centuries: we have examined all documents relating to secular or religious organizations, in whatever place, whether of the Catholic, Anglican or any other religious tradition, in organized parishes, missions and special entries in public or private archives.

Most of these registries have been consulted on site in each parish, or in the Archives nationales du Québec; we have examined registries of the Tadoussac mission at the archdiocese of Quebec, and those of Notre-Dame-des-Anges at the Hôpital-Général de Québec. Where forts on the periphery of Quebec are concerned, we have consulted the exhaustive collection of documents relating to civil status published by Madame Marthe Faribault-Beauregard in her two-volume *La population des forts français d'Amérique* (Éditions Bergeron). In some cases, we have benefited from the generous collaboration of the *Programme de recherche en démographie historique* of the Université de Montréal or the publication of some documents in the *Revue d'histoire de l'Amérique française* and the *Wisconsin Historical Collection*.

Private archives held by institutions
Several institutions hold archives containing information about slavery and aboriginal or black slaves:

ARCHDIOCESE OF QUEBEC
Book of abjurations, 1757-1826,
Catalogue or registry of confirmations, 1659-1749,
Two notebooks relating to the Tadoussac mission:

Miscellaneorum Liber, 1691-1775, and a registry of baptisms, marriages and burials, 1759-1784.

Hôpital-Général de Montréal

Registre de l'entrée des Pauvres à l'Hôpital-Général de Ville-Marie.
Registre des Pauvres décédés dans l'Hôpital-Général de Montréal à Ville-Marie, 1725 : covers the years 1725-1759.
Registre des sépultures, 1759-1776 : this registry goes well beyond this period, but we have only consulted it up to 1835.

Hôpital-Général de Québec

Registres des pauvres invalids reçus à l'Hôpital-Général de Québec sur la fondation de Mgr. de Saint-Vallier : from 1746 to 1941.
Décès, 1728-1783 : registry of the Notre-Dame-des-Anges parish, which contains baptisms and marriages and goes well beyond 1783; we have only consulted it up to 1840.

Hôtel-Dieu de Montréal

Registre des noms des militaires traités dans l'Hôtel-Dieu de Montréal depuis 1756 jusqu'à 1760; the subsequent registry only starts in the year 1829.

Hôtel-Dieu de Québec

Registre journalier des malades : we have consulted several record-books from the creation of the this registry in 1689 until the early 19th century.
Registre des sépultures faites dans le cimetière des Pauvres de l'Hôtel-Dieu, 1741-1795.
Registre mortuaire: we have examined this registry of funerals from its creation in 1723 until 1840.

Notre-Dame-de-Montréal

Premières communions et confirmations, 1756 à 1851: the list of communicants starts in 1756, and of confirmations in 1767.
Congrégation des hommes de Ville-Marie: Livre des élections ou

Livre des portiers. 1804-1868.

Congrégation des hommes de Ville-Marie. Notebook from 1805 containing lists, accounts and inventories.

Notre-Dame-de-Québec

Catalogue des noms de ceux qui ont été confirmés par Monseigneur Jean-Olivier Briand, évêque de Québec le 14 août 1779. This catalogue covers the period up to October 1825; a second catalogue takes the record up to 1853.

Confrérie de Sainte-Anne, 1658-1845. Regulations, deliberations, accounts.

Confrérie du scapulaire Mont-Carmel, 1807-1850. Lists, accounts.

Registre de la Sainte-Famille, 1664-1873. Lists, regulations, deliberations.

Recensement général des habitans de Québec, 1716. Incomplete census, published by Father Beaudet in 1887.

Séminaire de Montréal

Notarial deed of March 24th 1761, registered by the notary Panet: an emancipated black slave reverts to slavery in order to marry a black slave woman.

Séminaire de Québec

Document dated August 20th 1638 in the *Faribault Documents* about Couillart's black slave.

Original documents relating to civil status at the Saint-Joseph-des-Miamis trading post, with an (inaccurate) copy in Viger's *Saberdache*, vol. S (red binding).

Séminaire des Trois-Rivières

In the Hart fonds, deeds of sale from 1779 and 1786.

Private archives held by individuals

John Leblanc Collection

Excepts from civil status registries in Philipsburg.

NEILSON COLLECTION

Papers of the printers Brown and Gilmore: letters 1763-1768 and account books: *Memorial 1763-1774*; *Cash Book, 1765-1795*; *Account Book, 1779-1786*.

ROBERT-LIONEL SÉGUIN COLLECTION

Notes from civil status registeries, taken during research on slavery in the Vaudreuil region.

PRINTED SOURCES
Censuses

Censuses of Detroit and Michigan, in Michigan Census 1710-1830 Under the French, British and Americans, edited by Donna Valley Russell, Detroit Society for Genealogical Research, Detroit, 1882, 291 pp. Maps.

Census of Quebec for 1666, see Marcel Trudel, *La population du Canada en 1666. Recensement reconstitué*, Sillery, le Septentrion, 1995, 379 pp; for 1681, see Benjamin Sulte, Histoire des Canadiens-Français, vol. 5, pp. 63-90. For 1783,
see *RAC*, 1889, pp. 39-52.

Parish censuses in Quebec, for 1716 see Beaudet, *Recensement de la ville de Québec pour 1716*, Québec, Côté, 1887. For 1744, see *RAPQ*, 1939-1940, pp. 1-154. For 1792, see *RAPQ*, 1948-1949, pp. 9-55. For 1795, *Ibid.*, pp. 59-105. For 1798, *Ibid.*, pp. 109-156. For 1805, *Ibid.*, pp. 159-214.

Census of the *gouvernement* of Québec in 1762, see *RAPQ*, 1925-1926, pp. 1-143; of the *gouvernement* of Trois-Rivières in 1760 and 1762, see *RAPQ*, 1946-1947, pp. 5-53; of the *gouvernements* of Montreal and Trois-Rivières in 1765, see *RAPQ*, 1936-1937, pp. 1-121.

Newspapers

British American Register, The. Bilingual newspaper printed by John Neilson from January 8th to August 6th 1803.

Canadien, Le. French newspaper printed and published by Charles Roit from November 22nd 1806 to March 14th 1810. A second newspaper called the *Canadien* came out from June 1817 to March 1818; a third from January 1820 to 1825; a fourth was brought out by Étienne Parent from May 7th 1831 until 1893.

Courrier de Québec, Le. Weekly appearing from January 3rd 1807 to December 31st 1808.

Cours du temps, Le. Bilingual weekly appearing from June 23rd 1794 to July 27th 1795.

Gazette du commerce et littéraire, La. Newspaper brought out by Fleury Mesplet from June 3rd 1778 to June 2, 1779.

Journal of the House of Assembly of Lower Canada. Printed at Quebec by John Neilson starting in 1792. We have consulted this work up to 1833.

Montreal Gazette (La Gazette de Montréal). Bilingual weekly printed by Fleury Mesplet from 1785 to 1794, by Edward Edwards from 1795 to 1808, and by Charles Brown starting in 1808. Another newspaper with the same name was published by Louis Roy from 1795 to 1797, and then by J.M. Roy and John Bennett.

Quebec Gazette (La Gazette de Québec). Bilingual weekly printed by William Brown from 1764 to 1789, by Samuel Neilson from 1789 to 1793, and by John Neilson starting in 1793.

Quebec Herald Miscellany and Advertiser, The. English newspaper appearing twice weekly, from 1789 to 1792; published by William Moore.

Quebec Magazine (The). Le Magasin du Québec. Monthly magazine brought out by Samuel Neilson, from 1792 to 1794.

Spectateur canadien, Le. Newspaper founded in 1813.

Relations, Memoirs, Correspondence

Askin, John. *The John Askin Papers*, edited by Milo M. Quaife, the Detroit Library Commission, 1927 and 1931, 2 vols. Illustrations.

Bégon, Élisabeth. *Lettres au cher fils.* Montreal, Boréal, 1994, 429 pp.

Buade de Frontenac, Louis, "Correspondence échangée entre la

Cour de France et le gouverneur de Frontenac," in *RAPQ*, 1926-1927, pp. 1-144; 1927-1928, pp. 1-211; 1928-1929, pp. 247-384.

Casgrain C.E. and her son Father H.-R. Casgrain. *Mémoires de famille*, Rivière-Ouelle, 1891, 275 pp.

Dollier de Casson, François. *Histoire de Montréal*, critical edition by Marcel Trudel and Marie Baboyant, Montreal, Hurtubise HMH in the collection "Cahiers du Québec – Histoire," 1992, 342 pp. Some English quotations have been taken from the bilingual edition of this work, translated and edited by Ralph Flenley, London & Toronto, J.M. Dent & Sons, 1928.

Franquet, Louis. *Voyages et mémoires sur le Canada*, Quebec, A. Côté, 1889, 212 pp.

Gaultier de Lavérendrye, Pierre. *Journals and Letters of Pierre Gaultier de Lavérendrye and His Sons*, edited by L.I. Burpee, Toronto, Champlain Society, 1927, 548 pp. Maps.

Kalm, Pehr. *Voyage de Pehr Kalm au Canada en 1749*. Montreal, 1977, 674 pp. Translated and annotated by Jacques Rousseau, Guy Béthune and Pierre Morisset.

Lahontan, baron de. *Voyages du baron de Lahontan dans l'Amérique septentrionale*, Amsterdam, 2 vols.

Nau, François, S.J. *Lettres*, in *RAPQ*, 1926-1927, pp. 261-330.

Relations des Jésuites, The Jesuit Relations and Allied Documents, edited by R.G. Thwaites, Cleveland, 1896-1901, 73 vols.

Roberts, Kenneth. *March to Quebec: Journals of the Members of Arnold's Expedition*, New York, Doubleday, Doran & Co., 1940, 722 pp.

Rocquebrune, Robert de. *Testament de mon enfance. Récit*, Paris, Plon, 1951. 245 pp.

Talon, Jean. "Lettres de 1665 à 1677" in *RAPQ*, 1930-1931, pp. 1-182.

Vaudreuil, Philippe Rigaud de, Governor. *Correspondence entre M. de Vaudreuil et la Cour*, in *RAPQ*, 1938-1939, pp. 12-179; 1939-1940, pp 355-463; 1942-1943, pp. 399-443.

Vitry, Pierre, S.J. "Journal" in *Nova Francia*, vol. 4 (1929), pp. 146-170.

Youville, Madame d'. "Lettres" in Albertine Ferland-Angers, *Mère d'Youville, 1701-1771*, Montreal, Librairie Beauchemin, 1945. 385 pp.

Aubert de Gaspé, Philippe. *Les Anciens Canadiens*, Quebec, Desbarats et Desbishire, 1863. 411 pp.; by the same author, *Mémoires*, Quebec, N.S. Hardy, 1885; Quotations from *Yellow-Wolf & Other Tales of the Saint Lawrence*, Montreal, Véhicule Press, 1990 and *Canadians of Old*, Montreal, Véhicule Press, 1993, both both translated by Jane Brierley,

Boucault, Nicolas-Gaspard. *État present du Canada*, in *RAPQ*, 1920-1921, pp. 1-50.

Bougainville, Louis-Antoine de, *Mémoire sur l'état de la Nouvelle-France, 1757*, in *RAPQ*, 1923-1924, pp. 42-70.

Charlevoix, François-Xavier de, S.J. *Histoire et description générale de la Nouvelle-France avec le Journal historique d'un voyage fait par ordre du roi dans l'Amérique septentrionale*, Paris, Pierre-François Giffart, 1744, 6 vols. Maps.

Chartier de Lotbinière, M.-E.-G.-A. *Inventaire*, in *RAPQ*, 1951-1953, pp. 383-394.

Code Noir (Le) ou Recueil des réglements rendus jusqu'à présent, concernant le gouvernement, l'administration de la justice, la police, la discipline et le commerce des nègres dans les colonies françaises, Paris, Prault, 1767, 446 pp.

Coleman, Emma Lewis. *New England Captives Carried to Canada Between 1677 and 1760 During the French and Amerindian Wars*, Portland, Southworth Press, 1925. 2 vols.

Documents Relative to the Colonial History of the State of New York [...], Albany, edited by E.B. O'Callaghan, 1853-1887, 15 vols. Maps.

Édits, ordonnances royaux [...], Quebec, E.-R. Fréchette, 1854-1856, 3 vols.

Kirby, William. *Le Chien D'Or, The Golden Dog : A Legend of Quebec.* New York, Montreal, Lovell, Adam, Wesson and Co., 1877, 678 pp.

Margry, P.-A. *Mémoires et documents pour servir à l'histoire des origines françaises des pays d'outre-mer.* Paris, 1879-1888, 6 vols.

Papiers Contrecoeur et autres documents concernant le conflit anglo-français sur l'Ohio de 1745 à 1756, edited by Fernand Grenier,

Quebec, Presses de l'Université Laval, 1952, 485 pp. vol. I.

Riddell, William Renwick. *Michigan Under British Rule Law and Law Courts, 1760-1796*. Lansing, Michigan Historical Commission, 1926, 1926, 493 pp.

Saint-Vallier, Mgr. de. *Catéchisme du diocèse de Québec*. Paris, Urbain Coustelier, 1702. 522 pp.

_____. Mgr. de. *Rituel du diocèse de Québec*. Paris, Simon Langlois, 1703. 604 pp.

INVENTORIES, DICTIONARIES, DIRECTORIES

Congés et permis déposés et enregistrés à Montréal sous le Regime français, by E.Z. Massicotte, in *RAPQ*, 1921-1922, pp. 189-225.

Dictionary of Canadian Biography. Toronto and Quebec, University of Toronto Press and Presses de l'université Laval, vols. I to V published 1966-1983.

Inventaires des greffes des notaires du Regime français. Quebec, 1942-1976, 27 vols. Other typewritten notarized documents examined in the Gagnon room of the Municipal Library of Montreal.

Inventaire des jugements et deliberations du Conseil supérieur de la Nouvelle-France de 1717 à 1760. Beauceville, L'Éclaireur, 1932-1935, 7 vols.

Inventaire des ordonnances des intendants de la Nouvelle-France conservées aux Archives provinciales de Québec. Beauceville, L'Éclaireur, 1919, 4 vols.

Inventaire d'une collection de pièces manuscrites judiciaires, notariales, etc., conservées aux Archives judiciaires (Palais de justice) de Québec. Three typewritten notebooks.

Répertoires des actes de baptême, mariage, sépulture et des recensements du Québec ancien. Montreal, Presses de l'Université de Montréal, 1980, 7 vols. on the 17th century, edited by Hubert Charbonneau and Jacques Légaré.

Répertoires des engagements pour l'Ouest conservés dans les archives judiciaires de Montréal, in *RAPQ*, 1929-1930, pp. 191-466; 1930-1931, pp. 353-453; 1931-1932, pp. 143-265; 1932-1933,

245-304; edited by E.-Z. Massicotte.

Tanguay, Cyprien, Father. *Dictionnaire généalogique des familles canadiennes*. Montreal, Eusèbe Sénécal, 1871-1890, 7 vols. Tanguay was the first to develop a systematic inventory of slaves, although he restricted himself to the Hôpital-Général de Montréal and records at Michilimackinac. The third volume contains an appendix listing 135 slaves. In the fourth volume, Tanguay provided the names of 117 individuals under the headings *Nègres* (Negros) and *Panis* (Panis). He had the bad habit of calling anonymous slaves *Joseph* and *Marie*, depending on their gender, even when original records indicated these slaves were anonymous. In addition, he extrapolated from the approximate age of slaves their original date of baptism: some of his claims were simply made up, for example where he claims that a slave about 10 years old, buried in 1740, was baptised in 1730, whereas the slave may have reached New France at an uncertain date and may have been baptised much later.

Trudel, Marcel. *Dictionnaire des esclaves et de leurs propriétaires au Canada français*. Montreal, Éditions Hurtubise HMH, in the collection "Cahiers du Québec – Histoire," 1990, pp. xviii-490.

STUDIES

Specialized Studies (on slavery in Quebec)

Bail, Micheline. *L'Esclave*. Montreal, Libre Expression, 1999. A fictional history of the 1734 tragedy of the Negro slave Marie-Angélique.

Fehmiu Brown, Paul. *Ces Canadiens oubliés*, vol. I, Montreal, Éditions Aquaris, 1981. Historical drama on slavery in Quebec.

Hémond, Robert, "Joseph Lerenard," in *MSG*, June 1985, pp. 112-122. The descendants of this aboriginal slave from the 18th to the 20th centuries.

H.-Lapalice, O.-M. "Les esclaves noirs à Montréal sous l'Ancien Regime," in *Canadian Antiquarian and Numismatic Journal*,

3rd series, vol. XII, 1, January 1915, pp. 136-158. An important contribution to the history of slavery in a single location.

Mackey, Frank. *Done With Slavery: The Black Fact in Montreal, 1760-1840*. Montreal and Kingston, McGill-Queen's University Press, 2010.

McPherson Lemoyne, James. "Slavery at Quebec," in *Canadian Antiquarian and Numismatic Journal*, IV, 4, April 1876, pp. 158-160. Brief notes on slavery.

Neilson, Hubert. "Slavery in Old Canada Before and After the Conquest," in *Transactions of the Literary and Historical Society of Quebec*, XXVI, 1906, pp. 19-45. The author was the grandson of printer John Neilson (who had a slave) and scolded historians for remaining silent about slavery: he rightly criticized Garneau for distorting original documents in order to exonerate the French regime.

Pâquet, Mgr. L.-A. "L'esclavage au Canada," in *TRSC*, VII, 1913, pp. 139-149. Very brief study of slavery in Canada and elsewhere in the world.

Peabody, Sue and Keila Grinberg, *Slavery, Freedom and the Law in the Atlantic World:A Brief History with Documents*. New York, Bedford/St. Martin's, 2007.

Séguin, Robert-Lionel. "L'esclavage dans la Presqu'Île," in *BRH*, 55, 1949, pp. 91-94, 168. The author only dealt with the Vaudreuil-Soulanges region.

_____. "On a pratiqué l'esclavage dans la région de Vaudreuil jusqu'en 1800," in the *Petit Journal*, May 3th 1956, pp. 30 and 53. Brief report on the catalogue Séguin was developing.

Sulte, Benjamin. "L'esclavage au Canada, » in *Revue Canadienne*, vol. 61, 1911, 315-344.pp

Trudel, Marcel. "Quand les Québécois pratiquaient l'esclavage," in a work by the same author, *Mythes et réalités dans l'histoire du du Québec*, Montreal, Éditions Hurtubise HMH, 2003, pp. 175-192.

Trudel, Marcel. *Dictionnaire des esclaves et de leurs propriétaires au*

Canada français, Montreal, Éditions Hurtubise HMH, 1990, pp. xxviii-490 (3rd revised edition, with an accompanying CD-ROM).

Vente des esclaves par actes notariés sous les Regimes français et anglais, in *RAPQ*, 1921-1922, pp. 109-123. A collection of documents preceded by a review of studies on slavery.

Viger, Jacques and Louis-Hippolyte Lafontaine. "De l'esclavage en Canada," in *Mémoires de la Société historique de Montréal*, I, 1859, pp. 1-63; II, 1859, title page (Addenda page). The first historical work on slavery in Quebec.

Various studies

Ahern, N.J. and Georges. *Notes pour servir à l'histoire de la medicine dans le Bas-Canada*. Quebec, 1923, 563 pp.

Archibald, A.G. "Story of Deportation of Negroes from Nova Scotia to Sierra Leone," in *Collections of the Nova Scotia Historical Society*, VII (1889-1891), pp. 129-154.

Atherton, W.H. *Montreal 1535-1914*. Montreal, S.J. Clark, 1914. 3 vols.

Audet, F.-J. *Les Députés de Montréal (villes et comtés), 1792-1867*, Montreal, Éditions des Dix, 1943, 455 pp.

Audet F.-J. and Édouard Fabre-Surveyer. *Les Députés au premier Parlement du Bas-Canada, 1792-1796*, volume I, Montreal, Éditions des Dix, 1946, 316 pp.

Bélanger, Gaétan. *Le scandale qui a secoué la Nouvelle-France*, Montreal, Lanctôt éditeur, 2005, 312 pp. A work of fiction.

Boucher de Labruère, Montarville. "Le 'livre de raison' des seigneurs de Montarville," in *Cahiers des Dix*, IV, 1939, pp. 243-270.

Brymner, D. "The Jamaica Maroons, How They Came to Nova Scotia. How They Left It," in *TRSC*, I, 1895, pp. 81-90.

Côté, Paul and Constantina Mitchell. *Winter Passage*, California, Behler Publi cations, 2005, 214 pp. A work of fiction.

Delanguez, Jean, S.J. *Louis Jolliet. Vie et voyages (1645-1700)*, Montreal, Études de l'Institut d'histoire de l'Amérique française, 1950, 435 pp.

Denissen, Christian. *Genealogy of the French Families of the Detroit River Region, 7101-1911*, Detroit, Detroit Society for Genealogical Research, 1976, 2 vols.

Detroit in Perspective. Limited edition typewritten document, provided by the researcher Jean Dargis.

Ducassé, André. *Les Négriers ou le traffic des esclaves*, Paris, Hachette, 1948. 253 pp.

Fabre-Surveyer, Édouard. "From Montreal to Indiana," in *TRSC*, 39, 1945, pp. 45-83. On the Lacelle family.

Hill, Daniel G. *The Freedom-Seekers: Blacks in Early Canada*. The Book Society of Canada Limited, 1981. 242 pp.

Histoire de la Congrégation de Notre-Dame de Montréal. Montreal, 1910-1974, 11vols.

Jack, J. Allen. "The Loyalists and Slavery in New Brunswick," in *TRSC*, IV, 1898, II, pp. 137-185.

Lajeunesse, E.-J. *The Windsor Border Region: Canada's Southernmost Frontier*. Toronto, The Champlain Society, 1960, pp. cxxxix-376.

Langdon, Fred. "The Negro Migration to Canada After the Passing of the Fugitive Slave Act," in *The Journal of Negro History*, V, 1, 1920.

Laperrière, Auguste. *Les Abeilles canadiennes*, Ottawa, A. Bureau, 1881, 401 pp.

Lefebvre, Jean-Jacques. "La descendance de Pierre Boucher (1617-1722)," in *MSG*, V, June 2nd 1952, pp. 69-96.

----. *Saint-Constant et Saint-Philippe de Laprairie, 1744-1946*, Hull, Éditions L'Éclair, 1947, 43 pp.

Lemoine, James McPherson. *Picturesque Quebec: A Sequel to Quebec Past and Present*. Montreal, Dawson Brothers, 1882, 535 pp.

Martin, Gaston. *Histoire de l'esclavage dans les colonies françaises*. Paris, Presses universitaires de France, 1948, 318 pp.

Massicotte, E.-Z. "L'incendie du vieux Montéral en 1721," in *BRH*, 32, 1926, pp. 583-601.

Moran, J. *The Moran Family: 200 Years in Detroit*. Alved of Detroit, 1949.

Piquefort, Jean (pseudonym of Adolphe-Basile Routhier). "Portraits et pastels littéraires," in *Les Guêpes canadiennes*, pp. 255-401. See Laperrière.

Riddell, W.R. "Le Code Noir," in *TRSC*, XIX, 1925, II, p. 33-38.

Saint-Pierre, T. "Histoire des Canadiens du Michigan et du comté d'Essex (Ontario)," Montreal, *Gazette*, 1895.

Severance, F.H. *An Old Frontier of France: the Niagara Region and Adjacent Lakes Under French Control*, New York, 1917, 2 vols.

Smith, T.W. "The Slave in Canada," in *Collections of the Nova Scotia Historical Society*, X, 1896-1898, pp. 1-161.

Sulte, Benjamin. *Histoire des Canadiens-Français, 1608-1880*. Montreal, Wilson et Cie., 1882-1884, 8 vols.

Swanton, John R. *The Amerindian Tribes of North America*. Washington, 1952, 726 pp.

"The Slave in Canada," in *The Journal of Negro History*, vol. 3, 1920.

Viau, Roland. *Ceux de Nigger Rock*. Montreal, Libre expression, 2003, 180 pp.

Williams, Dorothy W. *Blacks in Montreal 1628-1986*. Montreal, Éditions Yvon Blais, 1989, 147 pp.

Winks R.W. *The Blacks in Canada: A History*. Montreal, New Haven and London, McGill-Queen's University Press and Yale University Press, 1971, pp. xvii-546.

Withrow, W.H. "The Underground Railway," in *TRSC*, 8, 1902, II, pp. 49-72.

Translator's note: in some cases the bibliography and footnotes refer to French editions of English-language works and documents, since these are the ones Marcel Trudel actually examined.

Index

Many slaves listed in the index went by the same name (Joseph, Marie, Pierre, et al.). In such cases, to make it clear which particular slaves he was referring to, Marcel Trudel indicated the date of the historical document identifying each slave, as well as the slave's ethnic origin as described in seventeenth, eighteenth and nineteenth century documents ("Chickasaw, Eskimo, Iroquois, Métis, mulatto, Negro, Panis" etc.). Some of these ethnic descriptions are no longer in use.

Montreal) 195

Bois d'ébène (Ebony slaves) 10, 17, 29, 33, 36, 37, 65, 74, 88, 97, 256

Bonaventure (Panis) 208

Bondfield, Acklom Rickaby (merchant) 150, 153

Bondfield family 150, 153

Bossu (Captain) 19

Boston, Massachusetts 86

Boston, Robert (Negro) 199

Boüat, François-Marie (merchant and judge) 52

Boucher de Boucherville family 224

Boucher de Boucherville, Pierre 226

Boucher de Labruère, Dr. 252

Boucher de Labruère, Pierre-Charles 98

Boucher de Laperrière, François 195

Boucher de Niverville family, 111

Boucher de Niverville, Jean-Baptiste 138

Boucher de Niverville, Joseph-Claude 171

Bougainville, Louis-Antoine de (French mathematician, officer and explorer) 10, 11, 64, 65, 69, 70

Bouillet de Lachassaigne, Jean (Governor of Trois-Rivières and Montreal) 105

Bouquet, Henry (officer) 174

Bourassa, Daniel 205

Bourassa family 104

Bourassa, René (voyageur) 185, 186, 217

Bourassa (voyageur) 144

Bourdon family 229

Bourdon, Joseph (Panis) 197

Bourdon *dit* Content, Jean-Baptiste (Panis) 138

Boutin, Mr. 156

Bradshaw, Nancy (Negro) 124

Brochet nation 67, 126, 256

Brooks, John 91

Brothers of Charity (Frères de la Charité) 114, 258

Brousse, Mr. 173

Brown, Caesar (Negro) 139, 198

Brown, William (printer of the *Quebec Gazette*) 86, 90, 92, 110, 129, 131, 144, 163, 164, 168

Bruce (Negro) 95, 168

Brunet, Louis 225

Bulkley, Marie (Negro) 89, 90, 93, 238, 251

Burglary 92, 161, 165-168, 173, 182, 183, 185, 261

Burials, slave (*see* Slave burials)

Burning of Montreal during a slave escape 174-177

Burns (merchant) 91

Burton, Ralph, British Military Governor of Trois-Rivières 188

Butcher, Benjamin (Negro) 198

Butchers, slave-owning 91, 99, 107, 134

Cabassié, Joseph (bourgeois) 208

Cadet, Joseph-Michel 107

Cahokia nation 66, 256

Cailhaut *dit* Baron, Jean 199

Caldwell, William (officer) 154

Caleb (Negro) 129

Callières, Louis-Hector (Governor General of New France) 34

Calvinists (*see* Presbyterians)

Campbell, Donald (Colonel) 174, 209, 214

Campbell, William 91, 93

Campeau family 104, 107, 118, 259

Campeau, François 140

Campeau, Jean-Baptiste (notary) 109

Decouagne, Thérèse 174
Deerfield, Massachusetts 25, 159
Dejean, Philippe (merchant and
   judge) 166
Delagarde, Pierre-Paul-François
   (Sulpician) 112
Delzenne, Ignace-François (mer-
   chant-goldsmith) 98, 107
Demers, Marie 224
Denonville, Jacques-René de Brisay
   de (Marquis and Governor of
   New France) 26, 29, 31, 32, 69,
   254
Denys de Laronde family 108
Denys de Laronde, Joseph 186
Desbois, Marie-Catherine (Panis),
   223
Deschaillons seigneurie 173
Desforges *dite* Saint-Maurice,
   Marie-Geneviève 225
Detroit (formerly New France,
   then Province of Quebec, now
   Michigan) 62, 66, 68, 79, 83, 87-
   89, 106, 112, 113, 126, 135, 137,
   140-142, 148, 154, 166, 167, 174,
   190, 191, 194, 197, 198, 203, 204,
   208, 214, 216, 222, 240, 258
Diane (Negro) 74
Dickson, John (Negro) 199
*Dictionnaire des esclaves et de leurs
   propriétaires*, 13, 59, 257, 270
Dillon, Richard (hotelier) 86, 240,
   245
Doctors, slave-owning 91, 93, 99,
   144, 258
Dollier de Casson, François
   (Sulpician and historian) 20, 21,
   22, 125
Donnacona (Iroquoian chief of
   Stadacona, on site of present-
   day Quebec City) 20

Don Quichotte (Amerindian) 20
Dorchester, Lord (Guy Carleton,
   British Governor of the Prov-
   ince of Quebec and Governor
   General of British North Amer-
   ica), 166
Dorothée (Panis, 1790) 204
Dorothée (Panis, 1790 daughter of
   the aforementioned) 204
Dosquet, Pierre-Herman, Bishop
   of Quebec 112
Douaire de Bondy family 106
Doyon family 24, 229, 230
Doyon, Nicolas (Panis) 24, 225, 226
Doyon (slave name) 24
Doyon *dit* Laframboise, Nicolas
   (Panis) 225
Drummond (Negro) 130
Duchesne (slave name) 158
Duchesne, René 158
Duchesne *dit* LeRoide, André 231
Duchesne *dite* LeRoide, Marie-
   Geneviève 231
Duclos, Marie-Élisabeth 154
Dufrost de Lajemmerais, Marie-
   Marguerite or "Mother d'You-
   ville" 85, 99, 114, 149, 258
Dufy-Charest, Joseph (merchant)
   75
Dumas, Alexandre (Member of
   the Assembly of Lower Canada)
   247, 248
Dumoulin, François (merchant)
   156
Dunière, Gaspard (priest) 112
Dunière, Louis (merchant and
   Member of the Assembly of
   Lower Canada) 237, 238
Duperron-Bâby family 114, 266
Duperron-Bâby, Jacques (merchant)
   127, 154, 216

Fort Saint-Joseph des Miamis (French fort, now Niles, Michigan) 203
Fortier, Michel 193
Fortune (Negro) 130
Foucher, Louis-Charles (notary and Solicitor General of Lower Canada) 85, 249
Fox nation (also known as Outagamies) 48, 53, 55, 60-62, 68, 94, 113, 114, 116, 122-125, 135, 136, 142, 146, 147, 149, 151, 152, 155, 159, 171, 202, 225, 257, 260, 266
France 15, 19, 20, 22, 29, 31, 33, 36, 43, 44-46, 50-52, 54-56, 64, 69, 74, 112-114, 121, 126, 136, 162, 165, 182, 211, 220, 231, 236, 244, 251, 255, 258, 268, 269
Francheville, Widow 174, 177, 202, 204
François (Amerindian 1692) 24
François (Amerindian 1695) 25
François (Fox) 125
François (Negro, 1696) 33
François (Negro, 1729) 215
François (Negro, 1740) 143
François (Negro, 1786) 112
François-Denis (Negro) 151
François-Dominique dit Mentor (Negro) 199
François-Prisque (Panis) 209
Françoise (Panis, 1759) 208
Françoise (Panis, 1778), 128
Françoise (Sioux) 113
Françoise-Charlotte (Negro) 138
Franquet, Louis (officer and military engineer) 69, 70, 113
Fraser, James 132-134, 240, 245, 246, 251
Fréchette, Louis-Honoré (poet) 266

Fréchette, Pierre (priest) 112, 148
Frement, Samuel (Negro) 74
French West Indies (Antilles, Caribbean, "Islands of French America") 29, 30, 36, 39, 43, 46, 52-55, 68, 75, 77, 87, 90, 96, 116, 121-123, 127, 134, 143, 150, 161, 162, 164, 172, 178, 180, 181, 183-185, 195, 207, 209, 211, 213, 215, 254-256, 261, 262, 269
Frères de la Charité (see Brothers of Charity)
Frontenac, Louis de Buade (Count and Governor General of New France) 22, 23, 32, 69, 104
Fugitive slaves (runaway slaves) 7, 21, 54, 55, 72, 76, 94, 121, 128, 132, 133, 161, 163, 164, 177, 236, 239, 240, 242, 243, 256, 265
Fur trade 10, 25, 27, 47, 48, 51, 73, 76, 84, 94, 103, 107, 108, 116, 118, 126, 127, 162, 167, 229, 255, 57, 259, 268

Gabrielle dite Arthémise (Panis) 196
Gadois-Mogé, Jacques 61
Gage, Thomas (British Military Governor of Montreal) 188, 189
Galley slaves 12, 55, 69, 169, 170
Galliffet, François (officer) 105
Gallinée, René-François de (Sulpician) 21
Gamelin family 106, 187
Gamelin, Geneviève 187, 189
Gamelin, Ignace (merchant) 158, 174, 204, 210, 212, 213, 218
Gamelin, Joseph-Jacques (merchant) 73, 187
Gamelin, Lajemmerais, Christophe 212

Garault *dit* St-Onge, Pierre 123
Gareau, Marie 226
Garneau, François-Xavier (historian) 7, 51, 103, 111, 113, 268, 269
Garneau, Hector de Saint Denys (publisher of a revised edition of his great-grandfather's works) 51
Gaspé peninsula (mountainous region on the St. Lawrence River and Gulf) 168
Gastineau-Duplessis, Louis 152, 229
Gaudet, Dominique (merchant) 89, 106, 194, 210, 212, 213, 215, 218
Gaudin, Marie-Madeleine 201
Gaultier de Landreville, Jean 99
Gaultier de Lavérendrye Louis-Joseph (fur trader and explorer) 108
Gaultier de Lavérendrye, Pierre (fur trader and explorer) 27, 51, 58, 67, 97, 108
Gazette de Montréal (now the *Montreal Gazette*) 110, 127, 241, 251
Gendron *dit* Potvin Simon 209
Geneviève (Panis) 154
Gent, Joseph (sailor) 241, 251
Giffard, Joseph 23
Giles, Cato (Negro) 199
Gill, William 131
Gilles (Panis) 60
Gilles-Hyacinthe (Fox) 60, 135, 151, 152
Gilmore, Thomas (printer of the *Quebec Gazette*) 110, 286
Girardin family 154
Gladwin, Henry (officer) 174
Glandons, Maurice-Louis de (notary) 90

Godefroy de Saint-Paul, Jean-Amador 25
Gouin, Claude (surveyor) 109, 194
Gouin family 107
Gouin, Thérèse 148
Gourdon *dit* Lachasse, Jean-Baptiste 156
Governors, slave-owning 21, 27, 34, 35, 52, 56, 59, 60, 75, 91, 93, 97, 104-106, 108, 123, 125, 152, 156, 171, 212, 214, 221, 254, 258
Grant, William (bourgeois and Member of the Assembly of Lower Canada) 130, 134, 237, 238, 247-249
Grasset de Saint-Sauveur, André (merchant) 114, 251, 266
Grave, Henri-François (priest) 152
Green Bay, Wisconsin (*see* Baie des Puants)
Gregory, George (merchant) 217
Greysolon Dulhut, Daniel (French explorer) 23, 27, 254
Griffiths, John (Negro) 199
Grondines, Les (settlement on the St. Lawrence River upstream from Quebec City) 222
Guérout, Pierre-Guillaume (Member of the Assembly of Lower Canada) 129, 237
Guillet family 136
Guillet, Joseph 136
Guinea (West African nation) 15, 33, 36, 75
Guy, Pierre (merchant) 74, 98, 106

Habeas Corpus 190, 191, 242, 243, 245, 261
Hackett, Thomas (merchant) 212
Hall, Elias 90
Hamelin, Charles (merchant) 68,

143, 222
Hamelin family 68, 222
Hamelin, Jacques 222
Hamelin, Louis 222
Hart, Aaron (fur trader and seign-
eur) 94
Havy, François (merchant) 149
Hébert, Guillemette 16
Henri-Thérèse (Sioux) 153
Hertel family 108
Hertel de Rouville, Pierre-Antoine
(officer) 108
Hervieux, Pierre-Jean-Baptiste
(merchant) 154, 213
Héry, Charles 156
Hill, Nancy (Negro) 212
Hipps, George (butcher) 91, 133,
134
Historical distortions about slav-
ery in Canada 7, 51, 103, 111-113,
268-271
Hocquart, Gilles (Intendant of New
France) 46, 49, 51-54, 60, 75, 87,
105, 135, 151, 152, 176, 181, 182,
184, 186, 193, 210, 255, 260
Hôpital-Général de Montréal (a
hospital in Montreal) 114, 134,
135, 136, 148, 149, 152, 153, 251,
252, 262, 266
Hôpital-Général de Québec (a hospital in Quebec City) 57, 74,
114, 134, 258
Hostages 12, 62, 68
Hôtel-Dieu de Montréal (a hospital in Montreal) 58, 114, 134, 98,
258, 262
Hôtel-Dieu de Québec (a hospital
in Quebec City) 24, 25, 33, 34,
38, 45, 58-60, 71, 74, 75, 112-
114, 125, 134, 135, 142, 167,
171, 173, 175, 198, 211, 238, 252

Houlacous, Mathieu 23
House of Commons (Great Brit-
ain) 234, 235
Hoyle, Rosseter (merchant) 132
Huart Dormicourt, Marc-Antoine
(Chevalier) 53, 87, 111, 180-186,
191, 261
Hubert, Augustin-David (priest)
193
Hubert (slave name) 193
Hubert-Lacroix family 104, 106
Hubert-Lacroix, Jacques 106
Hudson Bay 37, 69
Huguenots 12, 149, 150 (see also
Presbyterians)
Hunter, Joseph (Negro) 198
Huot, François (Member of the
Assembly of Lower Canada) 250
Huppé, Jean-Marie 240
Huron nation 10, 21, 23, 26, 68, 221
Hutchins, Dorothy (Negro) 142, 218

Ignace (Panis) 25
Illinois Country 26, 74, 127, 174,
197
Illinois nation 19, 24, 48, 66, 68,
113, 256
Innkeepers, slave-owning 86, 107,
195, 199, 243, 245
Intendants, slave-owning 52, 60,
75, 105, 135, 151, 158
Inuit nation (referred to in old
documents as "Eskimos") 70, 125
Iowa nation 65, 256
Iroquois nation 10, 18, 21-23, 25,
26, 48, 68, 69, 100, 104, 221, 257
Iroquois Country 21
Isaac (Negro) 168, 240
Isabella (mulatto) 91, 93, 97, 133,
134
"Islands of French America" (see

French West Indies)
Ismael (Negro) 95, 125, 130

Jack (Negro) 134
Jack (Negro, 1778) 130
Jack (Negro, 1792) 130, 237
Jack (Negro, 1796) 195, 196
Jackson, Nicolas (Negro) 199
Jackson, Robert (Negro) 142, 218
Jacob (mulatto) 130
Jacob (Panis) 128, 133
Jacobs, Mary 100
Jacques (Amerindian) 205
Jacques (Negro, 1694) 33, 45
Jacques (Negro, 1757) 123, 212
Jacques (Negro, 1794) 195
Jacques (Negro, 1806) 238
Jacques (Panis, 1687) 24
Jacques (Panis, 1699) 25
Jacques (Panis, 1712) 198
Jacques (Panis, 1734) 55, 143, 169, 170, 191, 200
Jacques (Sioux) 194
Jacques-Caton (Negro) 216
Jacques-César (Negro) 199, 204, 210, 212, 218, 252
Jacquin *dit* Philibert, Widow 207
Janis, Antoine (voyageur) 194, 196
Janis family 64
Janis, Hyacinthe 122
Janis, Widow 194, 196
Janot-Lachapelle, Widow 123
Janson (officer) 198
Jarret de Verchères family 108, 114
Jarret de Verchères, Madeleine 85, 98
Jasmin (Negro) 213
Jean (Arkansas) 25
Jean (Panis, 1718) 197
Jean-Baptiste (Amerindian) 140
Jean-Baptiste (Arkansas) 25

Jean-Baptiste (Fox) 122
Jean-Baptiste (Negro, 1783) 139
Jean-Baptiste (Negro, 1791) 139
Jean-Baptiste (Negro, 1808) 148
Jean-Baptiste (Panis, 1710) 197
Jean-Baptiste (Panis, 1722) 123
Jean-Baptiste (Panis, 1749) 154
Jean-Baptiste-Christophe (Chickasaw) 159
Jean-Baptiste-Pompée (Negro) 112
Jean-Baptiste-Thomas (Negro) 166
Jean-Barthélemy (Negro) 199
Jean-François (Negro) 209, 218
Jean-Louis (mulatto) 94
Jeanne (Negro) 209, 218
Jeannot (Negro) 74
Jenny (Negro) 140
Jews, 94, 99, 129
Joachim (Negro) 213
Joe (Negro) 92, 110, 129, 131, 144, 163, 164, 168
Johnson, Benjamin (Negro) 168
Johnson, William 174
Johnson and Purss (merchants) 132, 133
Johnton, Jean-Baptiste (Negro) 252
Joinville, Pierre 233, 238
Jolibois family 198
Jolliet, François (merchant) 126
Jolliet, Louis (explorer) 22, 23, 27, 104, 254
Joncaire de Chabert family 108
Jones, John (auctioneer) 168
Jones, Nicholas 199
Jones, Titus (Negro) 35, 73
Joseph (mulatto) 199
Joseph (Negro, 1729) 215
Joseph (Negro, 1746) 213
Joseph (Negro, 1748) 154
Joseph (Negro, 1750) 212, 213

Joseph (Negro, 1757) 214
Joseph (Paducah) 125
Joseph (Panis, 1712) 162
Joseph (Panis, 1723) 123
Joseph (Panis, 1754) 112
Joseph-François (Negro, 1741) 149
Joseph-Gaspard (Panis) 152
Joseph-Hippolyte (Negro) 213
Joseph-Hippolye dit l'Espiègle
    (Negro) 213
Joseph-Louis dit Pompée (Negro)
    249
Joseph-Marie (Negro) 75
Joseph-Nicolas (Missouri) 122
Joseph dit Neptune (Negro) 75,
    212
Joseph Hisme (Negro) 34
Jourdain-Labrosse, Dominique
    (sculptor) 109
Juchereau, Commander 26
Juchereau-Duchesnay, Antoine
    (seigneur and Member of the
    Assembly of Lower Canada)
    152, 196, 207, 212, 237, 238
Juchereau-Duchesnay family 108,
    111
Juchereau de Saint-Denys, Nicolas
    23
Judges, slave-owning 7, 105, 106,
    258
Judith (Negro) 241, 242
Jupiter (Negro) 156
Just, Madeleine 47, 85

Kansa nation 65, 66, 256
Kansas basin 65, 66, 256
Kaskaskia (French then British
    settlement on the Mississippi
    River, in what is now Illinois) 79,
    113, 258
Kellings, Jollock (Negro) 217

Kerry (lawyer) 246
Kidnapping 12, 169, 170, 201
Kirby, William 267
Kirke, the brothers 15, 17, 20, 162

L'Assomption (settlement north-
    east of Montreal) 267
Lacelle, Jacques-François (caterer)
    66, 107
Lachenaie (settlement north of
    Montreal) 47
Lachine (settlement on the St.
    Lawrence River on island of
    Montreal) 21, 23, 24, 28, 43, 66,
    114, 139, 156, 198, 212, 213, 216
Lacorne family 108, 109, 259
Lacorne, Louis-François (cheva-
    lier) 88, 213, 252
Lacorne, Louis, the Elder 109
Lacorne-Dubreuil, François-Josué
    109
Lacorne de Lacolombière Antoine
    109
Lacorne Saint-Luc, Luc (officer)
    109, 123, 156, 187, 212
Lafitau, Joseph-François (Jesuit
    ethnographer) 10, 18
Lafleur, Pierre-Dominique (Negro)
    207, 225, 261
LaFontaine, Louis-Hippolyte
    (baronet and first Prime Minis-
    ter of the United Province of
    Canada) 269
Laframboise (slave name) 225
Lafrenière, Jacques 93
Lafricain, Joseph (Negro) 124, 199
Lagord, John 233
Lagotherie family 209
Lahontan, Baron Louis-Armand de
    (French explorer and author)
    10, 18, 26

Mississippi basin 14, 22, 23, 25, 26, 36, 65, 66, 68, 71, 79, 104, 113, 203, 256

Mittleberger, John 132

Mix, Samuel 98

Mohican nation 25, 26, 69, 257

Mondina *dit* Olivier family 196

Mondina *dit* Olivier, Marie-Élisabeth 196

Monplaisir family 229

Monplaisir (slave name) 229

Monsaige, Jean (Negro) 237

Montagnais nation 10, 20, 48, 62, 69, 70, 142, 167, 191, 222, 257

Montpetit, Gaspard 226

Montreal (island town of New France and subsequently of Quebec) 8, 10, 18, 20-25, 33, 35, 37, 46, 47, 49, 57, 58, 66, 67, 69, 74, 77, 84, 86, 87, 89, 90, 91, 92, 100, 101, 105, 110, 112, 114, 116, 123, 125-127, 129, 130, 132, 134, 135, 137, 139, 141, 143, 147-149, 153, 154, 156-158, 162, 165-169, 173-177, 180, 183, 186-191, 195, 198, 200, 202, 204, 207, 209, 210, 212, 213, 221-223, 241, 242, 244, 245, 247, 251, 252, 255, 257, 258, 261, 262, 265-267, 270

Moore, William (printer of the *Quebec Herald*) 110, 127

Morand, Nicolas (carpenter) 110

Moreau de Lataupine, Pierre 24

Morin, Samuel 127

Mouet de Langlade, Charles 125, 205

Mouet de Langlade, Charles (son of the aforementioned) 125, 205

Mounier, Mr. 52, 53

Mulattos 10, 85, 86, 90, 91, 93-95, 97, 105, 110, 127, 130, 132, 134,
144, 145, 156, 166, 199, 227-230, 240, 251, 264, 266

Murder 173, 174, 190, 200, 261

Murray, James (British Governor of the Province of Quebec) 91, 105

Napoleon I (French emperor) 140

Naskapi nation 70

Natchez nation, 66, 151 256

Navarre, Robert 109

Navetier, Pierre (Sulpician) 176

Nègre *dit* Latreille, Joseph 71

Nègre *dit* Saint-Jean, Jean-Baptiste 71

Neilson family 251

Neilson, Hugh (Colonel and grandson of John Neilson, printer of the *Quebec Gazette*) 270

Neilson, John (printer of the *Quebec Gazette*) 110, 270

Neilson, Samuel (printer of the *Quebec Gazette* and brother of John Neilson) 164

Nemo (Negro) 131, 133

Nepveu, Jacques 47, 85

Nero (Negro) 132, 155

Neuville (settlement on the St. Lawrence River upstream from Quebec City) 140

New England 11, 12, 30, 31, 37, 56, 73, 95, 173, 175, 187, 188, 200

New England captives carried to Canada 12, 159, 187, 188

New Orleans (Louisiana) 75, 115, 177, 258

New York 30, 73, 77, 187, 240, 241

Nicolas (Panis, 1709) 173, 174, 200

Nicolas (Panis, 1757) 209

Niverville de Montizambert (officer) 74

Véhicule Press